Classic

EXPLORATION STORIES

Classic
EXPLORATION STORIES

EDITED *by*

STEPHEN BRENNAN

THE LYONS PRESS
GUILFORD, CONNECTICUT
AN IMPRINT OF THE GLOBE PEQUOT PRESS

The Lyons Press is an imprint of
The Globe Pequot Press.

10 9 8 7 6 5 4 3 2 1

Printed in the United States of America

ISBN 1–59228–285–7

Library of Congress Cataloging-in-Publication Data
is available on file.

for Thomas the Finn

Contents

CONTENTS

Introduction

The Gnats are gnown; We don't the land,
For the Eye altering alters all;
The senses roll themselves in fear,
And the flat Earth becomes a Ball.

—William Blake
"The Mental Traveler"

The need to explore is bred deep within us. For our earliest ancestors, it was a matter of daily survival. Where to find food, shelter, and—who are those other people over there? This impulse to scout out, to discover, to explore is so fixed in our DNA that even in these more settled times, when classic exploration has become something of a specialized activity, each of us retains this need to explore, this compulsion to find out. Thus, we take ourselves off to exotic locales; vacation in remote woodlands; climb (most of us) small mountains. We hike trails with our families, and we tour distant cities. We are very likely, and pretty much on a whim, to cram the whole brood into the backseat and, before you can say, "GPS," hit the highway. We can't help ourselves—the need-to-know, the itch to go, is that strong in us.

One stratagem we have devised in response to this urge is to loan the idea out as metaphor. History, then, we say is an *exploration* of the past (a *voyage* through time rather than space). We *search* for a cure for cancer. We *map* the genome. We make a fetish of it. We *scout out* the best restaurants. We *delve into* private matters, we *explore* relationships, we *discover* things about ourselves. And if the scale of our personal investigations and discoveries be not so great as compared to landing on the moon, or seeking a northwest passage, or first charting the south coast of Australia, it doesn't matter; we get it. Adam and Eve probably had no business checking out that forbidden fruit tree, but we understand the impulse.

Were we to attempt a kind of psychic map of our collective human consciousness, and thereon locate the headwaters of this idea of exploration, we might just discover that it lies at the nexus of some other very human attributes. Love of adventure, certainly—to be away and at risk (at venture), dependent, finally, only upon our own resources to see us through—is a thing that resonates deep in us. There is Romance, the lure of the exotic, be it only a snow-blinding tundra, or a particularly nasty stretch of white-water rapids. We romanticize the explorer himself; we picture him as a man (or woman) sunbaked and windblown. There's a wary look in his keen eye. He has faced, confronted, and charted the unknown. He is a man with answers. Often mystery is involved—not whodunit, but where is it, and what's it like? If you boldly go where no man has gone before, you can expect that the mysterious will be taking some hand in your journey. The explorer knows this, and it makes him smile. This is what he lives for. This is who he is. The need to discover is all well and good, but an explorer is one who does something about it, actually takes action to find answers. He acts for us all, and for this we do him honor. We invest him with a mythic aspect; we call him "Hero."

The reality of exploration is all this, and other things as well. By the middle of the classic Age of Discovery, western man generally saw exploration in terms of *what* was to be investigated. Expeditions were high-mindedly categorized as geographic, hydrographic (oceanographic), cartographic, ethnographic; science married to adventure (and armed to the teeth), a heady mix of altruism and selfish pleasure; because to the last, the voyager delights in the torments and dangers of his undertaking, though he may wrap himself in a flag of scientific disinterestedness. These may be counted as only two of the motivations for the pathfinder, but there are at least as many *reasons* to undertake as there are *kinds* of explorations. Our hero may have immediate gain or prospective profit uppermost in his mind as he sets out upon his voyage. Or fame may be his aim, self-promotion, a place in the history books, or a column-and-a-half in the *New York Times*. The chance for personal advancement, either up the ranks or within society as a whole, is also a great motivator. There may be some national interest at stake, some possible land grab or takeover. There may be resources begging to be exploited, trade routes secured, or conquest planned. All this may serve to underpin or make an expedition possible, but all of it is ancillary to the main ethos of the explorer, which is to go there, put his eyeballs on it, and get answers. We recognize that any explorer who hazards his life, and the lives of his comrades, merely to be the "first to see it," or to have "one for the record books," or "because it's there," is getting in the face of the Deity, and tempting fate to a pretty marked degree. What do we do? We applaud him for it. Quite right, too. He's acting for us all.

Nearly as strong as the need to discover, is the need to tell. Eve did not keep her investigations a secret from Adam; she had a story to relate, and she told it. When Columbus, thinking he had landed in Japan, instead "discovered" America, his first thought probably was: "Better tell Isabel." The scout needs to get his reconnaissance product back to HQ, or it has little value. It's no accident, then, that the explorer is much given to keeping logs and journals. In this sense, the story of an exploration becomes the story of the person who tells it.

My aim in assembling this selection is to sample texts that illustrate various aspects of the *classic exploration story*. All are true stories; half were written by participants, the explorers themselves. Firsthand narratives are particularly revealing, not just in their description of some never-before-seen wonder, but also as to the qualities and the characters of the heroes themselves. "The Famous Perry Expedition to Japan" reveals John S. Sewall to be a careful, slightly pretentious young man, with the eye for detail of a first-rate clerk, which in fact he is. The very funny "Down Through Italy by Rail" is an example of Mark Twain at his drollest. But the canny reader senses something cynical and smug, something impatiently dismissive, in the attitude of this original Connecticut Yankee. It is, perhaps, just what you'd expect when the man of the New World discovers the Old. Meet the naturalist Alfred Russel Wallace in "The Malay Archipelago." Wallace is the fellow many people believe ought to have co-credit with Charles Darwin for the idea of the origin of species, but, due to the machinations of Darwin and his adherents, never has. I suggest the reader compare the two men by turning next to "Chiloe and Concepion: Great Earthquake," from Darwin's *Voyage of the Beagle*. In the sampling from James Boswell's *A Journal of a Tour of the Hebrides*, Doctor Samuel Johnson sets out to observe life in 1760s western Scotland, while Boswell, acting as his guide, sets out to observe Johnson. They quarrel, and both men discover a new dimension to their friendship. This is exploration as an inner journey as well as outer. In the light of our explorations we rediscover ourselves.

The other stories in this collection may properly be called chronicles, as they are told by nonparticipants, and based on stories that are received, handed down, or ferreted out. As such, they illustrate various other aspects of the classic exploration story. For example, in "Major Burnham, Chief of Scouts," we have the exploration story as hero-worship; just as in "Northmen Voyage to Vinland" and "Chronicle of the Voyages of Saint Brendan" we have it as legend. "Stanley's Last Great Expedition" may be an imperialist apology dressed up as adventure, just as "Kit Carson and John Fremont" *is* history, and a buddy story too. In "Cavelier de La Salle," Francis Parkman debunks the tradition that held La Salle as the first European to set eyes on the Mississippi River.

One question rarely asked is: How does it feel to be the one who is being explored? For answers we must use our intuition. Imagine for a moment, that a flying saucer has landed out back, and your yard is now chockablock with alien beings. They are noisy, unintelligible and rather green. They poke at you, they measure everything, they root around in your trash, and they trample your garden while collecting samples. They menace your dog. This encounter is likely to be a troubling, life-changing experience for everyone involved; and you cannot be blamed if you find yourself asking these strangers the four questions most often put by people who are themselves the objects of exploration:

"Who are you?"

"Where do you come from?"

"How did you get here?"

And often enough, and perhaps most importantly:

"When will you leave?"

Stephen Brennan
March 2004

Chronicle of the Voyages of Saint Brendan

R emember Brendan, later called *Saint,* born in the land of Munster, hard by Loch Lein. A holy man of fierce abstinence, known for his great works and the father of almost three thousand monks, he lived at Clonfert then, where we knew him at the first and last.

One night there came to visit him a holy abbot called Barrind, later called *Saint,* and each of them was joyful of the other. And when Brendan began to tell the abbot of the many wonders he had seen voyaging in the sea and visiting in diverse lands, Barrind began to sigh and anon he threw himslf prostrate on the ground and prayed hard and wept. And Brendan comforted him the best he could, and lifting him up said: "Brother Abbot, have you not come to be joyful with us, to speak the word of God and to give us heart? Therefore for God's love, do not be afraid, but tell us what marvels you have seen in the great ocean, that encompasses all the world."

So Barrind began to tell Brendan and all the gathered monks of a great wonder.

"I have a son, his name is Meroc, who had a great desire to seek about by ship in diverse countries to find a solitary place wherein he might dwell secretly out of the business of the world, in order to better serve God quietly in devotion. I counseled him to sail to an island in the sea, nearby the mountain of stones, which everybody knows. So he made ready and sailed there with his monks. And when he came there, he liked the place full well, and there settled where he and his monks served our Lord devoutly. And then I saw in a vision that this monk Meroc was sailed right far westward into the sea more than three days sailing, and suddenly to those voyagers there came a dark cloud of fog that overcovered them, so that for a great part of the day they saw no light; then as our Lord willed, the fog passed away, and they saw a fair island, and thereward they drew. In that island was joy and mirth enough and all the earth of that island shone as brightly as the sun, and there were the fairest trees and herbs that ever any man saw, and here were many precious stones shining bright, and every herb was ripe, and every tree full of fruit; so that it was a glorious sight and a

heavenly joy to abide there. Then there came to them
a fair young man, and courteously he welcomed
them all, and called every monk by his name, and
said they were much bound to praise the name of
our Lord Jesu, who would of his grace show them
that glorious place, where it is always day and never
night, and that this place is called the garden of paradise. But by this island is another island whereon
no man may come. And the fair young man said to
them, 'You have been here half a year without meat
or drink or sleep.' They supposed they had been
there only half an hour, so merry and joyful they
were. The young man told them that this was the
place where Adam and Eve lived first, and ever
would have lived, if they had not broken the commandment of God. Then the fair young man brought
them to their ship again and said they might no
longer abide there, and when they were all shipped,
suddenly the young man vanished away out of their
sight. And then within a short time after, by the purveyance of the Lord Jesu, Meroc and the brothers
returned to their own island where I and the other
brothers received them goodly, and demanded where
they had been so long. And they said that they had
been in the Land of the Blest, before the gates of
Paradise. And they asked of us, 'Cannot you tell from
the sweetness of our clothes that we have been in
Paradise?' And I and the other brothers said, 'We

believe you have been in God's Paradise, but we don't know where this Paradise is.'"

At this we all lay prostrate and said, "The Lord God is just in all his works and merciful and loving to his servants, once again he has nourished our wonder with his holy spirit."

On the day following Barrind's visit, Brendan gathered twelve of the brothers and closed us up in the oratory saying, "If it is God's will, I will seek that holy land of which the brother Abbott spoke. Does this appeal to you? What do you think?"

We answered Brendan thus, "Not our will, but God's. To know God's will, we leave our families, give away what we possess, put away the lives we led and follow you, if it is the will of God."

To better know the will of God we fasted forty days, tho not oftener than for three days running. And during this time we sought the blessing of the holy father Edna, later called *Saint*, in his western island. We stayed there three days and three nights only.

Old Edna's blessing got, we took ourselves to a lonely inlet place we called Brendan's Butt, for he had known this spot as a boy and there sat many hours, looking away out over the ocean to the west, his butt upon a seat of stone. Here we built a vessel sufficient for a voyage of seven years. With iron tools we ribbed and framed it of ash and oak, the stepping for the mast was oak, and covered it in ox hides, tanned, stitched together and greased with lard. Therein we put provisions for a forty days journey and many spares of ox hide, and then we got ourselves aboard and here lived devoutly twelve days, afloat but well in sight of land.

On the day set for our departure we received the sacrament and got ourselves aboard, when just as Brendan blessed us all, there came another two of his monks who prayed him that they might come with us. And he said, "You may sail with us, but one of you shall die and go to hell ere we return." Even so, they would go with us.

And then Brendan bade the brethren raise the sail, and forth we voyaged in God's name, so that on the morrow we were out of sight of any land. For eleven days and nights we sailed plain, and then we saw an island afar from us. We sailed thitherward as fast as we could, and soon a great reach of stone appeared above all the water, and for three days we worked our way around the island before we found an inlet fit for a landing. At last we found a little haven and there we beached our leather boat.

Suddenly, bounding up to us, there came a fair hound who laid down at Brendan's feet cheering him. So Brendan said to us, "Be of good heart, for the Lord has sent his messenger to lead us into some good place." And the hound brought us to a fair hall, where we found tables spread with good meat and drink. Brendan said grace and then we brethren sat down and ate and drank. And there were beds made ready for us that we might sleep after our long labor. But Brendan did not sleep, but prayed the night away upon his knees.

On the morrow we returned again to our skin boat and sailed a long time in the sea before we found any land. At last, by the purveyance of God, we saw a full fair island of green pasture, whereon were the whitest sheep that we had ever seen. And every sheep was as big as an ox. Just after dragging our ship ashore, we were welcomed by a goodly old man who said, "This is the Isle of Sheep. Here it is never cold but ever summer. This is why the sheep are so huge, they feed all year on the best grasses and herbs anywhere." When the old man took his leave he told us, "Voyage on, and by God's grace, you soon will come upon a place like paradise, whereon you ought to spend your Eastertide."

We sailed forth and soon came upon an island, but because of shallows and broken stone and the fury of the seas, we bore off and beached our skin ship instead upon a rock, where nothing grew, a small desolate island. Or so we thought, for when we lit the fire so that we might bake our grain and dress our meat, the island began to move under us. And all a panic then, amazed and full of fear, we threw ourselves into the boat, and pulled and twisted at the oars, swatting and thumping one another in our haste to be away. And lo, the island seemed to dip and we floated free and soon were well away. And all that night we spied the beacon of our fire leaping and dancing in the cold, dark ocean. Brendan must have smelled the terror on us, for he said, "Do not be afraid. It is only a great fish, the biggest in the sea. He labors night and day to swallow his own tail, but he cannot because of his great size. He is called Jasconius."

And then anon we oared three days and nights before we sighted any land and the weariness was heavy on us. But soon after, as God would, we saw a fair island, full of flowers, herbs, and trees, whereof we thanked God of his good grace, and then anon we found a little stream and followed it, walking our hide boat well in land. And then anon we found a full fair well, and thereby grew a mighty tree, full of boughs, and on every bough sat a white bird, and they so thick upon the tree, their number being so great, and their song being so merry that it was a heavenly noise to hear. Then Brendan fell to his knees and wept for joy, and made his prayers devoutly unto our Lord God that he might understand the meaning of the bird song. And then at once a white bird flew from the tree to Brendan. She flapped and fluttered, she hooked and danced and called, and made a merry noise full like a fiddle. It seemed to us, no holy hymn ever was so joyful. And Brendan said, "If you are the messengers of God, tell me why you sit so thick upon the tree and why you sing so merrily?"

And the bird said, "Once upon a time, we were angels in heaven, but when our master Lucifer fell down into hell for his high pride, we fell with him for our offenses, some higher, some lower, depending on the quality of their trespass; and because our trespass was but little, our Lord has sent us here, out of all pain to live in great joy and mirth, here to serve him on this tree in the best manner that we can. Today is Sunday, can you not guess why we are all white as snow?"

And when we all remembered, we fell upon our knees and hymned praise to our good Lord Jesu Christ. And the white bird sang to Brendan, "It is twelve month past that you departed from your abbey. In the seventh year you shall come unto the place of your desire. For each of those years you shall spend the Eastertide here with us, as you do today."

Then all the birds began to sing evensong so merrily that it was truly a heavenly noise to hear. And after supper Brendan and all of us went to bed, and slept well, and on the morrow we rose early, to hear the birds sing matins, and later prime and all such services of the holy rule.

We all abided there with Brendan eight full weeks, til after Trinity Sunday when we again sailed for the Isle of Sheep, and there we victualed well and were blessed again by the old man, and returned again to our leather boat, and waited for the wind to blow fair. And ere we put out, the bird of the tree came again to us, and danced upon our prow and flapped and fluttered and sang, "I am come to tell you that you shall sail from here to an island whereon there is an abbey of twenty-four monks, and there you shall hold your Christmas, but Eastertide, do not forget, you spend with us." And then the bird flew off.

The wind with us now, we sailed forth into the ocean, but soon fell a great tempest on us, which we were greatly troubled by for a long time and sorely belabored. And we saw, by the purveyance of God, a little island afar off, and full meekly we prayed to our Lord to send us thither in safety. It took eleven days, and in this time we monks were so weary of the long pull and the mountain gray oceans that we set little price upon our lives, and cried continually to our Lord to show us mercy and bring us to that little island in safety. And by the purveyance of God we came at last into a little haven, but so narrow that only one ship might come in. And after we had come to anchor, the brethren went ashore, and when we had long walked about, at last we found two fair wells; one was of fair clear water, and the other was somewhat troubly and thick. At this we thanked our Lord full humbly that had brought us here, and made to drink the water, but Brendan charged us thus, "Take no water without license. If we abstain us a while longer, our Lord will purvey for us in the best wise."

And soon after came to us a good old hoar-haired man, who welcomed us full meekly and kissed Brendan, but did not speak, and by this we understood that he observed a rule of silence. And he led us past many a fair well til we came to an abbey, where we were received with much honor and solemn procession. And then the abbott welcomed Brendan and all our fellowship, and kissed him full meekly, but did not speak. And he drew Brendan by the hand, and led us into a fair hall, and sat us down in a row on benches; and the abbott of that place, in observance of the new commandment, washed all our feet with fair clear water. And afterward, in silence still, led us into the refractory, there to seat ourselves among the brothers of the abbey. And anon came one who served us well of meat and drink. For every monk had set before him a fair white loaf and white roots and herbs, which we found right delicious, tho none of us could name; and we drank of the water of the fair clear well that we had seen before when first we came ashore, that Brendan had forbade us. And then the abbott came, and breaking silence, prayed us eat and drink, "For every day the Lord sends a good old man that covers this table with meat and drink for us. But we know not how it comes, for we do nothing to procure it, and yet our Lord feeds us. And we are twenty-four monks in number, yet every day of the week he sends us twelve loaves, and every Sunday and feast day, twenty-four loaves, and the bread we leave at dinner we eat at supper. And now at your coming our Lord has sent us forty-eight loaves, that all of us may be merry together as brethren. And we have lived twenty-nine years here in this abbey: tho we did first come out of the abbey of Saint Patrick in Ireland eighty years ago. And here in this land it is ever fair weather, and none of us is ever sick since we came here."

And then Brendan and the abbott and all the company went into the church, and we said evensong together, and devoutly. And when we looked upward at the crucifix, we saw our Lord hanging on a cross made of fine crystal and curiously wrought; and in the choir were twenty-four seats for twenty-four monks, and seven unlit tapers, and the abbott's seat was made close upon the altar in the middle of the choir. And then Brendan asked the abbott, "How long have you kept silence one with another?"

And the abbott answered Brendan, "For this twenty-nine years, no one has spoken to another."

And Brendan wept for joy at this, and desired of the abbott, "That we might all dwell here with you."

And the abbott answered Brendan, "That will not do, for our Lord has showed to you in what manner you will be guided til the seventh year is done, and after that term you will return with your monks to Ireland in safety; except that one of the two monks that came last to you will dwell in the island of anchorites, and the other will burn in hell."

And as we knelt with Brendan in the church, we saw a bright shining angel fly in at the window that lighted all the tapers in the church and flew out again and then to heaven. And Brendan marveled greatly how fair the light burned but wasted not. And the abbott said to us that it is written how

Moses saw a bush afire, yet it burned not, "and therefore marvel not, for the might of our Lord is now as great as ever it was."

And when we had dwelled there even til Christmas was gone two live days and eight days more, we took leave of this holy abbott and his convent, and returned again to our skinned-ship. And then we sailed from thence toward the island of the abbey of Saint Hillary, but aching cold and furious tempests troubled us til just before the start of Lent, when we bespied an island, not far off; and then we pulled for it but weakly, our strength all spent, our stomaches empty, our bodies raw with thirst. And when at last we gained the island, and dragged our battered boat upon the beach, we found a well of clear water, and diverse roots that grew about it, and multitudes of sweet fleshed fish that swarmed in the river that flowed to the sea. And Brendan said, "Let us gather up this bounty which the Lord makes a gift to us, and then let us renew our bodies with meat and drink, and our spirits in hymns devoutly sung."

And we obeyed Brendan, and we dug many roots and put them in the fire to bake, likewise we netted many fish and cleaned and baked them also. But when we made to drink, our holy father Brendan said, "Of this clear water drink only what is meet for your good health, lest this gift of God do you some harm."

And after grace was said, we fell to meat and drink, and then when we had eaten and drunk, we began to sing the holy office and promptly, one by one, each man fell to sleep. Tho Brendan did not sleep, but prayed three days and nights upon his knees, and full devoutly for our awakening. And so at length we did awaken, and those of us who had drank three cups of that clear water slept three days and nights, and those who drank two cups slept two, and one cup only one day and night. And Brendan gathered us about the fire and said, "Brothers, we see here how a gift of God may do us harm. As Lent is neigh, let us now get ourselves to sea; take only meat and drink for one meal every three days, as is the rule, enough to last this holy season out."

And then again we pulled our hide boat upon God's ocean, and for three full days the wind blew foul, and then a sudden all grew still. The wind blew not and the sea calmned and flattened and seemed to set into a thing solid. And Brendan said, "Brothers, lay off your oars, let us drift; and in this show true submission to the will of God."

And then we drifted twenty days. And this was a time of meditation and prayer, and of perfect observance of the rule, and of good fellowship amoung the brethren. Then at last by the purveyance of the Lord, the wind arose and blew fresh til Palm Sunday.

And then at last we came again unto the Isle of Sheep, and were received again by the old man, who brought us again into the fair hall, and served us. And after soup on Holy Thursday, he washed our feet, and gave us each the kiss of peace, alike our Lord had done with his disciples. And on the Friday of the passion of our Lord we sacrificed the lamb of innocence, and on the Saturday we did all holy rite and prayed together full devoutly, that we might find ourselves prepared for the miracle of the resurrection of our Lord Jesu. And at eventide we toiled our skin vessel into the sea, and as Brendan bid us, pulled our ashen oars against the seas that blow shorewards at eventide. And Brendan made his seat upon the oaken tiller and captained us unto a place in the sea that he did chose. And on that Easter vigil, just at the hour of lauds, when all the world is blue with first light, he bid us lay upon our oars, and Brendan asked unto us, "Do you not know where it is you are?"

And we did not know, but Brendan did know; and lo, we seemed to rise up heavenward, and the seas fell away from our frail craft, and we beheld ourselves again upon Jasconius back. And we beheld the smear of char where twelve months past we laid a fire to bake our meat, and we were amazed, and Brendan seeing this said, "Do not be afraid."

And one by one we stepped out upon this living isle. And Brendan said, "How splendid is the will of our good Lord, that even savage monsters do his bidding and make this place upon a fish's back to keep the holy service of the resurrection."

And after Mass was said, and Brendan sacrificed the spotless lamb of innocence, we got ourselves again aboard our skin vessel, and lo Jasconius dove beneath the sea, and we sailed free. And on that same morning we gained the island where the tree of the birds was, and that same bird welcomed Brendan and sang full merrily. And there we dwelled from Easter til Trinity Sunday, as we had done the year before, in full great joy and mirth; and daily we heard the merry service of the birds sitting in the tree. And then the one bird told Brendan that he should return again at Christmas to the abbey of the monks, "and Easterday, do not forget, you spend with us. But every other day of your journey, you labor in the full great peril of the ocean, from year to year til the seventh year has been accomplished when you shall find the Land of the Blest, before the gates of Paradise, and dwell there forty days in full great joy and mirth; and after you shall return home in safety to your own abbey and there end your life and be admitted to blessed heaven, which our Lord bought you with his precious blood."

And then an angel of our Lord ordained all things needful to our voyage, in vitals and all other things necessary. And then we thanked our Lord for the great goodness that he had often shown us in our great need. And then we sailed forth in the great sea ocean, abiding in the mercy of our Lord through great troubles and tempests.

Northmen Voyage to Vinland

LEIF'S VOYAGE

This voyage is recorded in the Flato Manuscript. It contains the account of the voyage of Leif, son of Eric the Red, who, following out the hints of Biarne, sailed to discover the new land, which he called Vinland, on account of the quantity of vines that he found growing wild.

[A.D. 984] It is next to be told that Biarne Heriulfson came over from Greenland to Norway, on a visit to Earl Eric, who received him well. Biarne tells of this expedition of his, in which he had discovered unknown land; and people thought he had not been very curious to get knowledge, as he could not give any account of those countries, and he was somewhat blamed on this account. [A.D. 986] Biarne was made a Court man of the earl, and the summer after he went over to Greenland; and afterward there was much talk about discovering unknown lands. Leif, a son of Eric Red of Brattahlid, went over to Biarne Heriulfson, and bought the ship from him, and manned the vessel, so that in all, there were thirty-five men on board. Leif begged his father Eric to go as commander of the expedition; but he excused himself, saying he was getting old, and not so able as formerly to undergo the hardship of a sea voyage. Leif insisted that he among all their relations was the most likely to have good luck on such an expedition; and Eric consented, and rode from home with Leif, when they had got all ready for sea; but as they were getting near the ship, the horse on which Eric was riding, stumbled, and he fell from his horse and hurt his foot. "It is destined," said Eric, "that I should never discover more lands than this of Greenland, on which we live; and now we must not run hastily into this adventure." Eric accordingly returned home to Brattahlid, but Leif, with his comrades, in all thirty-five men, rigged out their vessel. There was a man from the south country called Tyrker, with the expedition [A.D. 1000] They put the ship in order, and went to sea when they were ready. They first came to the land which Biarne had last [first] discovered, sailed up to it, cast anchor, put out a boat and went on shore; but there was no grass to be seen. There were large snowy mountains up the country; but all the way from the sea up to these snowy ridges, the land was one field of snow, and it appeared to them a country of no advantages. Leif said: "It shall not be said of us, as it was of Biarne, that we did not come upon the land; for I will give the country a name, and call it Helluland. Then they went on board again and put to sea, and found another land. They sailed in toward it, put out a boat and landed. The country was flat, and overgrown with wood; and the strand far around, consisted of white sand, and low toward the sea. Then Leif said: "We shall give this land a name according to its kind, and called it Markland. Then they hastened on board, and put to sea again with the wind from the north-east, and were out for two days and made land. They sailed toward it, and came to an island which lay on the north side of the land, where they disembarked to wait for good weather. There was dew upon the grass; and, having accidently gotten some of the dew upon their hands and put it in their mouths, they thought that they had never tasted any thing so sweet as it was. Then they went on board and sailed into a sound that was between the island and a ness that went out northward from the land, and sailed westward past the ness. There was very shallow water in ebb tide, so that their ship lay dry; and there was a long way between their ship and the water. They were so desirous to get to the land that they would not wait till their ship floated, but ran to the land, to a place where a river comes out of a lake. As soon as their ship was afloat they took the boats, rowed to the ship, towed her up the river, and from thence into the lake, where they cast anchor, carried their beds out of the ship, and set up their tents. They resolved to put things in order for wintering there, and they erected a large house. They did not want for salmon, both in the river and in the lake; and they thought the salmon larger than any they had ever seen before. The country appeared to them of so good a kind, that it would not be necessary to gather fodder for the cattle for winter. There was no frost in winter, and the grass was not much withered. Day and night were more equal than in Greenland and Iceland; for on the shortest day the sun was in the sky between Eyktarstad and the Dagmalastad. Now when they were ready with their house building, [A.D. 1001] Leif said to his fellow travelers: "Now I will divide the crew into two divisions and explore the country. Half shall stay at home and do the work, and the other half shall search the land; but so that they do not go farther than they can come back in the evening, and that they do not wander from each other." This they continued to do for some time. Leif changed about, sometimes with them and sometimes with those at home. Leif was a stout and strong man and of manly appearance, and was, besides, a prudent and sagacious man in all respects.

It happened one evening that a man of the party was missing, and it was the south countryman, Tyrker. Leif was very sorry for this because Tyrker had long been in his father's house, and he loved Tyrker in his childhood. Leif blamed his comrades very much, and proposed to go with twelve men on an expedition to find him; but they had gone only a short way from the station when Tyrker came to meet them, and he was joyfully received. Leif soon perceived that his foster father was quite merry. Tyrker had a high forehead, sharp eyes, with a small face, and was little in size, and ugly; but was very dexterous in all feats. Leif said to him, "Why art thou so late, my foster father? and why didst thou leave thy comrades?" He spoke at first long in German, rolled his eyes and knit his brows; but they could not make out what he was saying. After a while, and some delay, he said in Norse, "I did not go much further than they; and yet I have something altogether new to relate, for I found vines and grapes." "Is that true, my foster father?" said Leif. "Yes, true it is," answered he, "for I was born where there was no scarcity of grapes." They slept all night, and the next morning Leif said to his men, "Now we shall have two occupations to attend to, and day about; namely, to gather grapes or cut vines, and to fell wood in the forest to lade our vessel." This advice was followed. It is related that their stern boat was filled with grapes, and then a cargo of wood was hewn for the vessel. Towards spring they made ready and sailed away, and Leif gave the country a name from its products, and called it Vinland. They now sailed into the open sea and had a fair wind until they came in sight of Greenland and the lands below the ice mountains. Then a man put in a word and said to Leif, "Why do you steer so close on the wind?" Leif replied: "I mind my helm and tend to other things too; do you notice anything?" They said that they saw nothing remarkable. "I do not know," said Leif, "whether I see a ship or a rock." Then they looked and saw that it was a rock. But he saw so much better than they, that he discovered men upon the rock. "Now I will," said Leif, "that we hold to the wind, that we may come up to them if they should need help; and if they should not be friendly inclined, it is in our power to do as we please and not theirs." Now they sailed under the rock, lowered their sails, cast anchor, and put out an-other small boat which they had with them. Then Tyrker asked who their leader was. He said his name was Thorer, and said he was a Northman; "But what is your name?" said he. Leif told him his name. "Are you the son of Eric the Red of Brattahlid?" he asked. Leif said that was so. "Now I will," said Leif, "take ye and all on board my ship, and as much of the goods as the ship will store." They took up this offer, and sailed away to Ericsfiord with the cargo, and from thence to Brattahlid, where they unloaded the ship. Leif offered Thorer and his wife, Gudrid, and three others, lodging with himself, and offering lodging elsewhere for the rest of the people, both of Thorer's crew and his own. Leif took fifteen men from the rock, and thereafter was called, Leif the Lucky. After that time Leif advanced greatly in wealth and consideration. That winter, sickness came among Thorer's people and he himself, and a great part of his crew, died. The same winter Eric Red died. This expedition to Vinland was much talked of, and Leif's brother, Thorvald, thought that the country had not been explored enough in different places. Then Leif said to Thorvald, "You may go, brother, in my ship to Vinland if you like; but I will first send the ship for the timber which Thorer left upon the rock." So it was done.

SECOND NARRATIVE

The same spring King Olaf, as said before, sent Gissur and Hialte to Iceland. The king also sent Leif to Greenland to proclaim Christianity there. The king sent with him a priest and some other religious men, to baptize the people and teach them the true faith. Leif sailed the same summer to Greenland; he took up out of the ocean the people of a ship who were on a wreck completely destroyed, and in a perishing condition. On this same voyage he discovered Vinland the Good, and came at the close of summer to Brattahlid, to his father Eric. After that time the people called him, Leif the Fortunate; but his father Eric said that these two things went against one another; that Leif had saved the crew of the ship, and delivered them from death, and that he had [brought] that bad man into Greenland, that is what he called the priest; but after much urging, Eric was baptized, as well as all the people of Greenland.

THIRD NARRATIVE

The same winter, Leif, the son of Eric the Red, was in high favor with King Olaf, and embraced Christianity. But the summer that Gissur went to Iceland, King Olaf sent Leif to Greenland, to proclaim Christianity. He sailed the same summer for Greenland. He found some men in the sea on a wreck, and helped them; the same voyage, he discovered Vinland the Good, and came at harvest time to Greenland. He brought with him a priest and other religious men, and went to live at Brattahlid with his father Eric. He was afterward called, Leif the Fortunate. But his father Eric said, that these two things were opposed to one another, because

Leif had saved the crew of the ship, and brought evil
men to Greenland, meaning the priests.

Thorvald Ericson's
Expedition

*The greater portion of this voyage appears to have been
performed during two summers, the expedition, after visiting the Bay of Boston, finally returning to Greenland on
account of the death of their leader.*

Now Thorvald [A.D. 1002] made ready for his
voyage with thirty men, after consulting his brother
Leif. They rigged their ship, and put to sea. Nothing
is related of this expedition until they came to Vinland, to the booths put up by Leif, where they secured the ship and tackle, and remained quiet all
winter and lived by fishing. In the spring [A.D.
1003] Thorvald ordered the vessel to be rigged, and
that some men should proceed in the long-boat
westward along the coast, and explore it during the
summer. They thought the country beautiful and
well wooded, the distance small between the forest
and the sea, and the strand full of white sand. There
were also many islands and very shallow water. They
found no abode for man or beast, but on an island
far toward the west they found a corn barn constructed of wood. They found no other traces of

human work, and came back in the autumn to Leif's booths. The following spring [A.D. 1004] Thorvald, with his merchant ship, proceeded eastward, and toward the north along the land. Opposite to a cape they met bad weather, and drove upon the land and broke the keel, and remained there a long time to repair the vessel. Thorvald said to his companions: "We will stick up the keel here upon the ness, and call the place Kialarness;" which they did. Then they sailed away eastward along the country, entering the mouths of the bays, to a point of land which was every where covered with woods. They moored the vessel to the land, laid out gangways to the shore, and Thorvald, with all his ship's company, landed. He said, "Here it is so beautiful, and I would willingly set up my abode here." They afterward went on board, and saw three specks upon the sand within the point, and went to them and found there were three skin boats with three men under each boat. They divided their men and took all of them prisoners, except one man, who escaped with his boat. They killed eight of them, and then went to the point and looked about them. Within this bay they saw several eminences, which they took to be habitations. Then a great drowsiness came upon them and they could not keep themselves awake, but all of them fell asleep. A sudden scream came to them, and they all awoke; and mixed with the

scream they thought they heard the words: "Awake,
Thorvald, with all thy comrades, if ye will save your
lives. Go on board your ship as fast as you can, and
leave this land without delay." In the same moment
an innumerable multitude, from the interior of the
bay, came in skin boats and laid themselves alongside. Then said Thorvald, "We shall put up our war
screens along the gunwales and defend ourselves as
well as we can, but not use our weapons much
against them." They did so accordingly. The
Skraellings shot at them for a while, and then fled
away as fast as they could. Then Thorvald asked if
anyone was wounded, and they said nobody was
hurt. He said: "I have a wound under the arm. An
arrow flew between the gunwale and the shield
under my arm: here is the arrow, and it will be my
death wound. Now I advise you to make ready with
all speed to return; but ye shall carry me to the point
which I thought would be so convenient for a
dwelling. It may be that it was true what I said, that
here would I dwell for a while. Ye shall bury me
there, and place a cross at my head and one at my
feet, and call the place Crossness." Christianity had
been established in Greenland at this time; but Eric
Red was dead before Christianity was introduced.
Now Thorvald died, and they did everything as he
had ordered. Then they went away in search of their
fellow voyagers, and they related to each other all

the news. They remained in their dwelling all winter, and gathered vines and grapes, and put them on board their ships. Toward spring, they prepared to return to Greenland, where they arrived with their vessel, and landed at Ericsfiord, bringing heavy tidings to Leif.

Thorstein Ericson's Attempt to Find Vinland

This expedition was wholly unsuccessful, and the leader finally died without reaching the desired land.

In the meantime it had happened in Greenland that Thorstein of Ericsfiord had married and taken to wife [A.D. 1005] Gudrid, the daughter of Thorbiorn, who had been married, as before related, to Thorer, the Eastman. Thorstein Ericson bethought him now that he would go to Vinland for his brother Thorvald's body. He rigged out the same vessel and chose an able and stout crew. He had with him twenty-five men and his wife Gudrid, and as soon as they were ready he put to sea. They quickly lost sight of the land. They drove about on the ocean the whole summer without knowing where they were, and in the first week of winter they landed at Lysifiord in Greenland, in the western settlement. Thorstein looked for lodgings for his men and got his whole ship's crew accomodated, but not himself

and wife, so that for some nights they had to sleep
on board. At that time Christianity was but recent in
Greenland. One day, early in the morning, some
men came to their tent and the leader asked them
what people were in the tent? Thorstein replies,
"Two; who is it that asks?" "Thorstein," was the
reply, "and I am called Thorstein the Black, and it is
my errand here to offer thee and thy wife lodging
beside me." Thorstein said he would speak to his
wife about it, and as she gave her consent he agreed
to it. "Then I shall come for you tomorrow with my
horses, for I do not want means to entertain you;
but few care to live in my house; I and my wife live
lonely, and I am very gloomy. I have also a different
religion from yours, although I think the one you
have the best." Now the following morning he
came for them with horses, and they took up their
abode with Thorstein Black, who was very friendly
toward them. Gudrid had a good outward appearance and was knowing, and understood well how to
behave with strangers. Early in the winter a sickness
prevailed among Thorstein Ericson's people, and
many of his shipmen died. He ordered that coffins
should be made for the bodies of the dead and that
they should be brought on board and stowed away
carefully, for he said, "I will transport all the bodies
to Ericsfiord in summer." It was not long before
sickness broke out in Thorstein Black's house, and

his wife, who was called Grimhild, fell sick first. She was very stout and as strong as a man, but yet she could not bear up against the illness. Soon after Thorstein Ericson also fell sick and they both lay ill in bed at the same time; but Grimhild, Thorstein Black's wife, died first. When she was dead, Thorstein went out of the room for a skin to lay over the corpse. Then Gudrid said, "My dear Thorstein, be not long away," which he promised. Then said Thorstein Ericson, "Our housewife is wonderful, for she raises herself up with her elbows, moves herself forward over the bed-frame, and is feeling for her shoes." In the same moment, Thorstein the Goodman, came back, and instantly, Grimhild laid herself down, so that it made every beam that was in the house crack. Thorstein now made a coffin for Grimhild's corpse, removed it outside, and buried it. He was a stout and strong man, but it required all his strength to remove the corpse from the house. Now Thorstein Ericson's illness increased upon him, and he died, which Gudrid his wife took with great grief. They were all in the room, and Gudrid had set herself upon a stool before the bench on which her husband Thorstein's body lay. Now Thorstein the Goodman took Gudrid from the stool in his arms, and set himself with her upon a bench just opposite to Thorstein's body, and spoke much with her. He consoled her, and promised to go with her in summer to Ericsfiord, with her husband Thorstein's corpse, and those of his crew. "And," said he, "I shall take with me many servants to console and assist." She thanked him for this. Thorstein Ericson then raised himself up and said, "Where is Gudrid?" And thrice he said this; but she was silent. Then she said to Thorstein the Goodman, "Shall I give answer or not?" He told her not to answer. Then went Thorstein the Goodman across the room, and sat down in a chair, and Gudrid set herself on his knee; and Thorstein the Goodman said: "What wilt thou make known?" After a while the corpse replies, "I wish to tell Gudrid her fate beforehand, that she may be the better able to bear my death; for I have come to a blessed resting place. This I have now to tell thee, Gudrid, that thou wilt be married to an Iceland man, and ye will live long together and from you will descend many men, brave, gallant and wise, and a well-pleasing race of posterity. Ye shall go from Greenland to Norway, and from thence to Iceland, where ye shall dwell. Long will ye live together, but thou wilt survive him; and then thou shalt go abroad, and go southward, and shall return to thy home in Iceland. And there must a church be built, and thou must remain there and be consecrated a nun, and there end thy days." And then Thorstein sank backward, and his corpse was put in order and carried to the ship. Thorstein the

‚man did all that he had promised. He sold in
‚ng [A.D. 1006] his land and cattle, and went
with Gudrid and all her goods; made ready the ship,
got men for it, and then went to Ericsfiord. The
body was buried at the church. Gudrid went to
Leif's at Brattahlid, and Thorstein the Black took his
abode in Ericsfiord, and dwelt there as long as he
lived; and was reckoned an able man.

Thorfinn Karlsefne's Expedition to Vinland

*This was in many respects the most important expedi-
tion to New England, both as regards the numbers engaged, and the information and experience derived. The
Saga of Karlsefne is occupied largely at the beginning with
accounts of various matters connected with social life; yet,
as such subjects are not essential to the treatment of the
voyage, they are all omitted, except the account of Thorfinn's
marriage with the widow of Thorstein Ericson.*

NARRATIVE OF THORFINN KARLSEFNE

There was a man named Thord who dwelt at
Hofda, in Hofda-Strand. He married Fridgerda,
daughter of Thorer the Idle, and of Fridgerda the
daughter of Kiarval, King of the Irish. Thord was the

son of Biarne Butter-Tub, son of Thorvald, son of
Aslak, son of Biarne Ironsides, son of Ragnar Lod-
brok. They had a son named Snorre, who married
Thorhild the Partridge, daughter of Thord Geller.
They had a son named Thord Horsehead. Thorfinn
Karlsefne was his son, whose mother's name was
Thoruna. Thorfinn occupied his time in merchant
voyages and was thought a good trader. One summer he fitted out his ship for a voyage to Greenland,
attended by Snorre Thorbrandson of Alptafiord, and
a crew of forty men. There was a man named Biarne
Grimolfson of Breidafiord, and another named
Thorhall Gamlason of Austfiord. These men fitted
out a ship at the same time to voyage to Greenland.
They also had a crew of forty men. This ship and
that of Thorfinn, as soon as they were ready, put to
sea. It is not said how long they were on the voyage;
it is only told that both ships arrived at Ericsfiord in
the autumn of that year. Leif and other people rode
down to the ships and friendly exchanges were
made. The captians requested Leif to take whatever
he desired of their goods. Leif, in return entertained
them well and invited the principal men of both
ships to spend the winter with him at Brattahlid.
The merchants accepted his invitation with thanks.
Afterward their goods were moved to Brattahlid,
where they had every entertainment that they could
desire; therefore their winter quarters pleased them

much. When the Yule feast began, Leif was silent and more depressed than usual. Then Karlsefne said to Leif: "Are you sick, friend Leif? you do not seem to be in your usual spirits. You have entertained us most liberally, for which we desire to render you all the service in our power. Tell me what it is that ails you." "You have received what I have been able to offer you," said Leif, "in the kindest manner and there is no idea in my mind that you have been wanting in courtesy; but I am afraid lest when you go away it may be said that you never saw a Yule feast so meanly celebrated as that which draws near at which you will be entertained by Leif of Brattahlid." "That shall never be the case, friend," said Karlsefne, "we have ample stores in the ship; take of these what you wish and make a feast as splendid as you please." Leif accepted this offer and the Yule began. So well were Leif's plans made, that all were surprised that such a rich feast could be prepared in so poor a country. After the Yule feast, Karlsefne began to treat with Leif, as to the marriage of Gudrid, Leif being the person to whom the right of betrothal belonged. Leif gave a favorable reply, and said she must fulfill that destiny which fate had assigned, and that he had heard of none except a good report of him; and in the end it turned out that Karlsefne married Gudrid, and their wedding was held at Brattahlid, this same winter [A.D. 1007].

The conversation often turned at Brattahlid, on
the discovery of Vinland the Good, and they said
that a voyage there had great hope of gain. After this
Karlsefne and Snorre made ready for going on a
voyage there the following spring. Biarne and
Thorhall Gamlason, before mentioned, joined with
a ship. There was a man named Thorvard, who married Freydis, natural daughter of Eric Red, and he
decided to go with them, as did also Thorvald, son
of Eric. Thorhall, commonly called the Hunter, who
had been the huntsman of Eric in the summer, and
his steward in the winter, also went. This Thorhall
was a man of immense size and of great strength,
and dark complexion and taciturn, and when he
spoke, it was always jestingly. He was always inclined
to give Leif evil advice. He was an enemy to Christianity. He knew much about desert lands; and was
in the same ship with Thorvord and Thorvald. These
used the ship which brought Thorbiorn from Iceland. There was in all, forty men and a hundred.
They sailed to the West district [of Greenland], and
thence to Biarney; hence they sailed south a night
and a day. Then land was seen, and they launched a
boat and explored the land; they found flat stones,
many of which were twelve ells broad. There were a
great number of foxes there. They called the land
Helluland. Then they sailed a day and a night in a
southerly course, and came to a land covered with

CLASSIC EXPLORATION STORIES

woods, in which there were many wild animals. Beyond this land to the southeast, lay an island on which they slew a bear. They called the island Bear island, and the land, Markland. Thence they sailed long south by the land and came to a cape. The land lay on the right [starboard] side of the ship, and there were long shores of sand. They came to land, and found on the cape, the keel of a ship, from which they called the place Kiarlarness, and the shores they also called Wonder-strand, because it seemed so long sailing by. Then the land became indented with coves, and they ran the ship into a bay, wither they directed their course. King Olaf Tryggvesson had given Leif two Scots, a man named Haki and a woman named Hekia; they were swifter of foot than wild animals. These were in Karlsefne's ship. When they had passed beyond Wonder-strand, they put these Scots ashore, and told them to run over the land to the south-west, three days, and discover the nature of the land, and then return. They had a kind of garment that they called kiafal, that was so made that a hat was on top, and it was open at the sides, and no arms; fastened between the legs with a button and strap, otherwise they were naked. When they returned, one had in his hand a bunch of grapes, and the other a spear of wheat. They went on board, and afterward the course was obstructed by another bay. Beyond this bay was an island, on each side of which was a rapid current, that they called the Isle of Currents. There was so great a number of eider ducks there, that they could hardly step without treading on their eggs. They called this place Stream Bay. Here they brought their ships to land, and prepared to stay. They had with them all kinds of cattle. The situation of the place was pleasant, but they did not care for any thing, except to explore the land. Here they wintered without sufficient food. The next summer [A.D. 1008], failing to catch fish, they began to want food. Then Thorhall the Hunter disappeared.

They found Thorhall, whom they sought three days, on the top of a rock, where he lay breathing, blowing through his nose and mouth, and muttering. They asked why he had gone there. He replied that this was nothing that concerned them. They said that he should go home with them, which he did. Afterward a whale was cast ashore in that place; and they assembled and cut it up, not knowing what kind of whale it was. They boiled it with water, and ate it, and were taken sick. Then Thorhall said: "Now you see that Thor is more prompt to give aid than your Christ. This was cast ashore as a reward for the hymn which I composed to my patron Thor, who rarely forsakes me." When they knew this, they cast all the remains of the whale into the sea, and commended their affairs to God. After which the air became milder, and opportunities were given for fishing. From that time there was an abundance of food; and there were beasts on the land, eggs in the island, and fish in the sea.

They say that Thorhall desired to northward around Wonder-strand to explore Vinland, but Karlsefne wished to go along the shore south. Then Thorhall prepared himself at the island, but did not have more than nine men in his whole company, and all the others went in the company of Karlsefne. When Thorhall was carrying water to his ship, he sang this verse:

People said when hither I
Came, that I the best
Drink would have, but the land
It justly becomes me to blame;
I, a warrior, am now obliged
To, bear the pail;
Wine touches not my lips,
But I bow down to the spring."
When they had made ready and were about to
    sail, Thorhall sang:
"Let us return
Thither where [our] country-men rejoice,
Let the ship try
The smooth ways of the sea;
While the strong heroes
Live on Wonder-strand
And there boil whales,
Which is an honor to the land.

Afterward he sailed north to go around Wonder-strand and Kiarlarness, but when he wished to sail westward, they were met by a storm from the west and driven to Ireland, where they were beaten and made slaves. As merchants reported, there Thorhall died.

It is said that Karlsefne, with Snorre and Biarne and his countrymen, sailed along the coast south. They sailed long until they came to a river flowing down from the land through a lake into the sea, where there were sandy shoals, where it was impossible to pass up, except with the highest tide. Karlsefne sailed up to the mouth of the river with his folk, and called the place Hop. Having come to the land, they saw that where the ground was low corn grew, and where it was higher, vines were found. Every river was full of fish.

They dug pits where the land began, and where the land was highest; and when the tide went down, there were sacred fish in the pits. There were a great number of all kinds of wild beasts in the woods. They stayed there half a month and enjoyed them-selves, and did not notice anything; they had their cattle with them. Early one morning, when they looked around, they saw a great many skin boats, and poles were swung upon them, and it sounded like reeds shaken by the wind, and they pointed to the sun. Then said Karlsefne, "What may this mean?" Snorre Thorbrandson replied, "It may be that this is a sign of peace, so let us take a white shield and hold it toward them." They did so. Thereupon they rowed toward them, wondering at them, and came to land. These people were swarthy and fierce, and had bushy hair on their heads; they had very large eyes and broad cheeks. They stayed there for a time, and gazed upon those they met, and afterward rowed away southward around the ness.

Karlsefne and his people had made their houses above the lake, and some of the houses were near the lake, and others more distant. They wintered there, and there was no snow, and all their cattle fed themselves on the grass. But when spring came [A.D. 1009] they saw one morning early, that a number of canoes rowed from the south around the ness; so many, as if the sea were sown with coal; poles were also swung on each boat. Karlsefne and his people then raised up the shield, and when they came together they began to trade. These people would rather have red cloth; for this they offered skins and real furs. They would also buy swords and spears, but this, Karlsefne and Snorre forbade. For a whole fur skin, the Skraellings took a piece of red cloth, a span long and bound it round their heads. Thus went on their traffic for a time. Next the cloth began to be scarce with Karlsefne and his people, and they cut it up into small pieces, which were not wider than a finger's breath, and yet the Skraellings gave just as much as before and more.

It happened that a bull, which Karlsefne had, ran out of the wood and roared aloud; this frightened the Skraellings, and they rushed to their canoes and rowed away toward the south. After that they were not seen for three whole weeks. But at the end of that time, a great number of Skraelling's ships were seen coming from the south like a rushing torrent, all the poles turned from the sun, and they all yelled very loud. Then Karlsefne's people took a red shield and held it toward them. The Skraellings leaped out of their vessels, and after this, they went against each other and fought. There was a hot shower of weapons, because the Skraellings had slings. Karlsefne's people saw that they raised upon a pole, a very large ball, something like a sheep's paunch, and of a blue color; this they swung from the pole over Karlsefne's men, upon the ground, and it made a great noise as it fell down. This caused great fear with Karlsefne and his men, so that they only thought of running away; and they retreated along the river, for it seemed to them that the Skraellings pressed them on all sides. They did not stop until they came to some rocks where they made a bold stand. Freydis came out and saw that Karlsefne's people fell back, and she cried out, "Why do you run, strong men as you are, before these miserable creatures whom I thought you would knock down like cattle? If I had arms, methinks I could fight better than any of you." They gave no heed to her words. Freydis would go with them, but she was slower because she was pregnant; still she followed after them in the woods. She found a dead man in the woods; it was Thorbrand Snorreson, and there stood a flat stone stuck in his head; the sword lay naked by his side. This she took up and made ready to defend herself. Then came the Skraellings toward her; she drew out her breasts from under her clothes and dashed them against the naked sword. By this the Skraellings became frightened and ran off to their ships and rowed away. Karlsefne and his men then came up and praised her courage. Two men fell on Karlsefne's side, but a number of the Skraellings. Karlsefne's band was overmatched. Next they went home to their dwelling and bound up their wounds, and considered what crowd that was that pressed upon them from the land side. It now seemed to them that it could have hardly been real people from the ships, but that these must have been optical illusions. The Skraellings also found a dead man and an axe lay by him; one of them took up the axe and cut wood with it, and then after another did the same and thought it was a fine thing and cut well. After that one took it and cut at a stone so that the axe broke, and then they thought that it was of no use because it would not cut stone, and they cast it away.

Karlsefne and his people now thought they saw, that although the land had many good qualities, they still would always be exposed to the fear of attacks from the original dwellers. They decided, therefore, to go away and to return to their own land. They coasted northward along the shore and found five Skraellings clad in skins, sleeping near the sea. They had with them vessels containing animal marrow mixed with blood. Karlsefne's people thought that these men had been banished from the land; they killed them. After that they came to a ness, and many wild beasts were there, and the ness was covered all over with dung from the beasts which had lain there during the night. Now they came back to Straumfiord, and there was a plenty of everything that they wanted to have. [It is thus that some men say that Biarne and Gudrid stayed behind and one hundred men with them, and did not go farther; but that Karlsefne and Snorre went southward with forty men with them, and were no longer in Hop than barely two months, and the same summer came back.] Karlsefne then went with one ship to seek Thorhall the Hunter, but the rest remained behind, and they sailed northward past Kiarlarness, and thence westward, and the land was upon their larboard hand. There were wild woods over all, as far as they could see, and scarcely any open places. When they had sailed long a river ran out of the land east and west. They sailed into the mouth of the river, and lay by its bank.

It chanced one morning that Karlsefne and his people saw opposite in an open place in the woods, a speck which glittered in their sight, and they called out towards it, and it was a Uniped, which thereupon hurried down to the bank of the river, where they lay. Thorvald Ericson stood at the helm, and the Uniped shot an arrow into his bowels. Thorvald drew out the arrow and said: "It has killed me! To a rich land we have come, but hardly shall we enjoy any benefit from it." Thorvald soon after died of his wound. Upon this the Uniped ran away to the northward. Karlsefne and his people went after him, and saw him now and then, and the last time they saw him, he ran out into a bay. Then they turned back, and a man sang these verses:

The people chased
A uniped
Down to the beach,
Behold he ran
Straight over the sea—
Hear thou, Thorfinn!

They drew off to the northward, and saw the country of the Unipeds, but they would not then expose their men any longer. They looked upon the mountain range that was at Hop, and that which they now found, as all one, and it also appeared to be of equal length from Straumfiord to both places. The third winter they were in Straumfiord. They now became, men to divided by party feeling, and the women were the cause of it, for those who were unmarried would injure those who were married, and hence arose great disturbance. There was born the first autumn, Snorre, Karlsefne's son, and he was three years old when they went away. When they sailed from Vinland they had a south wind, and then came to Markland, and found there, five Skraellings, one was bearded; two were females, and two boys; they took the boys, but the others escaped, and the Skraellings sank down in the ground. These boys they took with them; they taught them the language, and they were baptized. They called their mother Vathelldi, and their father, Uvaege. They said that two kings ruled over the Skraellings, and that one was named Avalldania, but the other Valldidia. They said that no houses were there. People lived in caves or in holes. They said there was a land on the other side, just opposite their country, where people lived who wore white clothes, and carried poles before them, and to these were fastened flags, and they shouted loud; and the people think that this was White-man's land, or Great Ireland.

Biarne Grimolfson was driven with his ship into the Irish ocean, and they came into a worm sea, and soon the ship began to sink under them. They had a boat which was smeared with sea oil, for the worms do not attack that. They went into the boat, and then saw that it could not hold them all. Then said Biarne: "As the boat will not hold more than half of our men, it is my counsel that lots should be drawn for those to go in the boat, for it shall not be according to rank." This, they all thought so generous an offer, that no one would oppose it. They then did so that lots were drawn, and it fell to Biarne to go in the boat, and the half of the men with him, for the boat had not room for more. But when they had gotten into the boat, an Icelandic man that was in the ship, and had come with Biarne from Iceland, said: "Dost thou mean, Biarne, to leave me here?" Biarne said: "So it seems." Then said the other: "Very different was the promise to my father, when I went with thee from Iceland, than thus to leave me, for thou said that we should both share the same fate." Biarne said, "It shall not be thus; go down into the boat, and I will go up into the ship, since I see that thou art so anxious to live." Then Biarne went up into the ship, and this man down into the boat, and after that they went on their voyage, until they came to Dublin, in Ireland, and there told these things; but it is most people's belief that Biarne and his companions were lost in the worm sea, for nothing was heard of them after that time.

THE ACCOUNT OF THORFINN

That same winter [A.D. 1006–7], there was much discussion about the affairs of Brattahlid; and they set up the game of chess, and sought amusement in the reciting of history, and in many other things, and were able to pass life joyfully. Karlsefne and Snorre resolved to seek Vinland, but there was much discussion about it. It turned out that Karlsefne and Snorre prepared their ships to seek Vinland the following summer. [A.D. 1007]. In this enterprise Biarne and Thorhall joined as comrades with their own ship and crew, who were their followers. There was a man named Thorvald, a relation of Eric. Thorhall was called the Hunter. He long had hunted with Eric in summer, and had the care of many things. Thorhall was of great stature, large and swarthy face, of a hard nature, taciturn, saying little of affairs, and nevertheless crafty and malicious, always inclined to evil, and opposed in his mind to the Christian religion, from its first introduction into Greenland. Thorhall indulged in trifling, but nevertheless Eric was used to his familiarity. He went in the ship with Thorvald, and was well acquainted with uninhabitable places. He used the ship in which Thorbiorn came; and Karlsefne engaged comrades for the expedition; and the best part of the sailors of Greenland were with him. They carried in their ships, forty and a hundred men. Afterward they sailed to West bygd and Biarney-isle. They sailed from Biarney-isle with a north wind, and were on the sea a day and night, when they found land, and, sending a boat to the shore, explored the land, where they found many flat stones of such great size, that they exceeded in length the size of two men. There were foxes there. They gave the land a name, and called it Helluland. After this, they sailed a night and a day with a north wind. They came to a land in which were great woods and many animals. South-west, opposite the land, lay an island. Here they found a bear, and called the island, Bear island. This land, where there were woods, they called Markland. After a voyage of a day and a night, they saw land, and they sailed near the land and saw that it was a cape; they kept close to the shore with the wind on the starboard side, and left the land upon the right side of the ship. There were places without harbors, long shores and sands. When they went to the shore with a boat, they found the keel of a ship, and they called the place Kiarlarness; and they gave the shore a name, and called it Wonder-strand, because they were so long going by. Then another bay extended into the land, and they steered into the bay. When Leif was with King Olaf Tryggvesson, he sent him to establish the Christian religion in Greenland; then the king gave him two Scots-folk, a man named Hake, and a woman named Hekia. The king told Leif to take them with his men, if he would have his commands done quickly, as they were swifter than beasts. These folk, Leif and Eric gave to Karlsefne, as followers. When they were come opposite Wonder-strand, they put the Scots on the shore, and told them to run southward and explore the country, and return before the end of three days. They were thus clothed having a garment called a Biafal; it was made so that a hat was on top, open at the sides, without arms, buttoned between the legs, and fastened with a button and a strap; and the rest was bare.

They came to anchor and lay by, until the three days passed, when they returned, one having in his hand a vine, and the other self-sown wheat. Karlsefne said that they had found a fruitful land. Afterward they were received into the ship, and they went on their way until a bay intersected the land. They steered the ship into the bay. On the outside was an island, and there was a great tide around the island. This they called Straumey. There was a great number of birds, and it was scarcely possible to find a place for their feet among the eggs. Then they steered into a long bay which they called Straum-fiord, where they landed from their ships and began to prepare habitations. They brought with them all kinds of cattle, and they found sufficient pasturage. There were mountains and the prospect was pleasant; but they cared for nothing except to explore the land; there was a great abundance of grass. Here they wintered, and the winter was severe, and they did not have stores laid up, they began to be in want of food and failed to catch fish. So they sailed over to the island, hoping that they might find means of subsistence either on what they could catch or what was cast ashore. But they found but little better fare though the cattle were better off. [A.D. 1008]. Afterward they prayed to God to send them food, which prayer was not answered as soon as desired. Then Thorhall disappeared and a search was made which lasted three days. On the morning of the fourth day Karlsefne and Biarne found him lying on the top of a rock; there he lay stretched out, with open eyes, blowing through his mouth, and muttering to himself. They asked him why he had gone there. He replied that it did not concern them and not to wonder as he was old enough to take care of himself without their troubling themselves with his affairs. They asked him to go home with them; this he did. After that a whale was cast up and they ran down to cut it up; nevertheless they did not know what kind it was. Neither did Karlsefne, though acquainted with whales, know this one. Then the cooks dressed the whale and they all ate of it and it made them all sick. Then Thorhall said, "It is clear now that the Red-beard is more prompt to give aid than your Christ. This food is a reward for a hymn which I made to my god Thor, who has seldom deserted me." When they heard this none would eat any more, and threw what was left from the rock, committing themselves to God. After this the opportunity was given of going after fish, and there was no lack of food. They sailed into Straumfiord and had abundance of food and hunting on the mainland, with many eggs and fish from the sea.

Now they began to consider where they should settle next. Thorhall, the Hunter, wished to go northward around Wonder-strand and Kiarlarness to explore Vinland, but Karlsefne wished to go southwest, thinking likely that there would be larger tracts of country the further they went south. Thorhall made ready at the island and only nine men went with him; all the rest of the ship folk went with Karlsefne. One day Thorhall was carrying water to his ship; he drank it and sang this verse:

People promised me when hither I
Came, then the best drink
I should have; but the country
I must denounce to all;
Here you are forced by hand
To bear the pail to the water,
I must bend me down to the spring;
Wine did not come to my lips.

Afterward they left the land and Karlsefne went with them to the island. Before they hoisted sail, Thorhall sang these verses:

Let us return
Home to our countrymen,
Let the vessel try
The broad path of the sea;
While the persevering
Men who praise the land
Are building and boil the whales
Here on Wonder-strand.

There upon they sailed northward around Wonder-strand and Kialarness. But when they wished to cruise westward, a storm came against them, and drove them to Ireland, where they were beaten and made slaves. There Thorhall passed his life.

Karlsefne, with Snorre and Biarne and the rest of his comrades, sailed south. They sailed long until they came to a river, which flowed from the land

through a lake, and passed into the sea. Before the
mouth of the river were great islands, and they were
not able to enter the river except at the highest tide.
Karlsefne sailed into the mouth of the river, and
called the land Hop. There they found fields, where
the land was low, with wild corn, and where the
land was high, were vines. Every river was full of
fish. They made pits in the sand, where the tide rose
highest, and at low tide, sacred fish were found in
these pits, and in the woods was a great number of
all kinds of beasts. Here they stayed half a month,
enjoying themselves, but observing nothing new.
Early one morning, on looking around, they saw
nine skin boats, in which were poles that, vibrating
toward the sun, gave out a sound like reeds shaken
by the wind. Then Karlsefne said: "What think you,
does this mean?" Snorre said: "It is possible that it is
a sign of peace; let us raise up a white shield and
hold it toward them," this they did. Then they rowed
toward them, wondering at them, and came to land.
These men were small of stature and fierce, having
a bushy head of hair, and very great eyes and wide
cheeks. They remained some time wondering at
them, and afterward rowed southward around the
cape. They built dwellings beyond the lake, others
made houses near the mainland, and others near the
lake. Here they spent the winter. No snow fell, and
all their cattle fed under the open sky. They decided

to explore all the mountains that were in Hop; which done, they went and passed the third winter [A.D. 1009] in Straum bay. At this time they had much contention among themselves, and the un- married women vexed the married. The first au- tumn, Snorre, Karlsefne's son, was born, and he [was three years old] when they went away. They had a south wind, and came to Markland, and found five Skraellings, of whom one was a man, and two women, and two were boys. Karlsefne took the boys, and the others escaped and sank into the earth. They carried the boys away with them, and taught them the language, and they were baptized. The name of their mother was Vatheldi, and their father, Uvaege. They said that two kings ruled over the Skraellinger's land; one was named Avalldania, and the other, Valldidia; that they had no houses, but lived in dens and caves. In another part of the coun- try, there was a region where the people wore white clothes, and shouted loud, and carried poles with flags. This they thought to be White-man's land.

After this they came into Greenland, and passed the winter with Leif, son of Eric Red. Biarne Gri- molfson was carried out into the Greenland sea, and came into a worm sea, which they did not observe, until their ship was full of worm holes. They con- sidered what should be done. They had a stern boat, smeared with oil. They say the wood covered with

oil, the worms will not bore. The result of the coun-
cil was, that as many should go into the boat as it
would hold. It then appeared that the boat would
not hold more than one-half of the men. Then
Biarne ordered that the men should go in the boat
by lot, and not according to rank. As it would not
hold all, they accepted the saying, and when the lots
were drawn, the men went out of the ship into the
boat. The lot was, that Biarne should go down from
the ship to the boat with one-half of the men. Then
those to whom the lot fell, went down from the
ship to the boat. When they had come into the boat,
a young Icelander, who was the companion of
Biarne, said: "Now thus do you intend to leave me,
Biarne?" Biarne replied, "That now seems necessary." He replied with these words: "Thou art not
true to the promise when I left my father's house in
Iceland." Biarne replied: "In this thing I do not see
any other way;" continuing, "What course can you
suggest?" He said, "I see this, that we change places
and thou come up here and I go down there."
Biarne replied: "Let it be so, since I see that you are
so anxious to live, and are frightened by the
prospect of death." Then they changed places, and
he descended into the boat with the men, and
Biarne went up into the ship. It is related that Biarne,
and the sailors with him in the ship, perished in the
worm sea. Those who went in the boat, went on

their course until they came to land, where they told all these things.

After the next summer, Karlsefne went to Iceland with his son Snorre, and he went to his own home at Reikianess. The daughter of Snorre, son of Karlsefne, was Hallfrida, mother to Bishop Thorlak Runolfson. They had a son named Thorbiorn, whose daughter was named Thoruna, mother of Bishop Biarne. Thorgeir was the name of the other son of Snorre, Karlsefne's son, father to Ingveld, and mother of the first bishop of Brand. And this is the end of the history.

THIRD NARRATIVE

That same summer came a ship from Norway to Greenland. The man was called Thorfinn Karlsefne who steered the ship. He was a son of Thord Hesthofde, a son of Snorre Thordarson, from Hofda. Thorfinn Karlsefne was a man of great wealth, and was in Brattahlid with Leif Ericsson. Soon he fell in love with Gudrid, and courted her, and she referred to Leif to answer for her. Afterward she was betrothed to him, and their wedding was held the same winter. At this time, as before, much was spoken about a Vinland voyage; and both Gudrid and others persuaded Karlsefne much to that expedition. Now this expedition was resolved upon, and they got ready a crew of sixty men, and five women; and then they made the agreement, Karlsefne and his people, that each of them should have equal share in what they made of gain. They had with them all kinds of cattle, having the intention to settle in the land, if they could. Karlsefne asked Leif for his houses in Vinland, but he said he would lend them, but not give them. Then they put to sea with the ship, and came to Leif's house safe, and carried up their goods. They soon had in hand a great and good prize, for a whale had been driven on shore, both large and excellent. They went to it and cut it up, and had no want of food. Their cattle went up into the land; but soon they were unruly, and gave trouble to them. They had one bull with them. Karlsefne let wood be felled and hewed for shipping it, and had it laid on a rock to dry. They had all the good of the products of the land, which were these: both grapes and wood, and other products. After that first winter, and when summer came [A.D. 1008], they were aware of Skraellings being there; and a great troop of men came out of the woods. The cattle were near to them, and the bull began to bellow and roar very loud. With that the Skraellings were frightened, and made off with their bundles,— and these were of furs and sables and all sorts of skins; and they turned and wanted to go into the houses, but Karlsefne defended the doors. Neither party understood the language of the other. Then the Skraellings took their bundles and opened them, and wanted to have weapons in exchange for them, but Karlsefne forbade his men to sell weapons. Next he adopted this plan with them, that he told the women to bear out milk and dairy products to them. When they saw these things, they would buy them and nothing else. Now the trade for the Skraellings was such, that they carried away their winnings in their stomachs; and Karlsefne and his comrades got both their bags and skin goods, and so they went away. Next it is to be told, that Karlsefne let a good strong fence be made around the habitation, and strengthened it for defense. At this time Gudrid, Karlsefne's wife, lay in of a male child, and the child was called Snorre. In the beginning of the next winter, came the Skraellings again to them, and in much greater numbers than before, and with the same kind of wares. Then said Karlsefne to the women, "Now ye shall carry out the same kind of foodas was best liked the last time, and nothing else. Then they saw that they threw their bundles in over the fence, while Gudrid sat in the door within, by the cradle of Snorre, her son. There came a shadow to the door, and a woman went in with a black kirtle on, rather short, with a snood around her head; clear, yellow hair; pale, with large eyes, so large that none ever saw such eyes in a human head. She went to where Gudrid was sitting, and said: "What art thou called?" "I am called Gudrid; and what art thou called?" "I am called Gudrid," said she. Then the goodwife, Gudrid, put out her hand to her, that she might sit down beside her. At the same time Gudrid heard a great noise, and the woman had vanished. At the same time one of the Skraellings was killed by one of Karlsefne's house men, because he was about to take one of their weapons; and they made off as soon as possible, leaving behind them goods and clothes. No one had seen this woman but Gudrid. "Now," says Karlsefne, "we must be cautious, and take counsel; for I think they will come the third time with hostility and many people. We shall now take the plan, that ten men go out to the ness and show themselves there, and the rest of our men shall go into the woods and make a clearance for our cattle against the time the enemy comes out of the forest; and we shall take the bull before us, and let him go in front." So it happened, that at the place where they were to meet, there was a lake on the one side, and the forest on the other. The plan which Karlsefne had laid down was adopted. The Skraellings came to the place where Karlsefne proposed to fight; and there was a battle there, and many of the Skraellings fell. There was one stout, handsome man among the Skraelling people, and Karlsefne thought that he must be their chief. One of the Skraellings had taken up an axe and looked at it a while, and wielded it against one of his comrades and cut him down, so that he fell dead instantly. Then the stout man took the axe, looked at it awhile, and threw it into the sea as far as he could. They then fled to the woods as fast as possible, and so ended the fight. Karlsefne stayed there with his men the whole winter; but toward spring he made known that he would not stay there any longer, and would return to Greenland. Now they prepared for their voyage and took much goods from thence— vines, grapes, and skin wares. They put to sea, and their ship came to Ericsfiord, and they there passed the winter.

The following summer [A.D. 1011], Karlsefne went to Iceland and Gudrid with him, and he went home to Reikianess. His mother felt that he had made a poor match, and for this reason Gudrid was not at home the first winter. But when she saw that Gudrid was a noble woman, she went home, and they got on well together. Halfrid was the daughter of Snorre Karlsefneson, mother to Bishop Thorlak Runolfson. Their son was named Thorbiorn, and his daughter, Thoruna, mother to Bishop Biorne. Thorgeir was the son of Snorre Karlsefneson, father to Ingveld, mother of the first Bishop Brand. Snorre Karlsefneson had a daughter, Steinun, who married Einar, son of Grundarketil, son of Thorvald Krok,

the son of Thorer, or Espihol; their son was
Thorstein Rauglatr. He was father to Gudrun, who
married Jorund of Keldum. Halla was their daughter, and she was mother to Flose, father of Valgerda,
who was the mother of Herr Erland Sterka, father
of Herr Hauk, the Lagman. Another daughter of
Flose was Thordis, mother of Fru Ingigerd the
Rich; her daughter was Fru Hallbera, Abbess of
Stad, in Reikianess. Many other distinguished men
in Iceland are the descendants of Karlsefne and
Thurid, who are not here mentioned. God be with
us. Amen.

Marco Polo

Know reader, that at the time when Baldwin II was Emperor of Constantinople, where a magistrate representing the Doge of Venice then resided, and in the year of our Lord 1250, Nicolo Polo, the father of the said Marco, and Maffeo, the brother of Nicolo, respectable and well-informed men, embarked in a ship of their own, with a rich and varied cargo of goods, and reached Constantinople in safety. After mature deliberation on the subject of their proceedings, it was determined, as the measure most likely to improve their trading capital, that they should prosecute their voyage into the Euxine or Black Sea. With this view they made purchases of many fine and costly jewels, and taking their departure from Constantinople, navigated that sea to a port named Soldaia, from whence they travelled on horseback many days until they reached the court of a powerful chief of the Western Tartars, named Barka VI who dwelt in the cities of Bolgara and Assara, and had the reputation of being one of the most liberal and civilized princes hitherto known amongst the tribes of Tartary. He expressed much satisfaction at the arrival of these travellers, and received them with marks of distinction. In return for which courtesy, when they had laid before him the jewels they brought with them, and perceived that their beauty pleased him, they presented them for his acceptance. The liberality of this conduct on the part of the two brothers struck him with admiration; and being unwilling that they should surpass him in generosity, he not only directed double the value of the jewels to be paid to them, but made them in addition several other rich presents.

The brothers having resided a year in the dominions of this prince, they became desirous of revisiting their native country, but were impeded by the sudden breaking out of a war between him and another chief, named Alaù, who ruled over the Eastern Tartars. In the fierce and very bloody battle that ensued between their respective armies, Alaù was victorious, in consequence of which, the roads being rendered unsafe for travellers, the brothers could not attempt to return by the way they came; and it was recommended to them, as the only practicable mode of reaching Constantinople, to proceed in an easterly direction, by an unfrequented route, so as to skirt the limits of Barka's territories. Accordingly they made their way to a town named Oukaka, situated on the confines of the kingdom of the Western Tartars. Leaving that place, and advancing still further, they crossed the Tigris, one of the four rivers of Paradise, and came to a desert, the extent of which was seventeen days' journey, wherein they found neither town, castle, nor any substantial building, but only Tartars with their herds, dwelling in tents on the plain. Having passed this tract, they arrived at length at a well-built city called Bokhara, in a province of that name, belonging to the dominions of Persia, and the noblest city of that kingdom, but governed by a prince whose name was Barak. Here, from inability to proceed further, they remained three years.

It happened while these brothers were in Bokhara, that a person of consequence and gifted with eminent talents made his appearance there. He was proceeding as ambassador from Alaù before mentioned, to the Grand Khan, supreme chief of all the Tartars. named Kublaï, whose residence was at the extremity of the continent, in a direction between north-east and east. Not having ever before had an opportunity, although he wished it, of seeing any natives of Italy, he was gratified in a high degree at meeting and conversing with these brothers, who had now become proficients in the Tartar language; and after associating with them for several days, and finding their manners agreeable to him, he proposed to them that they should accompany him to the presence of the Great Khan, who would be pleased by their appearance at his court, which had not hitherto been visited by any person from their country; adding assurances that they would be honourably received, and recompensed with many gifts. Convinced as they were that their endeavours to return homeward would expose them to the most imminent risks, they agreed to this proposal, and recommending themselves to the protection of the Almighty, they set out on their journey in the suite of the ambassador, attended by several Christian servants whom they had brought with them from Venice. The course they took at first was between the north-east and north, and an entire year was consumed before they were enabled to reach the imperial residence, in consequence of the extraordinary delays occasioned by the snows and the swelling of the rivers, which obliged them to halt until the former had melted and the floods had subsided. Many things worthy of admiration were observed by them in the progress of their journey, but which are here omitted, as they will be described by Marco Polo, in the sequel of the book.

Being introduced to the presence of the Grand Khan, Kublaï, the travelers were received by him

with the condescension and affability that belonged
to his character, and as they were the first Latins who
had made their appearance in that country, they were
entertained with feasts and honoured with other
marks of distinction. Entering graciously into conversation with them, he made earnest inquiries on
the subject of the western parts of the world, of the
emperor of the Romans, and of other Christian
kings and princes. He wished to be informed of their
relative consequence, the extent of their possessions,
the manner in which justice was administered in
their several kingdoms and principalities, how they
conducted themselves in warfare, and above all he
questioned them particularly respecting the Pope, the
affairs of the church, and the religious worship and
doctrine of the Christians. Being well instructed and
discreet men, they gave appropriate answers upon all
these points, and as they were perfectly acquainted
with the Tartar (Moghul) language, they expressed
themselves always in becoming terms; insomuch that
the Grand Khan, holding them in high estimation,
frequently commanded their attendance.

When he had obtained all the information that
the two brothers communicated with so much good
sense, he expressed himself well satisfied, and having
formed in his mind the design of employing them as
his ambassadors to the Pope, after consulting with his
ministers on the subject, he proposed to them, with

many kind entreaties, that they should accompany one of his officers, named Khogatal, on a mission to the see of Rome. His object, he told them, was to make a request to his holiness that he would send to him a hundred men of learning, thoroughly acquainted with the principles of the Christian religion, as well as with the seven arts, and qualified to prove to the learned of his dominions, by just and fair argument, that the faith professed by Christians is superior to, and founded upon more evident truth than, any other; that the gods of the Tartars and the idols worshipped in their houses were only evil spirits, and that they and the people of the East in general were under an error in reverencing them as divinities. He moreover signified his pleasure that upon their return they should bring with them, from Jerusalem, some of the holy oil from the lamp which is kept burning over the sepulchre of our Lord Jesus Christ, whom he professed to hold in veneration and to consider as the true God. Having heard these commands addressed to them by the Grand Khan, they humbly prostrated themselves before him, declaring their willingness and instant readiness to perform, to the utmost of their ability, whatever might be the royal will. Upon which he caused letters, in the Tartarian language, to be written in his name to the Pope of Rome, and these he delivered into their hands. He likewise gave orders that they should be

furnished with a golden tablet displaying the imperial cipher, according to the usage established by his
majesty; in virtue of which the person bearing it, together with his whole suite, are safely conveyed and
escorted from station to station by the governors of
all places within the imperial dominions, and are entitled, during the time of their residing in any city,
castle, town, or village, to a supply of provisions and
everything necessary for their accommodation.

Being thus honourably commissioned they took
their leave of the Grand Khan, and set out on their
journey, but had not proceeded more than twenty
days when the officer, named Khogatal, their companion, fell dangerously ill, in the city named Alau. In
this dilemma it was determined, upon consulting all
who were present, and with the approbation of the
man himself, that they should leave him behind. In the
prosecution of their journey they derived essential
benefit from being provided with the royal tablet,
which procured them attention in every place
through which they passed. Their expenses were
defrayed, and escorts were furnished. But notwithstanding these advantages, so great were the natural
difficulties they had to encounter, from the extreme
cold, the snow, the ice, and the flooding of the rivers,
that their progress was unavoidably tedious, and three
years elapsed before they were enabled to reach a sea-
port town in the lesser Armenia, named Laiassus.

Departing from thence by sea, they arrived at Acre in the month of April, 1269, and there learned, with extreme concern, that Pope Clement the Fourth was recently dead. A legate whom he had appointed, named M. Tebaldo de' Vesconti di Piacenza, was at this time resident in Acre, and to him they gave an account of what they had in command from the Grand Khan of Tartary. He advised them by all means to wait the election of another Pope, and when that should take place, to proceed with the objects of their embassy. Approving of this counsel, they determined upon employing the interval in a visit to their families in Venice. They accordingly embarked at Acre in a ship bound to Negropont, and from thence went on to Venice, where Nicolo Polo found that his wife, whom he had left with child at his departure, was dead, after having been delivered of a son, who received the name of Marco, and was now of the age of nineteen years. This is the Marco by whom the present work is composed, and who will give therein a relation of all those matters of which he has been an eye-witness.

In the meantime the election of a Pope was retarded by so many obstacles, that they remained two years in Venice, continually expecting its accomplishment; when at length, becoming apprehensive that the grand khan might be displeased at their delay, or might suppose it was not their intention to revisit his country, they judged it expedient to return to Acre;

and on this occasion they took with them young
Marco Polo. Under the sanction of the legate they
made a visit to Jerusalem, and there provided themselves with some of the oil belonging to the lamp of
the Holy Sepulchre, conformably to the directions of
the grand khan. As soon as they were furnished with
his letters addressed to that prince, bearing testimony
to the fidelity with which they had endeavoured to
execute his commission, and explaining to him that
the Pope of the Christian church had not as yet been
chosen, they proceeded to the before-mentioned port
of Laiassus. Scarcely however had they taken their departure, when the legate received messengers from
Italy, despatched by the College of Cardinals, announcing his own elevation to the Papal Chair; and
he thereupon assumed the name of Gregory the
Tenth. Considering that he was now in a situation
that enabled him fully to satisfy the wishes of the Tartar sovereign, he hastened to transmit letters to the
king of Armenia, communicating to him the event of
his election, and requesting, in case the two ambassadors who were on their way to the court of the
Grand Khan should not have already quitted his dominions, that he would give directions for their immediate return. These letters found them still in
Armenia, and with great alacrity they obeyed the
summons to repair once more to Acre; for which purpose the king furnished them with an armed galley;

sending at the same time an ambassador from himself, to offer his congratulations to the Sovereign Pontiff.

Upon their arrival, His Holiness received them in a distinguished manner, and immediately despatched them with letters papal, accompanied by two friars of the order of Preachers, who happened to be on the spot; men of letters and of science, as well as profound theologians. One of them was named Fra Nicolo da Vicenza, and the other, Fra Guielmo da Tripoli. To them he gave licence and authority to ordain priests, to consecrate bishops, and to grant absolution as fully as he could do in his own person. He also charged them with valuable presents, and among these, several handsome vases of crystal, to be delivered to the Grand Khan in his name, and along with his benediction. Having taken leave, they again steered their course to the port of Laiassus, where they landed, and from thence proceeded into the country of Armenia. Here they received intelligence that the soldan of Babylonia, named Bundokdari, had invaded the Armenian territory with a numerous army, and had overrun and laid waste the country to a great extent. Terrified at these accounts, and apprehensive for their lives, the two friars determined not to proceed further, and delivering over to the Venetians the letters and presents entrusted to them by the Pope, they placed themselves under the protection of the Master of the Knights Templars, and with him returned directly to the coast. Nicolo, Maffeo, and Marco, however, undismayed by perils or difficulties (to which they had long been inured), passed the borders of Armenia, and prosecuted their journey. After crossing deserts of several days' march, and passing many dangerous defiles, they advanced so far, in a direction between north-east and north, that at length they gained information of the grand khan, who then had his residence in a large and magnificent city named Clemen-fu. Their whole journey to this place occupied no less than three years and a half; but, during the winter months, their progress had been inconsiderable. The Grand Khan having notice of their approach whilst still remote, and being aware how much they must have suffered from fatigue, sent forward to meet them at the distance of forty days' journey, and gave orders to prepare in every place through which they were to pass, whatever might be requisite to their comfort. By these means, and through the blessing of God, they were conveyed in safety to the royal court.

Upon their arrival they were honourably and graciously received by the Grand Khan, in a full assembly of his principal officers. When they drew nigh to his person, they paid their respects by prostrating themselves on the floor. He immediately commanded them to rise, and to relate to him the circumstances of their travels, with all that had taken place in their negotiation with His Holiness the

Pope. To their narrative, which they gave in the regular order of events, and delivered in perspicuous
language, he listened with attentive silence. The letters and the presents from Pope Gregory were then
laid before him, and, upon hearing the former read,
he bestowed much commendation on the fidelity,
the zeal, and the diligence of his ambassadors; and receiving with due reverence the oil from the holy
sepulchre, he gave directions that it should be preserved with religious care. Upon his observing
Marco Polo, and inquiring who he was, Nicolo
made answer, "This is your servant, and my son;"
upon which the Grand Khan replied, "He is welcome, and it pleases me much," and he caused him
to be enrolled amongst his attendants of honour.
And on account of their return he made a great feast
and rejoicing; and as long as the said brothers and
Marco remained in the court of the Grand Khan,
they were honoured even above his own courtiers.

Marco was held in high estimation and respect by
all belonging to the court. He learnt in a short time
and adopted the manners of the Tartars, and acquired
a proficiency in four different languages, which he became qualified to read and write. Finding him thus
accomplished, his master was desirous of putting his
talents for business to the proof, and sent him on an
important concern of state to a city named Karazan,
situated at the distance of six months' journey from

the imperial residence; on which occasion he conducted himself with so much wisdom and prudence
in the management of the affairs entrusted to him,
that his services became highly acceptable. On his
part, perceiving that the Grand Khan took a pleasure
in hearing accounts of whatever was new to him respecting the customs and manners of people, and the
peculiar circumstances of distant countries, he endeavoured, wherever he went, to obtain correct information on these subjects, and made notes of all he saw
and heard, in order to gratify the curiosity of his master. In short, during seventeen years that he continued
in his service, he rendered himself so useful, that he
was employed on confidential missions to every part
of the empire and its dependencies; and sometimes
also he travelled on his own private account, but always with the consent, and sanctioned by the authority, of the Grand Khan. Under such circumstances it
was that Marco Polo had the opportunity of acquiring a knowledge, either by his own observation, or
what he collected from others, of so many things, until
his time unknown, respecting the eastern parts of the
world, and which he diligently and regularly committed to writing, as in the sequel will appear. And by this
means he obtained so much honour, that he provoked
the jealousy of the other officers of the court.

Our Venetians having now resided many years at
the imperial court, and in that time having realized

considerable wealth, in jewels of value and in gold, felt a strong desire to revisit their native country, and, however honoured and caressed by the sovereign, this sentiment was ever predominant in their minds. It became the more decidedly their object, when they reflected on the very advanced age of the Grand Khan, whose death, if it should happen previously to their departure, might deprive them of that public assistance by which alone they could expect to surmount the innumerable difficulties of so long a journey, and reach their homes in safety; which on the contrary, in his lifetime, and through his favour, they might reasonably hope to accomplish. Nicolo Polo accordingly took an opportunity one day, when he observed him to be more than usually cheerful, of throwing himself at his feet, and soliciting on behalf of himself and his family to be indulged with his majesty's gracious permission for their departure. But far from showing himself disposed to comply with the request, he appeared hurt at the application, and asked what motive they could have for wishing to expose themselves to all the inconveniences and hazards of a journey in which they might probably lose their lives. If gain, he said, was their object, he was ready to give them the double of whatever they possessed, and to gratify them with honours to the extent of their desires; but that, from the regard he bore to them, he must positively refuse their petition.

It happened, about this period, that a queen named Bolgana, the wife of Arghun, sovereign of India, died, and as her last request (which she likewise left in a testamentary writing) conjured her husband that no one might succeed to her place on his throne and in his affections, who was not a descendant of her own family, now settled under the dominion of the Grand Khan, in the country of Kathay. Desirous of complying with this solemn entreaty, Arghun deputed three of his nobles, discreet men, whose names were Ulatai, Apusca, and Goza, attended by a numerous retinue, as his ambassadors to the grand khan, with a request that he might receive at his hands a maiden to wife, from among the relatives of his deceased queen. The application was taken in good part, and under the directions of his majesty, choice was made of a damsel aged seventeen, extremely handsome and accomplished, whose name was Kogatin, and of whom the ambassadors, upon her being shown to them, highly approved. When everything was arranged for their departure, and a numerous suite of attendants appointed, to do honour to the future consort of king Arghun, they received from the grand khan a gracious dismissal, and set out on their return by the way they came. Having travelled for eight months, their further progress was obstructed and the roads shut up against them, by fresh wars that had broken out amongst the

Tartar princes. Much against their inclinations, there-fore, they were constrained to adopt the measure of returning to the court of the Grand Khan, to whom they stated the interruption they had met with.

About the time of their reappearance, Marco Polo happened to arrive from a voyage he had made, with a few vessels under his orders, to some parts of the East Indies, and reported to the Grand Khan the in-telligence he brought respecting the countries he had visited, with the circumstances of his own navigation, which, he said, was performed in those seas with the utmost safety. This latter observation having reached the ears of the three ambassadors, who were ex-tremely anxious to return to their own country, from whence they had now been absent three years, they presently sought a conference with our Venetians, whom they found equally desirous of revisiting their home; and it was settled between them that the for-mer, accompanied by their young queen, should ob-tain an audience of the Grand Khan, and represent to him with what convenience and security they might effect their return by sea, to the dominions of their master; while the voyage would be attended with less expense than the journey by land, and be performed in a shorter time; according to the experience of Marco Polo, who had lately sailed in those parts. Should His Majesty incline to give his consent to their adopting that mode of conveyance, they were

then to urge him to suffer the three Europeans, as
being persons well skilled in the practice of navigation, to accompany them until they should reach the
territory of King Arghun. The Grand Khan upon receiving this application showed by his countenance
that it was exceedingly displeasing to him, averse as
he was to parting with the Venetians. Feeling nevertheless that he could not with propriety do otherwise
than consent, he yielded to their entreaty. Had it
not been that he found himself constrained by the
importance and urgency of this peculiar case, they
would never otherwise have obtained permission to
withdraw themselves from his service. He sent for
them, however, and addressed them with much kind-
ness and condescension, assuring them of his regard,
and requiring from them a promise that when they
should have resided some time in Europe and with
their own family, they would return to him once
more. With this object in view he caused them to
be furnished with the golden tablet (or royal chop),
which contained his order for their having free and
safe conduct through every part of his dominions,
with the needful supplies for themselves and their attendants. He likewise gave them authority to act in
the capacity of his ambassadors to the Pope, the kings
of France and Spain, and the other Christian princes.

At the same time preparations were made for the
equipment of fourteen ships, each having four masts,

and capable of being navigated with nine sails, the construction and rigging of which would admit of ample description; but, to avoid prolixity, it is for the present omitted. Among these vessels there were at least four or five that had crews of two hundred and fifty or two hundred and sixty men. On them were embarked the ambassadors, having the queen under their protection, together with Nicolo, Maffeo, and Marco Polo, when they had first taken their leave of the Grand Khan, who presented them with many rubies and other handsome jewels of great value. He also gave directions that the ships should be furnished with stores and provisions for two years.

After a navigation of about three months, they arrived at an island which lay in a southerly direction, named Java, where they saw various objects worthy of attention, of which notice shall be taken in the sequel of the work. Taking their departure from thence, they employed eighteen months in the Indian seas before they were enabled to reach the place of their destination in the territory of king Arghun; and during this part of their voyage also they had an opportunity of observing many things, which shall, in like manner, be related hereafter. But here it may be proper to mention, that between the day of their sailing and that of their arrival, they lost by deaths, of the crews of the vessels and others who were embarked, about six hundred persons; and of the three ambassadors, only one, whose name was Goza, survived the voyage; while of all the ladies and female attendants one only died.

Upon landing they were informed that King Arghun had died some time before, and that the government of the country was then administered, on behalf of his son, who was still a youth, by a person of the name of Ki akato. From him they desired to receive instructions as to the manner in which they were to dispose of the princess, whom, by the orders of the late King, they had conducted thither. His answer was, that they ought to present the lady to Kasan, the son of Arghun, who was then at a place on the borders of Persia, which has its denomination from the Arbor secco, where an army of sixty thousand men was assembled for the purpose of guarding certain passes against the irruption of the enemy. This they proceeded to carry into execution, and having effected it, they returned to the residence of Ki-akato, because the road they were afterwards to take lay in that direction. Here, however, they reposed themselves for the space of nine months. When they took their leave he furnished them with four golden tablets, each of them a cubit in length, five inches wide, and weighing three or four marks of gold. Their inscription began with invoking the blessing of the Almighty upon the Grand Khan, that his name might be held in reverence for many years,

and denouncing the punishment of death and con-
fiscation of goods to all who should refuse obedience to the mandate. It then proceeded to direct that
the three ambassadors, as his representatives, should
be treated throughout his dominions with due honour, that their expenses should be defrayed, and that
they should be provided with the necessary escorts.
All this was fully complied with, and from many
places they were protected by bodies of two hundred
horse; nor could this have been dispensed with, as
the government of Ki-akato was unpopular, and the
people were disposed to commit insults and proceed
to outrages, which they would not have dared to
attempt under the rule of their proper sovereign. In
the course of their journey our travellers received
intelligence of the Grand Khan (Kublaï) having
departed this life; which entirely put an end to all
prospect of their revisiting those regions. Pursuing,
therefore, their intended route, they at length reached
the city of Trebizond, from whence they proceeded
to Constantinople, then to Negropont, and finally to
Venice, at which place, in the enjoyment of health
and abundant riches, they safely arrived in the year
1295. On this occasion they offered up their thanks
to God, who had now been pleased to relieve them
from such great fatigues, after having preserved them
from innumerable perils.

Cavelier de La Salle

[FRANCIS PARKMAN]

Among the burghers of Rouen was the old and rich family of the Caveliers. Though citizens and not nobles, some of their connections held high diplomatic posts and honorable employments at Court. They were destined to find a better claim to distinction. In 1643 was born at Rouen Robert Cavelier, better known by the designation of La Salle. His father Jean and his uncle Henri were wealthy merchants, living more like nobles than like burghers; and the boy received an education answering to the marked traits of intellect and character which he soon began to display. He showed an inclination for the exact sciences, and especially for the mathematics, in which he made great proficiency. At an early age, it is said, he became connected with the Jesuits; and, though doubt has been expressed of the statement, it is probably true.

La Salle was always an earnest Catholic; and yet, judging by the qualities which his after life evinced, he was not very liable to religious enthusiasm. It is nevertheless clear that the Society of Jesus may have had a powerful attraction for his youthful imagination. This great organization, so complicated yet so harmonious, a mighty machine moved from the centre by a single hand, was an image of regulated power, full of fascination for a mind like his. But, if it was likely that he would be drawn into it, it was no less likely that he would soon wish to escape. To find himself not at the centre of power, but at the circumference; not the mover, but the moved; the passive instrument of another's will, taught to walk in prescribed paths, to renounce his individuality and become a component atom of a vast whole,— would have been intolerable to him. Nature had shaped him for other uses than to teach a class of boys on the benches of a Jesuit school. Nor, on his part, was he likely to please his directors; for, self-controlled and self-contained as he was, he was far too intractable a subject to serve their turn. A youth whose calm exterior hid an inexhaustible fund of pride; whose inflexible purposes, nursed in secret, the confessional and the "manifestation of conscience" could hardly drag to the light; whose strong personality would not yield to the shaping hand; and who, by a necessity of his nature, could obey no initiative but his own,—was not after the model that Loyola had commended to his followers.

La Salle left the Jesuits, parting with them, it is said, on good terms, and with a reputation of excellent acquirement and unimpeachable morals. This last is very credible. The cravings of a deep ambition, the hunger of an insatiable intellect, the intense longing for action and achievement, subdued in him all other passions; and in his faults the love of pleasure had no part. He had an elder brother in Canada, the Abbé Jean Cavelier, a priest of St. Sulpice. Apparently, it was this that shaped his destinies. His connection with the Jesuits had deprived him, under the French law, of the inheritance of his father, who had died not long before. An allowance was made to him of three or, as is elsewhere stated, four hundred livres a year, the capital of which was paid over to him; and with this pittance he sailed for Canada, to seek his fortune, in the spring of 1666.

Next, we find him at Montreal. In another volume, we have seen how an association of enthusiastic devotees had made a settlement at this place. Having in some measure accomplished its work, it was now dissolved; and the corporation of priests, styled the Seminary of St. Sulpice, which had taken a prominent part in the enterprise, and, indeed, had

been created with a view to it, was now the propri-
etor and the feudal lord of Montreal. It was destined
to retain its seigniorial rights until the abolition of
the feudal tenures of Canada in our own day, and it
still holds vast possessions in the city and island.
These worthy ecclesiastics, models of a discreet and
sober conservatism, were holding a post with which
a band of veteran soldiers or warlike frontiersmen
would have been better matched. Montreal was perhaps the most dangerous place in Canada. In time of
war, which might have been called the normal condition of the colony, it was exposed by its position
to incessant inroads of the Iroquois, or Five Nations,
of New York; and no man could venture into the
forests or the fields without bearing his life in his
hand. The savage confederates had just received a
sharp chastisement at the hands of Courcelle, the
governor; and the result was a treaty of peace, which
might at any moment be broken, but which was an
inexpressible relief while it lasted.

The priests of St. Sulpice were granting out their
lands, on very easy terms, to settlers. They wished to
extend a thin line of settlements along the front of
their island, to form a sort of outpost, from which
an alarm could be given on any descent of the Iroquois. La Salle was the man for such a purpose. Had
the priests understood him,—which they evidently
did not, for some of them suspected him of levity,

the last foible with which he could be charged,—
had they understood him, they would have seen in
him a young man in whom the fire of youth glowed
not the less ardently for the veil of reserve that covered it; who would shrink from no danger, but
would not court it in bravado; and who would cling
with an invincible tenacity of gripe to any purpose
which he might espouse. There is good reason to
think that he had come to Canada with purposes
already conceived, and that he was ready to avail
himself of any stepping-stone which might help to
realize them. Queylus, Superior of the Seminary,
made him a generous offer; and he accepted it. This
was the gratuitous grant of a large tract of land at the
place now called La Chine, above the great rapids of
the same name, and eight or nine miles from Montreal. On one hand, the place was greatly exposed to
attack; and, on the other, it was favorably situated for
the fur-trade. La Salle and his successors became its
feudal proprietors, on the sole condition of delivering to the Seminary, on every change of ownership,
a medal of fine silver, weighing one mark. He entered on the improvement of his new domain with
what means he could command, and began to grant
out his land to such settlers as would join him.

Approaching the shore where the city of Montreal now stands, one would have seen a row of small
compact dwellings, extending along a narrow street,

parallel to the river, and then, as now, called St. Paul Street. On a hill at the right stood the windmill of the seigniors, built of stone, and pierced with loopholes to serve, in time of need, as a place of defence. On the left, in an angle formed by the junction of a rivulet with the St. Lawrence, was a square bastioned fort of stone. Here lived the military governor, appointed by the Seminary, and commanding a few soldiers of the regiment of Carignan. In front, on the line of the street, were the enclosure and buildings of the Seminary, and, nearly adjoining them, those of the Hôtel-Dieu, or Hospital, both provided for defence in case of an Indian attack. In the hospital enclosure was a small church, opening on the street, and, in the absence of any other, serving for the whole settlement.

Landing, passing the fort, and walking southward along the shore, one would soon have left the rough clearings, and entered the primeval forest. Here, mile after mile, he would have journeyed on in solitude, when the hoarse roar of the rapids, foaming in fury on his left, would have reached his listening ear; and at length, after a walk of some three hours, he would have found the rude beginnings of a settlement. It was where the St. Lawrence widens into the broad expanse called the Lake of St. Louis. Here, La Salle had traced out the circuit of a palisaded village, and assigned to each settler half an arpent, or about the third of an acre, within the enclosure, for which he was to render to the young seignior a yearly acknowledgment of three capons, besides six deniers—that is, half a sou—in money. To each was assigned, moreover, sixty arpents of land beyond the limits of the village, with the perpetual rent of half a sou for each arpent. He also set apart a common, two hundred arpents in extent, for the use of the settlers, on condition of the payment by each of five sous a year. He reserved four hundred and twenty arpents for his own personal domain, and on this he began to clear the ground and erect buildings. Similar to this were the beginnings of all the Canadian seigniories formed at this troubled period.

That La Salle came to Canada with objects distinctly in view, is probable from the fact that he at once began to study the Indian languages, and with such success that he is said, within two or three years, to have mastered the Iroquois and seven or eight other languages and dialects. Form the shore of his seigniory, he could gaze westward over the broad breast of the Lake of St. Louis, bounded by the dim forests of Chateauguay and Beauharnois; but his thoughts flew far beyond, across the wild and lonely world that stretched towards the sunset. Like Champlain, and all the early explorers, he dreamed of a passage to the South Sea, and a new road for commerce to the riches of China and Japan. Indians often came to his secluded settlement; and, on one occasion, he was visited by a band of the Seneca Iroquois, not long before the scourge of the colony, but now, in virtue of the treaty, wearing the semblance of friendship. The visitors spent the winter with him, and told him of a river called the Ohio, rising in their country, and flowing into the sea, but at such a distance that its mouth could only be reached after a journey of eight or nine months. Evidently, the Ohio and the Mississippi are here merged into one. In accordance with geographical views then prevalent, he conceived that this great river must needs flow into the "Vermilion Sea;" that is, the Gulf of California. If so, it would give him what he sought, a western passage to China; while, in any case, the populous Indian tribes said to inhabit its banks might be made a source of great commercial profit.

La Salle's imagination took fire. His resolution was soon formed; and he descended the St. Lawrence to Quebec, to gain the countenance of the governor for his intended exploration. Few men were more skilled than he in the art of clear and plausible statement. Both the governor, Courcelle, and the intendant, Talon, were readily won over to his plan; for which, however, they seem to have given him no more substantial aid than that of the governor's letters patent authorizing the enterprise. The cost was to be his own; and he had no money, having spent

it all on his seigniory. He therefore proposed that
the Seminary, which had given it to him, should buy
it back again, with such improvements as he had
made. Queylus, the Superior, being favorably disposed towards him, consented, and bought of him
the greater part; while La Salle sold the remainder,
including the clearings, to one Jean Milot, an iron-
monger, for twenty eight hundred livres With this
he bought four canoes, with the necessary supplies,
and hired fourteen men.

Meanwhile, the Seminary itself was preparing a
similar enterprise. The Jesuits at this time not only
held an ascendency over the other ecclesiastics in
Canada, but exercised an inordinate influence on the
civil government. The Seminary priests of Montreal
were jealous of these powerful rivals, and eager to
emulate their zeal in the saving of souls, and the con-
quering of new domains for the Faith. Under this
impulse, they had, three years before, established a
mission at Quinté, on the north shore of Lake Ontario, in charge of two of their number, one of
whom was the Abbé Fénelon, elder brother of the
celebrated Archbishop of Cambray. Another of them,
Dollier de Casson, had spent the winter in a hunting-
camp of the Nipissings, where an Indian prisoner,
captured in the North-west, told him of populous
tribes of that quarter, living in heathenish darkness.
On this, the Seminary priests resolved to essay their

conversion; and an expedition, to be directed by Dollier, was fitted out to this end.

He was not ill suited to the purpose. He had been a soldier in his youth, and had fought valiantly as an officer of cavalry under Turenne. He was a man of great courage; of a tall, commanding person; and of uncommon bodily strength, which he had notably proved in the campaign of Courcelle against the Iroquois, three years before. On going to Quebec to procure the necessary outfit, he was urged by Courcelle to modify his plans so far as to act in concert with La Salle in exploring the mystery of the great unknown river of the West. Dollier and his brother priests consented. One of them, Galinée, was joined with him as a colleague, because he was skilled in surveying, and could make a map of their route. Three canoes were procured, and seven hired men completed the party. It was determined that La Salle's expedition and that of the Seminary should be combined in one; an arrangement ill suited to the character of the young explorer, who was unfit for any enterprise of which he was not the undisputed chief.

Midsummer was near, and there was no time to lose. Ye the moment was most unpropitious, for a Seneca chief had lately been murdered by three scoundrel soldiers of the fort of Montreal; and, while they were undergoing their trial, it became known that three other Frenchmen had treacherously put to death several Iroquois of the Oneida tribe, in order to get possession of their furs. The whole colony trembled in expectation of a new outbreak of the war. Happily, the event proved otherwise. The authors of the last murder escaped; but the three soldiers were shot at Montreal, in presence of a considerable number of the Iroquois, who declared themselves satisfied with the atonement; and on this same day, the sixth of July, the adventurers began their voyage.

La Chine was the starting-point, and the combined parties, in all twenty-four men with seven canoes, embarked on the Lake of St. Louis. With them were two other canoes, bearing the party of Senecas who had wintered at La Salle's settlement, and who were now to act as guides. Father Gailnée recounts the journey. He was no woodsman: the river, the forests, the rapids, were all new to him, and he dilates on them with the minuteness of a novice. Above all, he admired the Indian birch canoes. "If God," he says, "grants me the grace of returning to France, I shall try to carry one with me." Then he describes the bivouac: "Your lodging is as extraordinary as your vessels; for, after paddling or carrying the canoes all day, you find mother earth ready to receive your wearied body. If the weather is fair, you make a fire and lie down to sleep without farther trouble; but, if it rains, you must peel bark from the trees, and make a shed by laying it on a frame of sticks. As for your food, it is enough to make you burn all the cookery books that ever were written; for in the woods of Canada one finds means to live well without bread, wine, salt, pepper, or spice. The ordinary food is Indian corn, or Turkey wheat as they call it in France, which is crushed between two stones and boiled, seasoning it with meat or fish, when you can get them. This sort of life seemed so strange to us, that we all felt the effects of it; and, before we were a hundred leagues form Montreal, not one of us was free from some malady or other. At last, after all our misery, on the second of August we discovered Lake Ontario, like a great sea with no land beyond it."

Thirty-five days after leaving La Chine, they reached Irondequoit Bay, on the south side of the lake. Here they were met by a number of Seneca Indians, who professed friendship and invited them to their villages, fifteen or twenty miles distant. As this was on their way to the upper waters of the Ohio, and as they hoped to find guides at the villages to conduct them, they accepted the invitation. Dollier, with most of the men, remained to guard the canoes; while La Salle, with Galinée and eight other Frenchmen, accompanied by a troop of Indians, set out on the morning of the twelfth, and reached the principal village before evening. It stood on a hill, in the midst of a clearing nearly two leagues in compass. A rude stockade surrounded it, and as the visitors drew near they saw a band of old men seated on the grass, waiting to receive them. One of these veterans, so feeble with age that he could hardly stand, made them an harangue, in which he declared that the Senecas were their brothers, and invited them to enter the village. The did so, surrounded by a crowd of savages, and presently found themselves in the midst of a disorderly cluster of large but filthy abodes of bark, about a hundred and fifty in number, the most capacious of which was assigned to their use. Here they made their quarters, and were soon overwhelmed by Seneca hospitality. Children brought them pumpkins and berries from the woods, and boy messengers came to summon them to endless feasts, where they were regaled with the flesh of dogs and with boiled maize seasoned with oil pressed from nuts and the seed of sunflowers.

La Salle had flattered himself that he knew enough Iroquois to hold communication with the Senecas; but he failed completely in the attempt. The priests had a Dutch interpreter, who spoke Iroquois fluently, but knew so little French, and was withal so obstinate, the he proved useless; so that it was necessary to employ a man in the service of the Jesuit Fremin, whose mission was at this village. What the party needed was a guide to conduct them to the Ohio; and soon after their arrival a party of warriors appeared, with a young prisoner belonging to one of the tribes of that region. Galinée wanted to beg or buy him from his captors; but the Senecas had other intentions. "I saw," writes the priest, "the most miserable spectacle I ever beheld in my life." It was the prisoner tied to a stake and tortured for six hours with diabolical ingenuity, while the crowd danced and yelled with delight, and the chiefs and elders sat in a row smoking their pipes and watching the contortions of the victim with an air of serene enjoyment. The body was at last cut up and eaten, and in the evening the whole population occupied themselves in scaring away the angry ghost by beating sticks against the bark sides of the lodges.

La Salle and his companions began to fear for their own safety. Some of their hosts wished to kill them in revenge for the chief murdered near Montreal; and, as these and others were at times in a frenzy of drunkenness, the position of the French became critical. They suspected that means had been used to prejudice the Senecas against them. Not only could they get no guides, but they were told that if they went to the Ohio the tribes of those parts would infallibly kill them. Their Dutch interpreter became disheartened and unmanageable, and, after staying a month at the village, the hope of getting farther on their way seemed less than ever. Their plan, it was clear, must be changed; and an Indian from Otinawatawa, a kind of Iroquois colony at the head of

Lake Ontario, offered to guide them to his village and show them a better way to the Ohio. They left the Senecas, coasted the south shore of the lake, passed the mouth of the Niagara, where they heard the distant roar of the cataract, and on the twenty-fourth of September reached Otinawatawa, which was a few miles north of the present town of Hamilton. The inhabitants proved friendly and La Salle received the welcome present of a Shawanoe prisoner, who told them that the Ohio could be reached in six weeks, and that he would guide them to it. Delighted at this good fortune, they were about to set out; when they heard, to their astonishment, of the arrival of two other Frenchmen at a neighboring village. One of the strangers was destined to hold a conspicuous place in the history of western discovery. This was Louis Joliet, a young man of about the age of la Salle. Like him, he had studied for the priesthood; but the world and the wilderness had conquered his early inclinations, and changed him to an active and adventurous fur-trader. Talon had sent him to discover and explore the copper-mines of Lake Superior. He had failed in the attempt, and was now returning. His Indian guide, afraid of passing the Niagara portage lest he should meet enemies, had led him from Lake Erie, by way of Grand River, towards the head of Lake Ontario; and thus it was that he met La Salle and the Sulpitians.

This meeting caused a change of plan. Joliet showed the priests a map which he had made, of such parts of the Upper Lakes as he had visited, and gave them a copy of it; telling them, at the same time, of the Pottawattamies, and other tribes of that region in grievous need of spiritual succor. The result was a determination on their part to follow the route which he suggested, notwithstanding the remonstrances of La Salle, who in vain reminded them that the Jesuits had preoccupied the field, and would regard them as intruders. They resolved that the Pottawattamies should no longer sit in darkness; while, as for the Mississippi, it could be reached, as they conceived, with less risk by this northern route than by that of the south.

La Salle was of a different mind. His goal was the Ohio, and not the northern lakes. A few days before, while hunting, he had been attacked by a fever, sarcastically ascribed by Galinée to his having seen three large rattlesnakes crawling up a rock. He now told his two colleagues that he was in no condition to go forward, and should be forced to part with them. The staple of La Salle's character, as his life will attest, was an invincible determination of purpose, which set at naught all risks and all sufferings. He had cast himself with all his resources into this enterprise, and, while his faculties remained, he was not a man to recoil from it. On the other hand, the masculine fibre of which he was made did not always withhold him from the practice of the arts of address, and the use of what Dollier de Casson styles *belles paroles.* He respected the priesthood, with the exception, it seems, of the Jesuits; and he was under obligations to the Sulpitians of Montreal. Hence there can be no doubt that he used his illness as a pretext for escaping from their company without ungraciousness, and following his own path in his own way.

On the last day of September, the priests made an altar, supported by the paddles of the canoes laid on forked sticks. Dollier said Mass; La Salle and his followers received the sacrament, as did also those of his late colleagues; and thus they parted, the Sulpitians and their party descending the Grand River towards Lake Erie, while La Salle, as they supposed, began his return to Montreal. What course he actually took we shall soon inquire; and meanwhile, for a few moments, we will follow the priests. When they reached Lake Erie, they saw it tossing like an angry ocean. They had no mind to tempt the dangerous and unknown navigation, and encamped for the winter in the forest near the peninsula called the Long Point. Here they gathered a good store of chestnuts, hickory-nuts, plums, and grapes; and built themselves a log cabin, with a recess at the end for an altar. They passed the winter unmolested, shooting game in abundance, and saying mass three times a week. Early in spring, they planted a large cross, attached to it the arms of France, and took formal possession of the country in the name of Louis XIV. This done, they resumed their voyage, and, after many troubles, landed one evening in a state of exhaustion on or near Point Pelée, towards the western extremity of Lake Erie. A storm rose as they lay asleep, and swept off a great part of their baggage, which, in their fatigue, they had left at the edge of the water. Their altar-service was lost with the rest, a misfortune which they ascribed to the jealousy and malice of the Devil. Debarred henceforth from saying Mass, they resolved to return to Montreal and leave the Pottawattamies uninstructed. They presently entered the strait by which Lake Huron joins Lake Erie; and, landing near where Detroit now stands, found a large stone, somewhat suggestive of the human figure, which the Indians had bedaubed with paint, and which they worshipped as a manito. In view of their late misfortune, this device of the arch-enemy excited their utmost resentment. "After the loss of our altar-service," writes Galinée, "and the hunger we had suffered, there was not a man of us who was not filled with hatred against this false deity. I devoted one of my axes to breaking him in pieces; and then, having fastened our canoes side by side, we carried the largest piece to the middle of the river, and threw it, with all the rest,

into the water, that he might never be heard of again.
God rewarded us immediately for this good action,
for we killed a deer and a bear that same day."

This is the first recorded passage of white men
through the Strait of Detroit; though Joliet had, no
doubt, passed this way on his return from the Upper
Lakes. The two missionaries took this course, with
the intention of proceeding to the Saut Sainte Marie,
and there joining the Ottawas, and other tribes of
that region, in their yearly descent to Montreal. They
issued upon Lake Huron; followed its eastern shores
till they reached the Georgian Bay, near the head of
which the Jesuits had established their great mission
of the Hurons, destroyed, twenty years before, by the
Iroquois; and, ignoring or slighting the labors of the
rival missionaries, held their way northward along
the rocky archipelago that edged those lonely coasts.
They passed the Manatoulins, and, ascending the
strait by which Lake Superior discharges its waters,
arrived on the twenty-fifth of May at Ste. Marie du
Saut. Here they found the two Jesuits, Dablon and
Marquette, in a square fort of cedar pickets, built by
their men within the past year, and enclosing a chapel
and a house. Near by, they had cleared a large tract of
land, and sown it with wheat, Indian corn, peas, and
other crops. The new-comers were graciously received, and invited to vespers in the chapel; but they
very soon found La Salle's prediction made good, and

saw that the Jesuit fathers wanted no help from St. Sulpice. Galinée, on his part, takes occasion to remark that, though the Jesuits had baptized a few Indians at the Saut, not one of them was a good enough Christian to receive the Eucharist; and he intimates that the case, by their own showing was still worse at their mission of St. Esprit. The two Sulpitians did not care to prolong their stay; and, three days after their arrival, they left the Saut: not, as they expected, with the Indians, but with a French guide, furnished by the Jesuits. Ascending French River to Lake Nipissing, they crossed to the waters of the Ottawa, and descended to Montreal, which they reached on the eighteenth of June. They had made no discoveries and no converts; but Galinée, after his arrival, made the earliest map of the Upper Lakes known to exist.

We return now to La Salle, only to find ourselves involved in mist and obscurity. What did he do after he left the two priests? Unfortunately, a definite answer is not possible; and the next two years of his life remain in some measure an enigma. That he was busied in active exploration, and that he made important discoveries, is certain; but the extent and character of these discoveries remain wrapped in doubt. He is known to have kept journals and made maps; and these were in existence, and in possession of his niece, Madeleine Cavelier, then in advanced age, as late as the year 1756; beyond which time the most diligent inquiry has failed to trace them. Abbé Faillon affirms that some of La Salle's men, refusing to follow him, returned to La Chine, and that the place then received its name, in derision of the young adventurer's dream of a westward passage to China. As for himself, the only distinct record of his movements is that contained in a paper, entitled "Histoire de Monsieur de La Salle." It is an account of his explorations, and of the state of parties in Canada previous to the year 1678; taken from the lips of La Salle himself, by a person whose name does not appear, but who declares that he had ten or twelve conversations with him at Paris, whither he had come with a petition to the Court. The writer himself had never been in America, and was ignorant of its geography; hence bounders on his part might reasonably be expected. His statements, however, are in some measure intelligible; and the following is the substance of them. After leaving the priests, La Salle went to Onondaga, where we are left to infer that he succeeded better in getting a guide than he had before done among the Senecas. Thence he made his way to a point six or seven leagues distant from Lake Erie, where he reached a branch of the Ohio; and, descending it, followed the river as far as the rapids at Louisville, or, as has been maintained, beyond its confluence with the Mississippi. His men now refused to go farther, and abandoned him, escaping to the English and the Dutch; where upon he retraced his steps alone. This must have been in the winter of 1669–70, or in the following spring; unless there is an error of date in the statement of Nicolas Perrot, the famous *voyageur,* who says that he met him in the summer of 1670, hunting on the Ottawa with a party of Iroquois.

But how was La Salle employed in the following year? The same memoir has its solution to the problem. By this it appears that the indefatigable explorer embarked on Lake Erie, ascended the Detroit to Lake Huron, coasted the unknown shores of Michigan, passed the Straits of Michilimackinac, and, leaving Green Bay behind him, entered what is described as an incomparably larger bay, but which was evidently the southern portion of Lake Michigan. Thence he crossed to a river flowing westward,— evidently the Illinois,—and followed it until it was joined by another river flowing from the north-west to the south-east. By this, the Mississippi only can be meant; and he is reported to have said that he descended it to the thirty-sixth degree of latitude; where he stopped, assured that it discharged itself not into the Gulf of California, but into the Gulf of Mexico; and resolved to follow it thither at a future day, when better provided with men and supplies.

The first of these statements,—that relating to the Ohio,—confused, vague, and in great part incorrect,

as it certainly is, is nevertheless well sustained as regards one essential point. La Salle himself, in a memorial addressed to Count Frontenac in 1677, affirms
that he discovered the Ohio, and descended it as far
as to a fall which obstructed it. Again, his rival, Louis
Joliet, whose testimony on this point cannot be suspected, made two maps of the region of the Mississippi and the Great Lakes. The Ohio is laid down on
both of them, with an inscription to the effect that it
had been explored by La Salle. That he discovered the
Ohio may then be regarded as established. That he
descended it to the Mississippi, he himself does not
pretend; nor is there reason to believe that he did so.

With regard to his alleged voyage down the Illinois,
the case is different. Here, he is reported to have made
a statement which admits but one interpretation,—
that of the discovery by him of the Mississippi prior
to its discovery by Joliet and Marquette. This statement is attributed to a man not prone to vaunt his
own exploits, who never proclaimed them in print,
and whose testimony, even in his own case, must
therefore have weight. But it comes to us through the
medium of a person strongly biased in favor of La
Salle, and against Marquette and the Jesuits.

Seven years had passed since the alleged discovery,
and La Salle had not before laid claim to it; although
it was matter of notoriety that during five years it
had been claimed by Joliet, and that his claim was

generally admitted. The correspondence of the governor and the intendant is silent as to La Salle's having penetrated to the Mississippi; though the attempt was made under the auspices of the latter, as his own letters declare; while both had the discovery of the great river earnestly at heart. The governor, Frontenac, La Salle's ardent supporter and ally, believed in 1672, as his letters show, that the Mississippi flowed into the Gulf of California; and, two years later, he announces to the minister Colbert its discovery by Joliet. After La Salle's death, his brother, his nephew, and his niece addressed a memorial to the king, petitioning for certain grants in consideration of the discoveries of their relative, which they specify at some length; but they do not pretend that he reached the Mississippi before his expeditions of 1679 to 1682. This silence is the more significant, as it is this very niece who had possession of the papers in which La Salle recounts the journeys of which the issues are in question. Had they led him to the Mississippi, it is reasonably certain that she would have made it known in her memorial. La Salle discovered the Ohio, and in all probability the Illinois also; but that he discovered the Mississippi has not been proved, nor, in the light of the evidence we have, is it likely.

Boswell and Johnson in the Hebrides

[JAMES BOSWELL]

D r Johnson had for many years given me hopes that we should go together, and visit the Hebrides. *Martin's Account* of those islands had impressed us with a notion that we might there contemplate a system of life almost totally different from what we had been accustomed to see; and, to find simplicity and wildness, and all the circumstances of remote time or place, so near to our native great island, was an object within the reach of reasonable curiosity. Dr Johnson has said in his Journey, 'that he scarcely remembered how the wish to visit the Hebrides was excited'; but he told me, in summer, 1763, that his father put *Martin's Account* into his hands when he was very young, and that he was much pleased with it. We reckoned there would be some inconveniencies and hardships, and perhaps a little danger; but these we were persuaded were magnified in the imagination of every body. When I was at Ferney, in 1764, I mentioned our design to Voltaire. He looked at me, as if I had talked of going to the North Pole, and said, 'You do not insist on my accompanying you?' 'No, sir.' 'Then I am very willing you should go.' I was not afraid that our curious expedition would be prevented by such apprehensions; but I doubted that it would not be possible to prevail on Dr Johnson to relinquish, for some time, the felicity of a London life, which, to a man who can enjoy it with full intellectual relish, is apt to make existence in any narrower sphere seem insipid or irksome. I doubted that he would not be willing to come down from his elevated state of philosophical dignity; from a superiority of wisdom among the wise, and of learning among the learned; and from flashing his wit upon minds bright enough to reflect it.

He had disappointed my expectations so long, that I began to despair; but in spring, 1773, he talked of coming to Scotland that year with so much firmness, that I hoped he was at last in earnest. I knew that, if he were once launched from the metropolis, he would go forward very well; and I got our common friends there to assist in setting him afloat. To Mrs Thrale in particular, whose enchantment over him seldom failed, I was much obliged. It was, 'I'll give thee a wind.' 'Thou art kind.'

Dr Samuel Johnson's character, religious, moral, political, and literary, nay his figure and manner, are, I believe, more generally known than those of almost any man; yet it may not be superfluous here to attempt a sketch of him. Let my readers then re-
ㅡㅡㅡ ㅡㅡㅡ ㅡㅡㅡ ㅡㅡㅡ ㅡㅡㅡ ㅡㅡㅡ ㅡㅡㅡ Christian,
of high Church of England and monarchical principles, which he would not tamely suffer to be questioned; steady and inflexible in maintaining the obligations of piety and virtue, both from a regard to the order of society, and from a veneration for the Great Source of all order; correct, nay stern in his taste; hard to please, and easily offended, impetuous and irritable in his temper, but of a most humane and benevolent heart; having a mind stored with a vast and various collection of learning and knowledge, which he communicated with peculiar perspicuity and force, in rich and choice expression. He united a most logical head with a most fertile imagination, which gave him an extraordinary advantage in arguing; for he could reason close or wide, as he saw best for the moment. He could, when he chose it, be the greatest sophist that ever wielded a weapon in the schools of declamation; but he indulged this only in conversation; for he owned he sometimes talked for victory; he was too conscientious to make

errour permanent and pernicious, by deliberately writing it. He was conscious of his superiority. He loved praise when it was brought to him; but was too proud to seek for it. He was somewhat susceptible of flattery. His mind was so full of imagery, that he might have been perpetually a poet. It has been often remarked, that in his poetical pieces, which it is to be regretted are so few, because so excellent, his style is easier than in his prose. There is deception in this: it is not easier, but better suited to the dignity of verse; as one may dance with grace, whose motions, in ordinary walking—in the common step— are awkward. He had a constitutional melancholy, the clouds of which darkened the brightness of his fancy, and gave a gloomy cast to his whole course of thinking: yet, though grave and awful in his deportment, when he thought it necessary or proper, he frequently indulged himself in pleasantry and sportive sallies. He was prone to superstition, but not to credulity. Though his imagination might incline him to a belief of the marvellous, and the mysterious, his vigorous reason examined the evidence with jealousy. He had a loud voice, and a slow deliberate utterance, which no doubt gave some additional weight to the sterling metal of his conversation. Lord Pembroke said once to me at Wilton, with a happy pleasantry, and some truth, that 'Dr Johnson's sayings would not appear so extraordinary, were it not for his bow-wow way': but I admit the truth of this only on some occasions. The Messiah, played upon the Canterbury organ, is more sublime than when played upon an inferior instrument: but very slight musick will seem grand, when conveyed to the ear through that majestick medium. WHILE THEREFORE DOCTOR JOHNSON'S SAYINGS ARE READ, LET HIS MANNER, BE TAKEN ALONG WITH THEM. Let it however be observed, that the sayings themselves are generally great; that, though he might be an ordinary composer at times, he was for the most part a Handel. His person was large, robust, I may say approaching to the gigantick, and grown unwieldy from corpulency. His countenance was naturally of the craft of an ancient statue, but somewhat disfigured by the scars of that evil, which, it was formerly imagined, the royal touch could cure. He was now in his sixty-fourth year, and was become a little dull of hearing. His sight had always been somewhat weak; yet, so much does mind govern, and even supply the deficiency of organs, that his perceptions were uncommonly quick and accurate. His head, and sometimes also his body, shook with a kind of motion like the effect of a palsy: he appeared to be frequently disturbed by cramps, or convulsive contractions, (Footnote: Such they appeared to me: but since the first edition, Sir Joshua Reynolds has observed to me, 'that Dr Johnson's

extraordinary gestures were only habits, in which he
indulged himself at certain times. When in company,
where he was not free, or when engaged earnestly
in conversation, he never gave way to such habits,
which proves that they were not involuntary', I still
however think, that these gestures were involuntary;
for surely had not that been the case, he would have
restrained them in the publick streets.) of the nature
of that distemper called St Vitus's dance. He wore a
full suit of plain brown clothes, with twisted-hair
buttons of the same colour, a large bushy greyish
wig, a plain shirt, black worsted stockings, and silver
buckles. Upon this tour, when journeying, he wore
boots, and a very wide brown cloth great coat, with
pockets which might have almost held the two volumes of his folio dictionary; and he carried in his
hand a large English oak stick. Let me not be cen-
sured for mentioning such minute particulars. Every
thing relative to so great a man is worth observing. I
remember Dr Adam Smith, in his rhetorical lectures
at Glasgow, told us he was glad to know that Milton
wore latchets in his shoes, instead of buckles. When
I mention the oak stick, it is but letting Hercules
have his club; and, by-and-by, my readers will find
this stick will bud, and produce a good joke.

His prejudice against Scotland was announced almost as soon as he began to appear in the world of

letters. In his London, a poem, are the following nervous lines:

For who would leave, unbrib'd, Hibernia's land
Or change the rocks of Scotland for the Strand
There none are swept by sudden fate away;
But all, whom hunger spares, with age decay.

The truth is, like the ancient Greeks and Romans, he allowed himself to look upon all nations but his own as barbarians: not only Hibernia, and Scotland, but Spain, Italy, and France, are attacked in the same poem. If he was particularly prejudiced against the Scots, it was because they were more in his way; because he thought their success in England rather exceeded the due proportion of their real merit; and because he could not but see in them that nationality which I believe no liberal-minded Scotsman will deny. He was indeed, if I may be allowed the phrase, at bottom much of a John Bull; much of a blunt 'true born Englishman'. There was a stratum of common clay under the rock of marble. He was voraciously fond of good eating; and he had a great deal of that quality called humour, which gives an oiliness and a gloss to every other quality.

I am, I flatter myself, completely a citizen of the world. In my travels through Holland, Germany,

Switzerland, Italy, Corsica, France, I never felt myself from home; and I sincerely love 'every kindred and tongue and people and nation'. I subscribe to what my late truly learned and philosophical friend Mr Crosbie said, that the English are better animals than the Scots; they are nearer the sun; their blood is richer, and more mellow: but when I humour any of them in an outrageous contempt of Scotland, I fairly own I treat them as children. And thus I have, at some moments, found myself obliged to treat even Dr Johnson.

To Scotland however he ventured; and he returned from it in great humour, with his prejudices much lessened, and with very grateful feelings of the hospitality with which he was treated; as is evident from that admirable work, his Journey to the Western Islands of Scotland, which, to my utter astonishment, has been misapprehended, even to rancour, by many of my countrymen.

[Editor's note: two weeks later, they are well on their way.]

Wednesday, 1st September

I awaked very early. I began to imagine that the landlord, being about to emigrate, might murder us to get our money, and lay it upon the soldiers in the barn. Such groundless fears will arise in the mind,

before it has resumed its vigour after sleep! Dr Johnson had had the same kind of ideas; for he told me
afterwards, that he considered so many soldiers, having seen us, would be witnesses, should any harm be
done, and that circumstance, I suppose, 'he considered as a security. When I got up, I found him sound
asleep in his miserable stye, as I may call it, with a
coloured handkerchief tied round his head. With
difficulty could I awaken him. It reminded me of
Henry the Fourth's fine soliloquy on sleep; for there
was here as 'uneasy a pallet' as the poet's imagination
could possibly conceive.

A red coat of the 15th regiment, whether officer,
or only serjeant, I could not be sure, came to the
house, in his way to the mountains to shoot deer,
which it seems the Laird of Glenmorison does not
hinder any body to do. Few, indeed, can do them
harm. We had him to breakfast with us. We got away
about eight. M'Queen walked some miles to give us
a convoy. He had, in 1745, joined the Highland army
at Fort Augustus, and continued in it till after the battle of Culloden. As he narrated the particulars of that
ill-advised, but brave attempt, I could not refrain from
tears. There is a certain association of ideas in my
mind upon that subject, by which I am strongly affected. The very Highland names, or the sound of a
bagpipe; will stir my blood, and fill me with a mix-
ture of melancholy and respect for courage; with pity

for an unfortunate and superstitious regard for antiq-
uity, and thoughtless inclination for war; in short,
with a crowd of sensations with which sober ration-
ality has nothing to do.

We passed through Glensheal, with prodigious
mountains on each side. We saw where the battle
was fought in the year 1719; Dr Johnson owned he
was now in a scene of as wild nature as he could see;
but he corrected me sometimes in my inaccurate
observations. 'There,' said I, 'is a mountain like a
cone.' JOHNSON. 'No, sir. It would be called so in
a book; and when a man comes to look at it, he sees
it is not so. It is indeed pointed at the top; but one
side of it is larger than the other.' Another mountain
I called immense. JOHNSON. 'No; it is no more
than a considerable protuberance.'

We came to a rich green valley, comparatively
speaking, and stopped a while to let our horses rest
and eat grass. (Dr Johnson, in his Journey, thus beautifully describes his situation here: 'I sat down on a
bank, such as a writer of romance might have delighted to feign. I had, indeed, no trees to whisper
over my head; but a clear rivulet streamed at my feet.
The day was calm, the air soft, and all was rudeness,
silence, and solitude. Before me, and on either side,
were high hills, which, by hindering the eye from
ranging, forced the mind to find entertainment for

itself. Whether I spent the hour well, I know not: for here I first conceived the thought of this narration.' The Critical Reviewers, with a spirit and expression worthy of the subject, say, 'We congratulate the publick on the event with which this quotation concludes, and are fully persuaded that the hour in which the entertaining traveller conceived this narrative will be annihilated, by every reader of taste, as a fortunate event in the annals of literature. Were it suitable to the talk in which we are at present engaged, to indulge ourselves in a poetical flight, we would invoke the winds of the Caledonian mountains to blow for ever, with their softest breezes, on the bank where our author reclined, and request of Flora, that it might be perpetually adorned with the gayest and most fragrant productions of the year.') We soon afterwards came to Auchnasheal, a kind of rural village, a number of cottages being built together, as we saw all along in the Highlands. We passed many miles this day without seeing a house, but only little summer-huts, called shielings. Evan Campbell, servant to Mr Murchison, factor to the Laird of Macleod in Glenelg, ran along with us to-day. He was a very obliging fellow. At Auchnasheal, we sat down on a green turf-seat at the end of a house; they brought us out two wooden dishes of milk, which we tasted. One of them was frothed like a syllabub. I saw a woman preparing it with such a stick as is used for chocolate, and in the same manner. We had a considerable circle about us, men, women and children, all M'Craas, Lord Seaforth's people. Not one of them could speak English. I observed to Dr Johnson, it was much the same as being with a tribe of Indians. JOHNSON. 'Yes, sir; but not so terrifying.' I gave all who chose it, snuff and tobacco. Governour Trapaud had made us buy a quantity at Fort Augustus, and put them up in small parcels. I also gave each person a bit of wheat bread, which they had never tasted before. I then gave a penny apiece to each child. I told Dr Johnson of this; upon which he called to Joseph and our guides, for change for a shilling, and declared that he would distribute among the children. Upon this being announced in Erse, there was a great stir; not only did some children come running down from neighbouring huts, but I observed one black-haired man, who had been with us all along, had gone off, and returned, bringing a very young child. My fellow traveller then ordered the children to be drawn up in a row; and he dealt about his copper, and made them and their parents all happy. The poor M'Craas, whatever may be their present state, were of considerable estimation in the year 1715, when there was a line in a song.

And aw the brave M'Craas are coming.

(The M'Craas, or Macraes, were since that time
brought into the king's army, by the late Lord
Seaforth. When they lay in Edinburgh castle in 1778,
and were ordered to embark for Jersey, they with a
number of other men in the regiment, for different
reasons, but especially an apprehension that they were
to be sold to the East-India Company, though enlisted not to be sent out of Great-Britain without
their own consent, made a determined mutiny and
encamped upon the lofty mountain, Arthur's Seat,
where they remained three days and three nights;
bidding defiance to all the force in Scotland. At last
they came down, and embarked peaceably, having
obtained formal articles of capitulation, signed by Sir
Adolphus Oughton, commander in chief, General
Skene, deputy commander, the Duke of Buccleugh,
and the Earl of Dunmore, which quieted them. Since
the secession of the Commons of Rome to the Mons
Sacer, a more spirited exertion has not been made. I
gave great attention to it from first to last, and have
drawn up a particular account of it. Those brave fellows have since served their country effectually at
Jersey, and also in the East Indies, to which, after
being better informed, they voluntarily agreed to go.)

There was great diversity in the faces of the circle
around us: Some were as black and wild in their appearance as any American savages whatever. One
woman was as comely almost as the figure of Sappho,

as we see it painted. We asked the old woman, the mistress of the house where we had the milk, (which by the bye, Dr Johnson told me, for I did not observe it myself, was built not of turf, but of stone,) what we should pay. She said, what we pleased. One of our guides asked her, in Erse, if a shilling was enough. She said, 'Yes.' But some of the men bade her ask more. This vexed me; because it shewed a desire to impose upon strangers, as they knew that even a shilling was high payment. The woman, however, honestly persisted in her price; so I gave her half a crown. Thus we had one good scene of life uncommon to us. The people were very much pleased, gave us many blessings, and said they had not had such a day since the old Laird of Macleod's time.

Dr Johnson was much refreshed by this repast. He was pleased when I told him he would make a good chief. He said, 'Were I a chief, I would dress my servants better than myself, and knock a fellow down if he looked saucy to a Macdonald in rags: but I would not treat men as brutes. I would let them know why all of my clan were to have attention paid to them. I would tell my upper servants why, and make them tell the others.'

We rode on well, till we came to the high mountain called the Rattakin, by which time both Dr Johnson and the horses were a good deal fatigued. It is a terrible steep climb, notwithstanding the road is formed slanting along it; however, we made it out. On the top of it we met Captain M'Leod of Balmenoch (a Dutch officer who had come from Sky) riding with his sword slung across him. He asked, 'Is this Mr Boswell?' which was a proof that we were expected. Going down the hill on the other side was no easy task. As Dr Johnson was a great weight, the two guides agreed that he should ride the horses alternately. Hay's were the two best, and the Doctor would not ride but upon one or other of them, a black or a brown. But, as Hay complained much after ascending the Rattakin, the Doctor was prevailed with to mount one of Vass's greys. As he rode upon it down hill, it did not go well; and he grumbled. I walked on a little before, but was excessively entertained with the method taken to keep him in good humour. Hay led the horse's head, talking to Dr Johnson as much as he could; and (having heard him, in the forenoon, express a pastoral pleasure on seeing the goats browzing) just when the Doctor was uttering his displeasure, the fellow cried, with a very Highland accent, 'See such pretty goats!' Then he whistled, WHU! and made them jump. Little did he conceive what Doctor Johnson was. Here now was a common ignorant Highland clown imagining that he could divert, as one does a child, DR SAMUEL JOHNSON! The ludicrousness, absurdity, and extraordinary contrast between what the fellow fancied, and the reality, was truly comick. It grew dusky; and we had a very tedious ride for what was called five miles; but I am sure would measure ten. We had no conversation. I was riding forward to the inn at Glenelg, on the shore opposite to Sky, that I might take proper measures, before Dr Johnson, who was now advancing in dreary silence, Hay leading his horse, should arrive. Vass also walked by the side of his horse, and Joseph followed behind: as therefore he was thus attended, and seemed to be in deep meditation, I thought there could be no harm in leaving him for a little while. He called me back with a tremendous shout, and was really in a passion with me for leaving him. I told him my intentions, but he was not satisfied, and said, 'Do you know, I should as soon have thought of picking a pocket, as doing so.' BOSWELL. 'I am diverted with you, sir.' JOHNSON. 'Sir, I could never be diverted with incivility. Doing such a thing, makes one lose confidence in him who has done it, as one cannot tell what he may do next.' His extraordinary warmth confounded me so much, that I justified myself but lamely to him; yet my intentions were not improper. I wished to get on, to see how we were to be lodged, and how we were to get a boat; all which I thought I could best settle myself, without his having any trouble. To apply his great mind to minute particulars, is wrong: it is like taking an immense balance, such as is kept on quays for weighing cargoes of ships, to weigh a guinea. I knew I had neat little scales, which would do better; and that his attention to every thing which falls in his way, and his uncommon desire to be always in the right, would make him weigh, if he knew of the particulars: it was right therefore for me to weigh them, and let him have them only in effect. I however continued to ride by him, finding he wished I should do so.

As we passed the barracks at Bernea, I looked at them wishfully, as soldiers have always every thing in the best order: but there was only a serjeant and a few men there. We came on to the inn at Glenelg. There was no provender for our horses: so they were sent to grass, with a man to watch them. A maid shewed us up stairs into a room damp and dirty, with bare walls, a variety of bad smells, a coarse black greasy fir table, and forms of the same kind; and out of a wretched bed started a fellow from his sleep, like Edgar in King Lear, 'Poor Tom's a-cold'. (It is amusing to observe the different im-ages which this being presented to Dr Johnson and me. The Doctor, in his Journey, compares him to a Cyclops.)

This inn was furnished with not a single article that we could either eat or drink; but Mr Murchi-son, factor to the Laird of Macleod in Glenelg, sent us a bottle of rum and some sugar, with a polite message, to acquaint us, that he was very sorry that he did not hear of us till we had passed his house, otherwise he should have insisted on our sleeping there that night; and that, if he were not obliged to set out for Inverness early next morning, he would have waited upon us. Such extraordinary attention from this gentleman, to entire strangers, deserves the most honourable commemoration.

Our bad accommodation here made me uneasy, and almost fretful. Dr Johnson was calm. I said, he was so from vanity. JOHNSON. 'No, sir, it is from philosophy.' It pleased me to see that the Rambler could practise so well his own lessons.

I resumed the subject of my leaving him on the road, and endeavoured to defend it better. He was still violent upon that head, and said, 'Sir, had you gone on, I was thinking that I should have returned with you to Edinburgh, and then have parted from you, and never spoken to you more.'

I sent for fresh hay, with which we made beds for ourselves, each in a room, equally miserable. Like Wolfe, we had a 'choice of difficulties'. Dr Johnson made things easier by comparison. At M'Queen's, last night, he observed, that few were so well lodged in a ship. To-night he said, we were better than if we had been upon the hill. He lay down buttoned up in his great coat. I had my sheets spread on the hay, and my clothes and great coat laid over me, by way of blankets.

Thursday, 2d September

I had slept ill. Dr Johnson's anger had affected me much. I considered that, without any bad intention, I might suddenly forfeit his friendship, and was impatient to see him this morning. I told him how uneasy he had made me, by what he had said, and reminded him of his own remark at Aberdeen, upon old friendships being hastily broken off. He owned, he had spoken to me in passion; that he would not have done what he threatened; and that, if he had, he should have been ten times worse than I; that forming intimacies, would indeed be 'limning the water', were they liable to such sudden dissolution; and he added, 'Let's think no more on't.' BOSWELL. 'Well then, sir, I shall be easy. Remember, I am to have fair warning in case of any quarrel. You are never to spring a mine upon me. It was absurd in me to believe you.' JOHNSON. 'You deserved about as much, as to believe me from night to morning.' After breakfast, we got into a boat for Sky. It rained much when we set off, but cleared up as we advanced. One of the boatmen, who spoke English, said, that a mile at land was two miles at sea. I then observed, that from Glenelg to Armidale in Sky, which was our present course, and is called

twelve, was only six miles: but this he could not understand. 'Well,' said Dr Johnson, 'never talk to me of
the native good sense of the Highlanders. Here is a
fellow who calls one mile two, and yet cannot comprehend that twelve such imaginary miles make in
truth but six.'

We reached the shore of Armidale before one
o'clock. Sir Alexander M'Donald came down to receive us. He and his lady (formerly Miss Bosville of
Yorkshire) were then in a house built by a tenant at
this place, which is in the district of Slate, the family mansion here having been burned in Sir Donald
Macdonald's time.

The most ancient seat of the chief of the Mac-
donalds in the Isle of Sky was at Duntulm, where
there are the remains of a stately castle. The principal residence of the family is now at Mugstot, at
which there is a considerable building. Sir Alexander and Lady Macdonald had come to Armidale in
their way to Edinburgh, where it was necessary for
them to be soon after this time.

Armidale is situated on a pretty bay of the narrow
sea, which flows between the main land of Scotland
and the Isle of Sky. In front there is a grand prospect
of the rude mountains of Moidart and Knoidart.
Behind are hills gently rising and covered with a
finer verdure than I expected to see in this climate,

and the scene is enlivened by a number of little clear brooks.

Sir Alexander Macdonald having been an Eton scholar, and being a gentleman of talents, Dr Johnson had been very well pleased with him in London. But my fellow traveller and I were now full of the old Highland spirit, and were dissatisfied at hearing of racked rents and emigration; and finding a chief not surrounded by his clan. Dr Johnson said, 'Sir, the Highland chiefs should not be allowed to go farther south than Aberdeen. A strong-minded man, like Sir James Macdonald, may be improved by an English education; but in general, they will be tamed into insignificance.'

We found here Mr Janes of Aberdeenshire, a naturalist. Janes said he had been at Dr Johnson's in London, with Ferguson the astronomer. JOHNSON. 'It is strange that, in such distant places, I should meet with any one who knows me. I should have thought I might hide myself in Sky.'

South Coast Discovery 1801

[EARNEST SCOT T]

That part of the coast lying between the south-west corner of the continent and Fowler's Bay, in the Great Australian Bight, had been traversed prior to this time. In 1791 Captain George Vancouver, in the British ship Cape Chatham, sailed along it from Cape Leeuwin to King George's Sound, which he discovered and named. He anchored in the harbour, and remained there for a fortnight. He would have liked to pursue the discovery of this unknown country, and did sail further east, as far as the neighbourhood of Termination Island, in longitude 122 degrees 8 minutes. But, meeting with adverse winds, he abandoned the research, and resumed his voyage to north-west America across the

Pacific. In 1792, Bruny Dentrecasteaux, with the French ships Recherche and Esperance, searching for tidings of the lost Laperouse, followed the line of the shore more closely than Vancouver had done, and penetrated much further eastward. His instructions, prepared by Fleurieu, had directed him to explore the whole of the southern coast of Australia; but he was short of water, and finding nothing but sand and rock, with no harbour, and no promise of a supply of what he so badly needed, he did not continue further than longitude 131 degrees 38½ minutes east, about two and a half degrees east of the present border line of Western and South Australia. These navigators, with the Dutchman Pieter Nuyts, in the early part of the seventeenth century, and the Frenchman St. Alouarn, who anchored near the Leeuwin in 1772, were the only Europeans known to have been upon any part of these southern coasts before the advent of Flinders; and the extent of the voyage of Nuyts is by no means clear.

Flinders laid it down as a guiding principle that he would make so complete a survey of the shores visited by him as to leave little for anybody to do after him. He therefore commenced his work im-mediately when he touched land, constructing his own charts as the ship slowly traversed the curves of the coast. The result was that many corrections and additions to the charts of Vancouver and Dentrecasteaux were made before the entirely new discoveries were commenced. In announcing this fact, Flinders, always generous in his references to good work done by his predecessors, warmly praised the charts prepared by Beautemps-Beaupre, "geographical engineer" of the Recherche. "Perhaps no chart of a coast so little known as this is, will bear a comparison with its original better than this of M. Beaupre," he said. His own charts were of course fuller and more precise, but he made no claim to superiority on this account, modestly observing that he would have been open to reproach if, after following the coast with an outline of M. Beaupre's chart before him, he had not effected improvements where circumstances did not permit so close an examination to be made in 1792.

Several inland excursions were made, and some of the King George's Sound aboriginals were encountered. Flinders noted down some of their words, and pointed out the difference from words for the same objects used by Port Jackson and Van Diemen's Land natives. An exception to this rule was the word used for calling to a distance—cau-wah! (come here). This is certainly very like the Port Jackson cow-ee, whence comes the one aboriginal word of universal employment in Australia to-day, the coo-ee of the townsman and the bushman alike, a call entered in the vocabulary collected by Hunter as early as 1790.

The method of research adopted by Flinders was similar to that employed on the Norfolk voyage. The ship was kept all day as close inshore as possible, so that water breaking on the shore was visible from the deck, and no river or opening could escape notice. When this could not be done, because the coast retreated far back, or was dangerous, the commander stationed himself at the masthead with a glass. All the bearings were laid down as soon as taken, whilst the land was in sight; and before retiring to rest at night Flinders made it a practice to finish up his rough chart for the day, together with his journal of observations. The ship hauled off the coast at dusk, but especial care was taken to come upon it at the same point next morning, as soon after daylight as practicable, so that work might be resumed precisely where it had been dropped on the previous day. "This plan," said Flinders, "to see and lay down everything myself, required constant attention and much labour, but was absolutely necessary to obtaining that accuracy of which I was desirous." When bays or groups of islands were reached, Flinders went ashore with the theodolite, took his angles, measured, mapped, and made topographical notes. The lead was kept busy, making soundings. The rise and fall of the tides were observed; memoranda on natural phenomena were written; opportunities were given for the naturalists to collect specimens, and for the artist to make drawings. The net was frequently drawn in the bays for examples of marine life. Everybody when ashore kept a look out for plants, birds, beasts, and insects. In short, a keenness for investigation, an assiduity in observation, animated the whole ship's company, stimulated by the example of the commander, who never spared himself in his work, and interested himself in that of others.

As in a drama, "comic relief" was occasionally interposed amid more serious happenings. The blacks were friendly, though occasionally shy and suspicious. In one scene the mimicry that is a characteristic of the aboriginal was quaintly displayed. The incident, full of colour and humour, is thus related by Flinders:

> Our friends, the natives, continued to visit us; and an old man with several others being at the tents this morning, I ordered the party of marines on shore, to be exercised in their presence. The red coats and white crossed belts were greatly admired, having some resemblance to their own manner of ornamenting themselves; and the drum, but particularly the fife, excited their astonishment; but when they saw these beautiful red and white men, with their bright muskets, drawn up in a line, they absolutely screamed with delight; nor were their wild gestures and vociferation to be silenced but by commencing the

exercise, to which they paid the most earnest and silent attention. Several of them moved their hands, involuntarily, according to the motions; and the old man placed himself at the end of the rank, with a short staff in his hand, which he shouldered, presented, grounded, as did the marines their muskets, without, I believe, knowing what he did. Before firing, the Indians were made acquainted with what was going to take place; so that the volleys did not excite much terror.

Seaman Smith was naturally much interested in the aboriginals, whose features were however to him "quite awful, having such large mouths and long teeth." They were totally without clothing, and "as soon as they saw our tents they run into the bushes with such activity that would pawl any European to exhibit. Because our men would not give them a small tommy-hawk they began to throw pieces of wood at them, which exasperated our men; but orders being so humane towards the natives that we must put up with anything but heaving spears." Furthermore, "they rubbd their skin against ours, expecting some mark of white upon their's, but finding their mistake they appeared surprised."

Pleasures more immediately incidental to geographical discovery—those pleasures which eager and enterprising minds must experience, however

severe the labour involved, on traversing portions of
the globe previously unknown to civilised man-
kind—commenced after the head of the Great
Bight was passed. From about the vicinity of Fowler's
Bay (named after the first lieutenant of the Investigator) the coast was virgin to geographical science.
Comparisons of original work with former charts
were no longer possible. The ship was traversing un
navigated waters, and the coasts delineated were
new to the world's knowledge. The quickening of
the interest in the work in hand, which touched
both officers and men of the expedition, can be felt
by the reader of Flinders' narrative. There was a consciousness of having crossed a line separating what
simply required verification and amplification, from
a totally fresh field of research. Every reach of coastline now traversed was like a cable, long buried in
the deep of time, at length hauled into daylight,
with its oozy deposits of seaweed, shell and mud
lying thick upon it.

Contingent upon discovery was the pleasure of
naming important features of the coast. It is doubtful whether any other single navigator in history applied names which are still in use to so many capes,
bays and islands, upon the shores of the habitable
globe, as Flinders did. The extent of coastline freshly
discovered by him was not so great as that first explored by some of his predecessors. But no former

navigator pursued extensive new discoveries so minutely, and, consequently, found so much to name; while the precision of Flinders' records left no doubt about the places that he named, when in later years the settlement of country and the navigation of seas necessitated the use of names. Compare, for instance, in this one respect, the work of Cook and Dampier, Vasco da Gama and Magellan, Tasman and Quiros, with that of Flinders. Historically their voyages may have been in some respects more important; but they certainly added fewer names to the map. There are 103 names on Cook's charts of eastern Australia from Point Hicks to Cape York; but there are about 240 new names on the charts of Flinders representing southern Australia and Tasmania. He is the Great Denominator among navigators. He named geographical features after his friends, after his associates on the Investigator, after distinguished persons connected with the Navy, after places in which he was interested. Fowler's Bay, Point Brown, Cape Bauer, Franklin's Isles, Point Bell, Point Westall, Taylor's Isle, and Thistle Island, commemorate his shipmates. Spencer's Gulf was named "in honour of the respected nobleman who presided at the Board of Admiralty when the voyage was planned and the ship was put in commission," and Althorp Isles celebrated Lord Spencer's heir. Cockburn, Nomenclature of South Australia, is mis-

taken in speculating that "there is a parish of Althorp in Flinders' native country in Lincolnshire
which probably accounts for the choice of the name
here." Althorp, which should be spelt without a final
"e," is not in Lincolnshire, but in Northampton-
shire. St. Vincent's Gulf was named "in honour of
the noble admiral" who was at the head of the Admiralty when the Investigator sailed from England,
and who had "continued to the voyage that countenance and protection of which Earl Spencer had
set the example." To Yorke's Peninsula, between the
two gulfs, was affixed the name of the Right Hon.
C.P. Yorke, afterwards Lord Hardwicke, the First
Lord who authorised the publication of Flinders'
Voyage. Thus, the ministerial heads of the Admiralty
in three Governments (Pitt's, Addington's and Spencer
Perceval's) came to be commemorated. It may be
remarked as curious that a naval officer so proud of
his service as Flinders was, should nowhere have
employed the name of the greatest sailor of his age,
Nelson. There is a Cape Nelson on the Victorian
coast, but that name was given by Grant.

In Spencer's Gulf we come upon a group of Lin-
colnshire place-names, for Flinders, his brother
Samuel, the mate, Fowler, and Midshipman John
Franklin, all serving on this voyage, were Lincolnshire
men. Thus we find Port Lincoln, Sleaford Bay, Louth
Bay, Cape Donington, Stamford Hill, Surfleet Point,

Louth Isle, Sibsey Isle, Stickney Isle, Spilsby Isle, Part-
ney Isle, Revesby Isle, Point Boston, and Winceby
Isle. Banks' name was given to a group of islands, and
Coffin's Bay must not be allowed to suggest any
gruesome association, for it was named after Sir Isaac
Coffin, resident naval commissioner at Sheerness,
who had given assistance in the equipment of the Investigator. A few names, like Streaky Bay, Lucky Bay,
and Cape Catastrophe, were applied from circumstances that occurred on the voyage. A poet of the antipodes who should, like Wordsworth, be moved to
write "Poems on the Naming of Places," would find
material in the names given by Flinders.

Interest in this absorbing work rose to something
like excitement on February 20th, when there were
indications, from the set of the tide, that an unusual
feature of the coast was being approached. "The tide
from the north-eastward, apparently the ebb, ran
more than one mile an hour, which was the more
remarkable from no set of the tide worthy to be noticed having hitherto been observed upon this
coast." The ship had rounded Cape Catastrophe, and
the land led away to the north, whereas hitherto it
had trended east and south. What did this mean?
Flinders must have been strongly reminded of his
experience in the Norfolk in Bass Strait, when the
rush of the tide from the south showed that the
north-west corner of Van Diemen's Land had been

turned, and that the demonstration of the Strait's existence was complete. There were many speculations as to what the signs indicated. "Large rivers, deep inlets, inland seas and passages into the Gulf of Carpentaria, were terms frequently used in our conversations of this evening, and the prospect of making an interesting discovery seemed to have infused new life and vigour into every man in the ship." The expedition was, in fact, in the bell-mouth of Spencer's Gulf, and the next few days were to show whether the old surmise was true—that Terra Australis was cloven in twain by a strait from the Gulf of Carpentaria to the southern ocean. It was, indeed, a crisis-time of the discovery voyage.

But before the gulf was examined, a tragedy threw the ship into mourning. On the evening of Sunday, February 21st, the cutter was returning from the mainland, where a party had been searching for water in charge of the Master, John Thistle. She carried a midshipman, William Taylor, and six sailors. Nobody on the ship witnessed the accident that happened; but the cutter had been seen coming across the water, and as she did not arrive when darkness set in, the fear that she had gone down oppressed everybody on board. A search was made, but ineffectually; and next day the boat was found floating bottom uppermost, stove in, and bearing the appearance of having been dashed against rocks. The loss of John Thistle was especially grievous to Flinders. The two had been companions from the very beginning of his career in Australia. Thistle had been one of Bass's crew in the whaleboat; he had been on the Norfolk when Van Diemen's Land was circumnavigated; and he had taken part in the cruise to Moreton Bay. His memory lives in the name of Thistle Island, on the west of the entrance to the gulf, and in the noble tribute which his commander paid to his admirable qualities. It would be wrong to deprive the reader of the satisfaction of reading Flinders' eulogy of his companion of strenuous years:

The reader will pardon me the observation that Mr. Thistle was truly a valuable man, as a seaman, an officer, and a good member of society. I had known him, and we had mostly served together, from the year 1794. He had been with Mr. Bass in his perilous expedition in the whaleboat, and with me in the voyage round Van Diemen's Land, and in the succeeding expedition to Glass House and Hervey's Bays. From his merit and prudent conduct, he was promoted from before the mast to be a midshipman and afterwards a master in His Majesty's service. His zeal for discovery had induced him to join the Investigator when at Spithead and ready to sail, although he had returned to England only three weeks before, after an absence of six years. Besides performing assiduously the duties of his situation, Mr. Thistle had made himself well acquainted with the practice of nautical astronomy, and began to be very useful in the surveying department. His loss was severely felt by me, and he was lamented by all on board, more especially by his messmates, who knew more intimately the goodness and stability of his disposition." (In a letter to Banks from Spithead on June 3rd, 1801, Flinders had written, "I am happy to inform you that the Buffalo has brought home a person formerly of the Reliance whom I wish to have as master. He volunteers, the captain of the ship agrees, and I have made application by to-day's post and expect his appointment by Friday." The reference was evidently to John Thistle.)

Taylor's Isle was named after the young midshipman of this catastrophe, and six small islands in the vicinity bear the names of the boat's crew. It is a singular fact that only two of the eight sailors drowned could swim. Even Captain Cook never learnt to swim!

Before leaving the neighbourhood, Flinders erected a copper plate upon a stone post at the head of Memory Cove, and had engraved upon it the names of the unfortunates who had perished, with a brief account of the accident. Two fragments of the original plate are now in the museum at Adelaide. In later years it was beaten down by a storm, and the South Australian Government erected a fresh tablet in Memory Cove to replace it.

A thorough survey of Port Lincoln was made while the ship was being replenished with water. Some anxiety had been felt owing to the lack of this necessity, and Flinders showed the way to obtain it by digging holes in the white clay surrounding a brackish marsh which he called Stamford Mere. The water that drained into the holes was found to be sweet and wholesome, though milky in appearance. As the filling of the casks and conveying them to the ship—to a quantity of 60 tons—occupied several days, the surveying and scientific employments were pursued diligently on land.

The discovery of Port Lincoln was in itself an event of consequence, since it is a harbour of singular commodiousness and beauty, and would, did it but possess a more prolific territory at its back, be a maritime station of no small importance. Nearly forty years later, Sir John Franklin, then Governor of Tasmania, paid a visit to Port Lincoln, expressly to renew acquaintance with a place in the discovery of which he had participated in company with a commander whose memory he honoured; and he erected on Stamford Hill, at his own cost, an obelisk in commemoration of Flinders. In the same way, on his first great overland arctic journey in 1821, Franklin remembered Flinders in giving names to discoveries.

It was on March 6th that the exploration of Spencer's Gulf commenced. As the ship sailed along the western shore, the expectations which had been formed of a strait leading through the continent to the Gulf of Carpentaria faded away. The coast lost its boldness, the water became more and more shallow, and the opposite shore began to show itself. The gulf was clearly tapering to an end. "Our prospect of a channel or strait cutting off some considerable portion of Terra Australis grew less, for it now appeared that the ship was entering into a gulph." On the 10th, the Investigator having passed Point Lowly, and having on the previous day suddenly come into two-and-a-half fathoms, Flinders decided to finish the exploration in a rowing boat, accompanied by Surgeon Bell. They rowed along the shore till night fell, slept in the boat, and resumed the journey early next morning (March 11th). At ten o'clock, the oars touched mud on each side, and it became impossible to proceed further. They had reached the head of the gulf, then a region of mangrove swamps and flat waters, but now covered by the wharves of Port Augusta, and within view of the starting point of the transcontinental railway.

The disappointment was undoubtedly great at not finding even a large river flowing into the gulf. The hope of a strait had been abandoned as the continually converging shores, shallow waters, and diminishing banks made it clear, long before the head was reached, that the theory of a bifurcated Terra Australis was impossible. But as Flinders completed his chart and placed it against the outline of the continent, he might fairly enjoy the happiness of having settled an important problem and of taking one more stride towards completing the map of the world.

The Investigator travelled down by the eastern shore, once hanging upon a near bank for half an hour, and by March 20th was well outside. The length of the gulf, from the head to Gambier Island, Flinders calculated to be 185 miles, and its width at the mouth, in a line from Cape Catastrophe, 48 miles. At the top it tapered almost to a point. The whole of it was personally surveyed and charted by Flinders, who was able to write that for the general exactness of his drawing he could "answer with tolerable confidence, having seen all that is laid down, and, as usual, taken every angle which enters into the construction."

The next discovery of importance was that of Kangaroo Island, separated from the foot-like southern projection of Yorke's Peninsula by Investigator Strait. The island was named on account of the quantity of kangaroos seen and shot upon it; for a supply of fresh meat was very welcome after four months of salt pork. Thirty-one fell to the guns of the Investigator's men. Half a hundredweight of heads, forequarters and tails were stewed down for soup, and as much kangaroo steak was available for officers and men as they could consume "by day and night." It was declared to be a "delightful regale."

The place where Flinders is believed to have first landed on Kangaroo Island is now marked by a tall cairn, which was spontaneously built by the inhabitants, the school children assisting, in 1906. An inscription on a faced stone commemorates the event. The white pyramid can be seen from vessels using Backstairs Passage.

A very short stay was made at Kangaroo Island on this first call. On March 24th Investigator Strait was crossed, and the examination of the mainland was resumed. The ship was steered north-west, and, the coast being reached, no land was visible to the eastward. The conclusion was drawn that another gulf ran inland, and the surmise proved to be correct. The new discovery, named St. Vincent's Gulf, was penetrated on the 27th, and was first explored on the eastern shore, not on the western as had been the case with Spencer's Gulf. Mount Lofty was sighted at dawn on Sunday, March 28th. The nearest part of the coast was three leagues distant at the time, "mostly low, and composed of sand and rock, with a few small trees scattered over it; but at a few miles inland, where the back mountains rise, the country was well clothed with forest timber, and had a fertile appearance. The fires bespoke this to be a part of the continent." The coast to the northward was seen to be very low, and the soundings were fast decreasing. From noon to six o'clock the Investigator ran north thirty miles, skirting a sandy shore, and at length dropped anchor in five fathoms.

On the following morning land was seen to the westward, as well as eastward, and there was "a hummocky mountain, capped with clouds, apparently near the head of the inlet." Wind failing, very little progress was made till noon, and at sunset the shores appeared to be closing round. The absence of tide gave no prospect of finding a river at the head of the gulf. Early on the morning of the 30th Flinders went out in a boat, accompanied by Robert Brown, and rowed up to the mud-flats at the head of the gulf. Picking out a narrow channel, it was found possible to get within half a mile of dry land. Then, leaving the boat, Flinders and Brown walked along a bank of mud and sand to the shore, to examine the country. Flinders ascended one of the foot-hills of the range that forms the backbone of Yorke's Peninsula, stretching north and south upwards of two hundred miles.

At dawn on March 31st the Investigator was got under way to proceed down the eastern side of Yorke's Peninsula. The wind was contrary, and the work could be done only "partially," though, of

course, sufficiently well to complete the chart. The
peninsula was described as "singular in form, having
some resemblance to a very ill-shaped leg and foot."
Its length from Cape Spencer to the northern junction with the mainland was calculated to be 105
miles. On April 1st Flinders was able to write that
the exploration of St. Vincent's Gulf was finished.

The general character of the country, especially on
the east, he considered to be superior to that on the
borders of Spencer's Gulf; and the subsequent development of the State of South Australia has justified
his opinion. He would assuredly have desired to
linger longer upon the eastern shore, could he have
foreseen that within forty years of the discovery there
would be laid there the foundations of the noble city
of Adelaide, with its fair and fruitful olive-groves,
vineyards, orchards and gardens, and its busy port,
whither flow the wheat of vast plains and the wool
from a million sheep leagues upon leagues away.

A second visit to Kangaroo Island was necessitated by a desire to make corrections in the Investigator's timekeepers, and on this occasion a
somewhat longer stay was made. The ship arrived
on April 2nd, and did not leave again till the 7th.

Very few aboriginals were seen upon the shores of
the two gulfs, and these only through a telescope. At
Port Lincoln some blacks were known to be in the
neighbourhood, but the expedition did not succeed

in getting into contact with them. Flinders scrupulously observed the policy of doing nothing to alarm them; and his remarks in this relation are characterised by as much good sense as humane feeling. Writing of a small party of natives who were heard calling but did not show themselves, probably having hidden in thick scrub to observe the boat's crew, he said:

No attempt was made to follow them, for I had always found the natives of this country to avoid those who seemed anxious for communication; whereas, when left entirely alone, they would usually come down after having watched us for a few days. Nor does this conduct seem to be unnatural; for what, in such case, would be the conduct of any people, ourselves for instance, were we living in a state of nature, frequently at war with our neighbours, and ignorant of the existence of any other nation? On the arrival of strangers so different in complexion and appearance to ourselves, having power to transplant themselves over, and even living upon, an element which to us was impossible, the first sensation would probably be terror, and the first movement flight. We should watch these extraordinary people from our retreats in the woods and rocks, and if we found ourselves sought and pursued by them, should conclude their designs to be inimical; but if, on the contrary, we saw them quietly employed in occupations which had no reference to us, curiosity would get the better of fear, and after observing them more closely, we should ourselves risk a communication. Such seemed to have been the conduct of these Australians; and I am persuaded that their appearance on the morning when the tents were struck was a prelude to their coming down; and that, had we remained a few days longer, a friendly communication would have ensued. The way was, however, prepared for the next ship which may visit this port, as it was to us in King George's Sound by Captain Vancouver and the ship Elligood; to whose previous visits and peaceable conduct we were most probably indebted for our early intercourse with the inhabitants of that place. So far as could be perceived with a glass, the natives of this port were the same in personal appearance as those of King George's Sound and Port Jackson. In the hope of conciliating their goodwill to succeeding visitors, some hatchets and various other articles were left in their paths, fastened to stumps of trees which had been cut down near our watering pits.

More wild life was seen at Kangaroo Island than in the gulf region. Thirty emus were observed on one day; kangaroos, as has been remarked, were plentiful; and a large colony of pelicans caused the name of Pelican Lagoon to be given to a feature of the island's eastern lobe. The marsupial, the seal, the emu, and the bag-billed bird that nature built in one of her whimsical moods, had held unchallenged possession for tens of thousands of years, probably never visited by any ships, nor even preyed upon by blacks. The reflections of Flinders upon Pelican Lagoon have a tinting of poetic feeling which we do not often find in his solid pages:

> Flocks of the old birds were sitting upon the beaches of the lagoon, and it appeared that the islands were their breeding places; not only so, but from the number of skeletons and bones there scattered it should seem that they had for ages been selected for the closing scene of their existence. Certainly none more likely to be free from disturbance of every kind could have been chosen, than these inlets in a hidden lagoon of an uninhabited island, situate upon an unknown coast near the antipodes of Europe; nor can anything be more consonant to the feelings, if pelicans have any, than quietly to resign their breath whilst surrounded by their progeny, and in the same spot where they first drew it. Alas, for the pelicans! their golden age is past; but it has much exceeded in duration that of man.

The picture of the zoological interests of Kangaroo Island is heightened by Flinders' account of the seals and marsupials. "Never perhaps has the dominion possessed here by the kangaroo been invaded before this time. The seal shared with it upon the shores, but they seemed to dwell amicably together. It not unfrequently happened that the report of a gun fired at a kangaroo, near the beach, brought out two or three bellowing seals from under bushes considerably further from the water side. The seal, indeed, seemed to be much the more discerning animal of the two; for its actions bespoke a knowledge of our not being kangaroos, whereas the kangaroo not unfrequently appeared to consider us to be seals." In the quotation, it may be as well to add, the usual spelling of "kangaroo" is followed, but Flinders invariably spelt it "kanguroo." The orthography of the word was not settled in his time; Cook wrote "kangooroo" and "kanguru," but Hawkesworth, who edited his voyages, made it "kangaroo."

The quantity of fallen timber lying upon the island prompted the curiosity of Flinders. Trunks of trees lay about in all directions "and were nearly of the same size and in the same progress towards decay; from whence it would seem that they had not fallen from age nor yet been thrown down in a gale of wind. Some general conflagration, and there were marks apparently of fire on many of them, is perhaps the sole cause which can be reasonably assigned; but whence came the woods on fire? There were no inhabitants upon the island, and that the natives of the continent did not visit it was demonstrated, if not by the want of all signs of such visits, yet by the tameness of the kangaroo, an animal which, on the continent, resembles the wild deer in timidity. Perhaps lightning might have been the cause, or possibly the friction of two dead trees in a strong wind; but it would be somewhat extraordinary that the same thing should have happened at Thistle's Island, Boston Island, and at this place, and apparently about the same time. Can this part of Terra Australis have been visited before, unknown to the world? The French navigator, Laperouse, was ordered to explore it, but there seems little probability that he ever passed Torres Strait.

Some judgment may be formed of the epoch when these conflagrations happened, from the magnitude of the growing trees; for they must have sprung up since that period. They were a species of eucalyptus, and being less than the fallen tree, had most probably not arrived at maturity; but the wood is hard and solid, and it may thence be supposed to grow slowly. With these considerations, I should be inclined to fix the period at not less than ten, nor more than twenty years before our arrival. This brings us back to Laperouse. He was in Botany Bay in the beginning of 1788, and, if he did pass through Torres Strait, and come round to this coast, as was his intention, it would probably be about the middle or latter end of that year, or between thirteen and fourteen years before the Investigator. My opinion is

not favourable to this conjecture; but I have furnished
all the data to enable the reader to form his own opinion upon the cause which might have prostrated the
woods of these islands.

The passage is worth quoting, if only for the interesting allusion to Laperouse, whose fate was, at
the time when Flinders sailed and wrote, an un
solved mystery of the sea. Captain Dillon's discovery
of relics at Vanikoro, in 1826, twelve years after the
death of Flinders, informed the world that the illus-
trious French navigator did not pass through Torres
Strait, but was wrecked in the Santa Cruz group.
The fire, so many signs of which were observed on
Kangaroo Island, was in all probability caused naturally in the heat of a dry summer.

Chiloe and Concepcion: Great Earthquake

[CHARLES DARWIN]

On January the 15th we sailed from Low's Harbour, and three days afterwards anchored a second time in the bay of S. Carlos in Chiloe. On the night of the 19th the volcano of Osorno was in action. At midnight the sentry observed something like a large star, which gradually increased in size till about three o'clock, when it presented a very magnificent spectacle. By the aid of a glass, dark objects, in constant succession, were seen, in the midst of a great glare of red light, to be thrown up and to fall down. The light was sufficient to cast on the water a long bright reflection. Large masses of molten matter seem very commonly to be cast out of the craters in this part of the Cordillera. I was assured that when the Corcovado is in eruption, great masses are projected upwards and are seen to burst in the air, assuming many fantastical forms, such as trees: their size must be immense, for they can be distinguished from the high land behind S. Carlos, which is no less than ninety-three miles from the Corcovado. In the morning the volcano became tranquil.

I was surprised at hearing afterwards that Aconcagua in Chile, 480 miles northwards, was in action on the same night; and still more surprised to hear that the great eruption of Coseguina (2700 miles north of Aconcagua), accompanied by an earthquake felt over a 1000 miles, also occurred within six hours of this same time. This coincidence is the more remarkable, as Coseguina had been dormant for twenty-six years; and Aconcagua most rarely shows any signs of action. It is difficult even to conjecture whether this coincidence was accidental, or shows some subterranean connection. If Vesuvius, Etna, and Hecla in Iceland (all three relatively nearer each other than the corresponding points in South America), suddenly burst forth in eruption on the same night, the coincidence would be thought remarkable; but it is far more remarkable in this case, where the three vents fall on the same great mountain-chain, and where the vast plains along the entire eastern coast, and the upraised recent shells along more than 2000 miles on the western coast, show in how equable and connected a manner the elevatory forces have acted.

Captain Fitz Roy being anxious that some bearings should be taken on the outer coast of Chiloe, it was planned that Mr. King and myself should ride to Castro, and thence across the island to the Capella de Cucao, situated on the west coast. Having hired horses and a guide, we set out on the morning of the 22nd. We had not proceeded far, before we were joined by a woman and two boys, who were bent on the same journey. Every one on this road acts on a "hail fellow well met" fashion; and one may here enjoy the privilege, so rare in South America, of travelling without firearms. At first, the country consisted of a succession of hills and valleys: nearer to Castro it became very level. The road itself is a curious affair; it consists in its whole length, with the exception of very few parts, of great logs of wood, which are either broad and laid longitudinally, or narrow and placed transversely. In summer the road is not very bad; but in winter, when the wood is rendered slippery from rain, travelling is exceedingly difficult. At that time of the year, the ground on each side becomes a morass, and is often overflowed: hence it is necessary that the longitudinal logs should be fastened down by transverse poles, which are pegged on each side into the earth. These pegs render a fall from a horse dangerous, as

the chance of alighting on one of them is not small.
It is remarkable, however, how active custom has
made the Chilotan horses. In crossing bad parts,
where the logs had been displaced, they skipped
from one to the other, almost with the quickness
and certainty of a dog. On both hands the road is
bordered by the lofty forest-trees, with their bases
matted together by canes. When occasionally a long
reach of this avenue could be beheld, it presented a
curious scene of uniformity: the white line of logs,
narrowing in perspective, became hidden by the
gloomy forest, or terminated in a zigzag which ascended some steep hill.

Although the distance from S. Carlos to Castro is
only twelve leagues in a straight line, the formation of
the road must have been a great labour. I was told that
several people had formerly lost their lives in at-
tempting to cross the forest. The first who succeeded
was an Indian, who cut his way through the canes in
eight days, and reached S. Carlos: he was rewarded by
the Spanish government with a grant of land. During
the summer, many of the Indians wander about the
forests (but chiefly in the higher parts, where the
woods are not quite so thick) in search of the half-
wild cattle which live on the leaves of the cane and
certain trees. It was one of these huntsmen who by
chance discovered, a few years since, an English vessel, which had been wrecked on the outer coast. The

crew were beginning to fail in provisions, and it is not probable that, without the aid of this man, they would ever have extricated themselves from these scarcely penetrable woods. As it was, one seaman died on the march, from fatigue. The Indians in these excursions steer by the sun; so that if there is a continuance of cloudy weather, they can not travel.

The day was beautiful, and the number of trees which were in full flower perfumed the air; yet even this could hardly dissipate the effects of the gloomy dampness of the forest. Moreover, the many dead trunks that stand like skeletons, never fail to give to these primeval woods a character of solemnity, absent in those of countries long civilized. Shortly after sunset we bivouacked for the night. Our female companion, who was rather good-looking, belonged to one of the most respectable families in Castro: she rode, however, astride, and without shoes or stockings. I was surprised at the total want of pride shown by her and her brother. They brought food with them, but at all our meals sat watching Mr. King and myself whilst eating, till we were fairly shamed into feeding the whole party. The night was cloudless; and while lying in our beds, we enjoyed the sight (and it is a high enjoyment) of the multitude of stars which illumined the darkness of the forest.

January 23rd.—We rose early in the morning, and reached the pretty quiet town of Castro by two o'clock. The old governor had died since our last visit, and a Chileno was acting in his place. We had a letter of introduction to Don Pedro, whom we found exceedingly hospitable and kind, and more disinterested than is usual on this side of the continent. The next day Don Pedro procured us fresh horses, and offered to accompany us himself. We proceeded to the south—generally following the coast, and passing through several hamlets, each with its large barn-like chapel built of wood. At Vilipilli, Don Pedro asked the commandant to give us a guide to Cucao. The old gentleman offered to come himself; but for a long time nothing would persuade him that two Englishmen really wished to go to such an out-of-the-way place as Cucao. We were thus accompanied by the two greatest aristocrats in the country, as was plainly to be seen in the manner of all the poorer Indians towards them. At Chonchi we struck across the island, following intricate winding paths, sometimes passing through magnificent forests, and sometimes through pretty cleared spots, abounding with corn and potato crops. This undulating woody country, partially cultivated, reminded me of the wilder parts of England, and therefore had to my eye a most fascinating aspect. At Vilinco, which is situated on the borders of the lake of Cucao, only a few fields were cleared; and all the inhabitants appeared to be Indians. This lake is twelve miles long, and runs in an east and west direction. From local circumstances, the sea-breeze blows very regularly during the day, and during the night it falls calm: this has given rise to strange exaggerations, for the phenomenon, as described to us at S. Carlos, was quite a prodigy.

The road to Cucao was so very bad that we determined to embark in a *periagua*. The commandant, in the most authoritative manner, ordered six Indians to get ready to pull us over, without deigning to tell them whether they would be paid. The periagua is a strange rough boat, but the crew were still stranger: I doubt if six uglier little men ever got into a boat together. They pulled, however, very well and cheerfully. The stroke-oarsman gabbled Indian, and uttered strange cries, much after the fashion of a pig-driver driving his pigs. We started with a light breeze against us, but yet reached the Capella de Cucao before it was late. The country on each side of the lake was one unbroken forest. In the same periagua with us, a cow was embarked. To get so large an animal into a small boat appears at first a difficulty, but the Indians managed it in a minute. They brought the cow alongside the boat, which was heeled towards her; then placing two oars under her belly, with their ends resting on the gunwale, by the aid of these levers they fairly tumbled the poor beast heels over head into the bottom of the boat, and then lashed her down with ropes. At Cucao we found an uninhabited hovel (which is the residence of the padre when he pays this Capella a visit), where, lighting a fire, we cooked our supper, and were very comfortable.

The district of Cucao is the only inhabited part on the whole west coast of Chiloe. It contains about thirty or forty Indian families, who are scattered along four or five miles of the shore. They are very much secluded from the rest of Chiloe, and have scarcely any sort of commerce except sometimes in a little oil, which they get from seal-blubber. They are tolerably dressed in clothes of their own manufacture, and they have plenty to eat. They seemed, however, discontented, yet humble to a degree which it was quite painful to witness. These feelings are, I think, chiefly to be attributed to the harsh and authoritative manner in which they are treated by their rulers. Our companions, although so very civil to us, behaved to the poor Indians as if they had been slaves, rather than free men. They ordered provisions and the use of their horses, without ever condescending to say how much, or indeed whether the owners should be paid at all. In the morning, being left alone with these poor people, we soon ingratiated ourselves by presents of cigars and mate. A lump of white sugar was divided between all present, and tasted with the greatest curiosity. The Indians ended all their complaints by saying, "And it is only because we are poor Indians, and know nothing; but it was not so when we had a King."

The next day after breakfast, we rode a few miles northward to Punta Huantamo. The road lay along a very broad beach, on which, even after so many fine days, a terrible surf was breaking. I was assured that after a heavy gale, the roar can be heard at night even at Castro, a distance of no less than twenty one sea miles across a hilly and wooded country. We had some difficulty in reaching the point, owing to the intolerably bad paths; for everywhere in the shade the ground soon becomes a perfect quagmire. The point itself is a bold rocky hill. It is covered by a plant allied, I believe, to Bromelia, and called by the inhabitants Chepones. In scrambling through the beds, our hands were very much scratched. I was amused by observing the precaution our Indian guide took, in turning up his trousers, thinking that they were more delicate than his own hard skin. This plant bears a fruit, in shape like an artichoke, in which a number of seed-vessels are packed: these contain a pleasant sweet pulp, here much esteemed. I saw at Low's Harbour the Chilotans making chichi, or cider, with this fruit: so true is it, as Humboldt remarks, that almost everywhere man finds means of preparing some kind of beverage from the vegetable kingdom. The savages, however, of Tierra del Fuego, and I believe of Australia, have not advanced thus far in the arts.

The coast to the north of Punta Huantamo is exceedingly rugged and broken, and is fronted by many breakers, on which the sea is eternally roaring. Mr. King and myself were anxious to return, if it had been possible, on foot along this coast; but even the Indians said it was quite impracticable. We were told that men have crossed by striking directly through the woods from Cucao to S. Carlos, but never by the coast. On these expeditions, the Indians carry with them only roasted corn, and of this they eat sparingly twice a day.

26th.—Re-embarking in the periagua, we returned across the lake, and then mounted our horses. The whole of Chiloe took advantage of this week of unusually fine weather, to clear the ground by burning. In every direction volumes of smoke were curling upwards. Although the inhabitants were so assiduous in setting fire to every part of the wood, yet I did not see a single fire which they had succeeded in making extensive. We dined with our friend the commandant, and did not reach Castro till after dark. The next morning we started very early. After having ridden for some time, we obtained from the brow of a steep hill an extensive view (and it is a rare thing on this road) of the great forest. Over the horizon of trees, the volcano of Corcovado, and the great flat-topped one to the north, stood out in proud pre-eminence: scarcely another peak in the long range showed its snowy summit. I hope it will be long before I forget this farewell view of the magnificent Cordillera fronting Chiloe. At night we bivouacked under a cloudless sky, and the next morning reached S. Carlos. We arrived on the right day, for before evening heavy rain commenced.

February 4th.—Sailed from Chiloe. During the last week I made several short excursions. One was to examine a great bed of now-existing shells, elevated 350 feet above the level of the sea: from among these shells, large forest-trees were growing. Another ride was to P. Huechucucuy. I had with me a guide who knew the country far too well; for he would pertinaciously tell me endless Indian names for every little point, rivulet, and creek. In the same manner as in Tierra del Fuego, the Indian language appears singularly well adapted for attaching names to the most trivial features of the land. I believe every one was glad to say farewell to Chiloe; yet if we could forget the gloom and ceaseless rain of winter, Chiloe might pass for a charming island. There is also something very attractive in the simplicity and humble politeness of the poor inhabitants.

We steered northward along shore, but owing to thick weather did not reach Valdivia till the night of the 8th. The next morning the boat proceeded to the town, which is distant about ten miles. We followed the course of the river, occasionally passing a few hovels, and patches of ground cleared out of the otherwise unbroken forest; and sometimes meeting a canoe with an Indian family. The town is situated on the low banks of the stream, and is so completely buried in a wood of apple-trees that the streets are merely paths in an orchard. I have never seen any country where apple-trees appeared to thrive so well as in this damp part of South America: on the borders of the roads there were many young trees evidently self-grown. In Chiloe the inhabitants possess a marvellously short method of making an orchard. At the lower part of almost every branch, small, conical, brown, wrinkled points project: these are always ready to change into roots, as may sometimes be seen, where any mud has been accidentally splashed against the tree. A branch as thick as a man's thigh is chosen in the early spring, and is cut off just beneath a group of these points, all the smaller branches are lopped off, and it is then placed about two feet deep in the ground. During the ensuing summer the stump throws out long shoots, and sometimes even bears fruit: I was shown one which had produced as many as twenty-three apples, but this was thought very unusual. In the third season the stump is changed (as I have myself seen) into a well-wooded tree, loaded with fruit. An old man near Valdivia illustrated his motto, "Necesidad es la madre del invencion," by giving an account of the several useful things he manufactured from his apples. After making cider, and likewise wine, he extracted from the refuse a white and finely flavoured spirit; by another process he procured a sweet treacle, or, as he called it, honey. His children and pigs seemed almost to live, during this season of the year, in his orchard.

February 11th.—I set out with a guide on a short ride in which, however, I managed to see singularly little, either of the geology of the country or of its inhabitants. There is not much cleared land near Valdivia: after crossing a river at the distance of a few miles, we entered the forest, and then passed only one miserable hovel, before reaching our sleeping-place for the night. The short difference in latitude, of 150 miles, has given a new aspect to the forest compared with that of Chiloe. This is owing to a slightly different proportion in the kinds of trees. The evergreens do not appear to be quite so numerous, and the forest in consequence has a brighter tint. As in Chiloe, the lower parts are matted together by canes: here also another kind (resembling the bamboo of Brazil and about twenty feet in height) grows in clusters, and ornaments the banks of some of the streams in a very pretty manner. It is with this plant that the Indians make their chuzos, or long tapering spears. Our resting-house was so dirty that I preferred sleeping outside: on these journeys the first night is generally very uncomfortable, because one is not accustomed to the tickling and biting of the fleas. I am sure, in the morning, there was not a space on my legs the size of a shilling which had not its little red mark where the flea had feasted.

12th.—We continued to ride through the uncleared forest; only occasionally meeting an Indian on horseback, or a troop of fine mules bringing alerce-planks and corn from the southern plains. In the afternoon one of the horses knocked up: we were then on a brow of a hill, which commanded a fine view of the Llanos. The view of these open plains was very refreshing, after being hemmed in and buried in the wilderness of trees. The uniformity of a forest soon becomes very wearisome. This west coast makes me remember with pleasure the free, unbounded plains of Patagonia; yet, with the true spirit of contradiction, I cannot forget how sublime is the silence of the forest. The Llanos are the most fertile and thickly peopled parts of the country, as they possess the immense advantage of being nearly free from trees. Before leaving the forest we crossed some flat little lawns, around which single trees stood, as in an English park: I have often noticed with surprise, in wooded undulatory districts, that the quite level parts have been destitute of trees. On account of the tired horse, I determined to stop at the Mission of Cudico, to the friar of which I had a letter of introduction. Cudico is an intermediate district between the forest and the Llanos. There are a good many cottages, with patches of corn and potatoes, nearly all belonging to Indians. The tribes dependent on Valdivia are "reducidos y cristianos." The Indians farther northward, about Arauco and Imperial, are still very wild, and not converted; but they have all much intercourse with the Spaniards. The padre said that the Christian Indians did not much like coming to mass, but that otherwise they showed respect for religion. The greatest difficulty is in making them observe the ceremonies of marriage. The wild Indians take as many wives as they can support, and a cacique will sometimes have more than ten: on entering his house, the number may be told by that of the separate fires. Each wife lives a week in turn with the cacique; but all are employed in weaving ponchos, etc., for his profit. To be the wife of a cacique, is an honour much sought after by the Indian women.

The men of all these tribes wear a coarse woolen poncho: those south of Valdivia wear short trousers, and those north of it a petticoat, like the chilipa of the Gauchos. All have their long hair bound by a scarlet fillet, but with no other covering on their heads. These Indians are good-sized men; their cheek-bones are prominent, and in general appearance they resemble the great American family to which they belong; but their physiognomy seemed to me to be slightly different from that of any other tribe which I had before seen. Their expression is generally grave, and even austere, and possesses much character: this may pass either for honest bluntness or fierce determination. The long black hair, the grave and much-lined features, and the dark complexion, called to my mind old portraits of James I. On the road we met with none of that humble politeness so universal in Chiloe. Some gave their "mari-mari" (good morning) with promptness, but the greater number did not seem inclined to offer any salute. This independence of manners is probably a consequence of their long wars, and the repeated victories which they alone, of all the tribes in America, have gained over the Spaniards.

I spent the evening very pleasantly, talking with the padre. He was exceedingly kind and hospitable; and coming from Santiago, had contrived to surround himself with some few comforts. Being a man of some little education, he bitterly complained of the total want of society. With no particular zeal for religion, no business or pursuit, how completely must this man's life be wasted! The next day, on our return, we met seven very wild-looking Indians, of whom some were caciques that had just received from the Chilian government their yearly small stipend for having long remained faithful. They were fine-looking men, and they rode one after the other, with most gloomy faces. An old cacique, who headed them, had been, I suppose, more excessively drunk than the rest, for he seemed extremely grave and very crabbed. Shortly before this, two Indians joined us, who were travelling from a distant mission to Valdivia concerning some lawsuit. One was a good-humoured old man, but from his wrinkled and mellow face looked more like an old woman than a man. I frequently presented both of them with cigars; and though ready to receive them, and I dare say grateful, they would hardly condescend to thank me. A Chilotan Indian would have taken off his hat, and given his "Dios le page!" The travelling was very tedious, both from the badness of the roads, and from the number of great fallen trees, which it was necessary either to leap over or to avoid by making long circuits. We slept on the road, and next morning reached Valdivia, whence I proceeded on board.

A few days afterwards I crossed the bay with a party of officers, and landed near the fort called Niebla. The buildings were in a most ruinous state, and the gun-carriages quite rotten. Mr. Wickham remarked to the commanding officer, that with one discharge they would certainly all fall to pieces. The poor man, trying to put a good face upon it, gravely replied, "No, I am sure, sir, they would stand two!" The Spaniards must have intended to have made this place impregnable. There is now lying in the middle of the court-yard a little mountain of mortar, which rivals in hardness the rock on which it is placed. It was brought from Chile, and cost 7000 dollars. The revolution having broken out, prevented its being applied to any purpose, and now it remains a monument of the fallen greatness of Spain.

I wanted to go to a house about a mile and a half distant, but my guide said it was quite impossible to penetrate the wood in a straight line. He offered, however, to lead me, by following obscure cattle-tracks, the shortest way: the walk, nevertheless, took no less than three hours! This man is employed in hunting strayed cattle; yet, well as he must know the woods, he was not long since lost for two whole days, and had nothing to eat. These facts convey a good idea of the impracticability of the forests of these countries. A question often occurred to me — how long does any vestige of a fallen tree remain? This man showed me one which a party of fugitive royalists had cut down fourteen years ago; and taking this as a criterion, I should think a bole a foot and a half in diameter would in thirty years be changed into a heap of mould.

February 20th.—This day has been memorable in the annals of Valdivia, for the most severe earthquake experienced by the oldest inhabitant. I happened to be on shore, and was lying down in the wood to rest myself. It came on suddenly, and lasted

two minutes, but the time appeared much longer.
The rocking of the ground was very sensible. The
undulations appeared to my companion and myself
to come from due east, whilst others thought they
proceeded from south-west: this shows how difficult
it sometimes is to perceive the directions of the vi-
brations. There was no difficulty in standing upright,
but the motion made me almost giddy: it was something like the movement of a vessel in a little cross-
ripple, or still more like that felt by a person skating
over thin ice, which bends under the weight of his
body. A bad earthquake at once destroys our oldest
associations: the earth, the very emblem of solidity,
has moved beneath our feet like a thin crust over a
fluid;—one second of time has created in the mind
a strange idea of insecurity, which hours of reflection would not have produced. In the forest, as a
breeze moved the trees, I felt only the earth tremble, but saw no other effect. Captain Fitz Roy and
some officers were at the town during the shock,
and there the scene was more striking; for although
the houses, from being built of wood, did not fall,
they were violently shaken, and the boards creaked
and rattled together. The people rushed out of doors
in the greatest alarm. It is these accompaniments that
create that perfect horror of earthquakes, experienced by all who have thus seen, as well as felt, their
effects. Within the forest it was a deeply interesting,

but by no means an awe-exciting phenomenon. The tides were very curiously affected. The great shock took place at the time of low water; and an old woman who was on the beach told me that the water flowed very quickly, but not in great waves, to high-water mark, and then as quickly returned to its proper level; this was also evident by the line of wet sand. The same kind of quick but quiet movement in the tide happened a few years since at Chiloe, during a slight earthquake, and created much cause-less alarm. In the course of the evening there were many weaker shocks, which seemed to produce in the harbour the most complicated currents, and some of great strength.

March 4th.—We entered the harbour of Con-cepcion. While the ship was beating up to the an-chorage, I landed on the island of Quiriquina. The major-domo of the estate quickly rode down to tell me the terrible news of the great earthquake of the 20th: — "That not a house in Concepcion or Talc-ahuano (the port) was standing; that seventy villages were destroyed; and that a great wave had almost washed away the ruins of Talcahuano." Of this latter statement I soon saw abundant proofs—the whole coast being strewed over with timber and furniture as if a thousand ships had been wrecked. Besides chairs, tables, book-shelves, etc., in great numbers, there were several roofs of cottages, which had been

transported almost whole. The storehouses at Talcahuano had been burst open, and great bags of cotton, yerba, and other valuable merchandise were
scattered on the shore. During my walk round the
island, I observed that numerous fragments of rock,
which, from the marine productions adhering to
them, must recently have been lying in deep water,
had been cast up high on the beach, one of those
was six feet long, three broad, and two thick.

The island itself as plainly showed the overwhelming power of the earthquake, as the beach did
that of the consequent great wave. The ground in
many parts was fissured in north and south lines,
perhaps caused by the yielding of the parallel and
steep sides of this narrow island. Some of the fissures
near the cliffs were a yard wide. Many enormous
masses had already fallen on the beach; and the inhabitants thought that when the rains commenced
far greater slips would happen. The effect of the vibration on the hard primary slate, which composes
the foundation of the island, was still more curious:
the superficial parts of some narrow ridges were as
completely shivered as if they had been blasted by
gunpowder. This effect, which was rendered conspicuous by the fresh fractures and displaced soil,
must be confined to near the surface, for otherwise
there would not exist a block of solid rock throughout Chile; nor is this improbable, as it is known that

the surface of a vibrating body is affected differently from the central part. It is, perhaps, owing to this same reason, that earthquakes do not cause quite such terrific havoc within deep mines as would be expected. I believe this convulsion has been more effectual in lessening the size of the island of Quiriquina, than the ordinary wear-and-tear of the sea and weather during the course of a whole century.

The next day I landed at Talcahuano, and afterwards rode to Concepcion. Both towns presented the most awful yet interesting spectacle I ever beheld. To a person who had formerly known them, it possibly might have been still more impressive; for the ruins were so mingled together, and the whole scene possessed so little the air of a habitable place, that it was scarcely possible to imagine its former condition. The earthquake commenced at half-past eleven o'clock in the forenoon. If it had happened in the middle of the night, the greater number of the inhabitants (which in this one province must amount to many thousands) must have perished, instead of less than a hundred: as it was, the invariable practice of running out of doors at the first trembling of the ground, alone saved them. In Concepcion each house, or row of houses, stood by itself, a heap or line of ruins; but in Talcahuano, owing to the great wave, little more than one layer of bricks, tiles, and timber with here and there part of a wall left standing, could be distinguished. From this circumstance Concepcion, although not so completely desolated, was a more terrible, and if I may so call it, picturesque sight. The first shock was very sudden. The major-domo at Quiriquina told me, that the first notice he received of it, was finding both the horse he rode and himself, rolling together on the ground. Rising up, he was again thrown down. He also told me that some cows which were standing on the steep side of the island were rolled into the sea. The great wave caused the destruction of many cattle; on one low island near the head of the bay, seventy animals were washed off and drowned. It is generally thought that this has been the worst earthquake ever recorded in Chile; but as the very severe ones occur only after long intervals, this cannot easily be known; nor indeed would a much worse shock have made any difference, for the ruin was now complete. Innumerable small tremblings followed the great earthquake, and within the first twelve days no less than three hundred were counted.

After viewing Concepcion, I cannot understand how the greater number of inhabitants escaped unhurt. The houses in many parts fell outwards; thus forming in the middle of the streets little hillocks of brickwork and rubbish. Mr. Rouse, the English consul, told us that he was at breakfast when the first movement warned him to run out. He had scarcely reached the middle of the court-yard, when one side of his house came thundering down. He retained presence of mind to remember, that if he once got on the top of that part which had already fallen, he would be safe. Not being able from the motion of the ground to stand, he crawled up on his hands and knees; and no sooner had he ascended this little eminence, than the other side of the house fell in, the great beams sweeping close in front of his head. With his eyes blinded, and his mouth choked with the cloud of dust which darkened the sky, at last he gained the street. As shock succeeded shock, at the interval of a few minutes, no one dared approach the shattered ruins, and no one knew whether his dearest friends and relations were not perishing from the want of help. Those who had saved any property were obliged to keep a constant watch, for thieves prowled about, and at each little trembling of the ground, with one hand they beat their breasts and cried "Misericordia!" and then with the other filched what they could from the ruins. The thatched roofs fell over the fires, and flames burst forth in all parts. Hundreds knew themselves ruined, and few had the means of providing food for the day.

Earthquakes alone are sufficient to destroy the prosperity of any country. If beneath England the now inert subterranean forces should exert those powers, which most assuredly in former geological ages they have exerted, how completely would the entire condition of the country be changed! What would become of the lofty houses, thickly packed cities, great manufactories, the beautiful public and private edifices? If the new period of disturbance were first to commence by some great earthquake in the dead of the night, how terrific would be the carnage! England would at once be bankrupt; all papers, records, and accounts would from that moment be lost. Government being unable to collect the taxes, and failing to maintain its authority, the hand of violence and rapine would remain uncontrolled. In every large town famine would go forth, pestilence and death following in its train.

Shortly after the shock, a great wave was seen from the distance of three or four miles, approaching in the middle of the bay with a smooth outline; but along the shore it tore up cottages and trees, as it swept onwards with irresistible force. At the head of the bay it broke in a fearful line of white breakers, which rushed up to a height of 23 vertical feet above the highest spring-tides. Their force must have been prodigious; for at the Fort a cannon with its carriage, estimated at four tons in weight, was moved 15 feet inwards. A schooner was left in the midst of the ruins, 200 yards from the beach. The first wave was followed by two others, which in their retreat carried away a vast wreck of floating objects. In one part of the bay, a ship was pitched high and dry on shore, was carried off, again driven on shore, and again carried off. In another part, two large vessels anchored near together were whirled about, and their cables were thrice wound round each other; though anchored at a depth of 36 feet, they were for some minutes aground. The great wave must have travelled slowly, for the inhabitants of Talcahuano had time to run up the hills behind the town; and some sailors pulled out seaward, trusting successfully to their boat riding securely over the swell, if they could reach it before it broke. One old woman with a little boy, four or five years old, ran into a boat, but there was nobody to row it out: the boat was consequently dashed against an anchor and cut in twain; the old woman was drowned, but the child was picked up some hours afterwards clinging to the wreck. Pools of salt-water were still standing amidst the ruins of the houses, and children, making boats with old tables and chairs, appeared as happy as their parents were miserable. It was, however, exceedingly interesting to observe, how much more active and cheerful all appeared than could have been expected. It was remarked with much truth, that from the destruction being universal, no one individual was humbled more than another, or could suspect his friends of coldness—that most grievous result of the loss of wealth. Mr. Rouse, and a large party whom he kindly took under his protection, lived for the first week in a garden beneath some apple-trees. At first they were as merry as if it had been a picnic; but soon afterwards heavy rain caused much discomfort, for they were absolutely without shelter.

In Captain Fitz Roy's excellent account of the earthquake, it is said that two explosions, one like a column of smoke and another like the blowing of a great whale, were seen in the bay. The water also appeared everywhere to be boiling; and it "became black, and exhaled a most disagreeable sulphureous smell." These latter circumstances were observed in the Bay of Valparaiso during the earthquake of 1822; they may, I think, be accounted for, by the disturbance of the mud at the bottom of the sea containing organic matter in decay. In the Bay of Callao, during a calm day, I noticed, that as the ship dragged her cable over the bottom, its course was marked by a line of bubbles. The lower orders in Talcahuano thought that the earthquake was caused by some old Indian women, who two years ago, being offended, stopped the volcano of Antuco. This silly belief is curious, because it shows that experience has taught them to observe, that there exists a relation between the suppressed action of the volcanos, and the trembling of the ground. It was necessary to apply the witchcraft to the point where their perception of cause and effect failed; and this was the closing of the volcanic vent. This belief is the more singular in this particular instance, because, according to Captain Fitz Roy, there is reason to believe that Antuco was noways affected.

The town of Concepcion was built in the usual Spanish fashion, with all the streets running at right angles to each other; one set ranging S.W. by W., and the other set N.W. by N. The walls in the former direction certainly stood better than those in the latter; the greater number of the masses of brickwork were thrown down towards the N.E. Both these circumstances perfectly agree with the general idea, of the undulations having come from the S.W., in which quarter subterranean noises were also heard; for it is evident that the walls running S.W. and N.E. which presented their ends to the point whence the undulations came, would be much less likely to fall than those walls which, running N.W. and S.E., must in their whole lengths have been at the same instant thrown out of the perpendicular; for the undulations, coming from the S.W., must have extended in N.W. and S.E. waves, as they passed under the foundations. This may be illustrated by placing books edgeways on a carpet, and then, after the manner suggested by Michell, imitating the undulations of an earthquake: it will be found that they fall with more or less readiness, according as their direction more or less nearly coincides with the line of the waves. The fissures in the ground generally, though not uniformly, extended in a S.E. and N.W. direction, and therefore corresponded to the lines of undulation or of principal flexure. Bearing in mind all these circumstances, which so clearly point to the S.W. as the chief focus of disturbance, it is a very interesting fact that the island of S. Maria, situated in that quarter, was, during the general uplifting of the land, raised to nearly three times the height of any other part of the coast.

The different resistance offered by the walls, according to their direction, was the N.E. presented a grand pile of ruins, in the midst of which door-cases and masses of timber stood up, as if floating in a stream. Some of the angular blocks of brickwork were of great dimensions; and they were rolled to a distance on the level plaza, like fragments of rock at the base of some high mountain. The side walls (running S.W. and N.E.), though exceedingly fractured, yet remained standing; but the vast buttresses (at right angles to them, and therefore parallel to the walls that fell) were in many cases cut clean off, as if by a chisel, and hurled to the ground. Some square ornaments on the coping of these same walls, were moved by the earthquake into a diagonal position. A similar circumstance was observed after an earthquake at Valparaiso, Calabria, and other places, including some of the ancient Greek temples. This twisting displacement, at first appears to indicate a vorticose movement beneath each point thus affected; but this is highly improbable. May it not be caused by a tendency in each stone to arrange itself in some particular position, with respect to the lines of vibration,—in a manner somewhat similar to pins on a sheet of paper when shaken? Generally speaking, arched doorways or windows stood much better than any other part of the buildings. Nevertheless, a poor lame old man, who had been in the habit, during trifling shocks, of crawling to a certain doorway, was this time crushed to pieces.

I have not attempted to give any detailed description of the appearance of Concepcion, for I feel that it is quite impossible to convey the mingled feelings which I experienced. Several of the officers visited it before me, but their strongest language failed to give a just idea of the scene of desolation. It is a bitter and humiliating thing to see works, which have cost man so much time and labour, overthrown in one minute; yet compassion for the inhabitants was almost instantly banished, by the surprise in seeing a state of things produced in a moment of time, which one was accustomed to attribute to a succession of ages. In my opinion, we have scarcely beheld, since leaving England, any sight so deeply interesting.

In almost every severe earthquake, the neighbouring waters of the sea are said to have been greatly agitated. The disturbance seems generally, as in the case

of Concepcion, to have been of two kinds: first, at
the instant of the shock, the water swells high up on
the beach with a gentle motion, and then as quietly
retreats; secondly, some time afterwards, the whole
body of the sea retires from the coast, and then re-
turns in waves of overwhelming force. The first
movement seems to be an immediate consequence
of the earthquake affecting differently a fluid and a
solid, so that their respective levels are slightly deranged: but the second case is a far more important
phenomenon. During most earthquakes, and especially during those on the west coast of America, it
is certain that the first great movement of the waters
has been a retirement. Some authors have attempted
to explain this, by supposing that the water retains its
level, whilst the land oscillates upwards; but surely
the water close to the land, even on a rather steep
coast, would partake of the motion of the bottom:
moreover, as urged by Mr. Lyell, similar movements
of the sea have occurred at islands far distant from
the chief line of disturbance, as was the case with
Juan Fernandez during this earthquake, and with
Madeira during the famous Lisbon shock. I suspect
(but the subject is a very obscure one) that a wave,
however produced, first draws the water from the
shore, on which it is advancing to break: I have observed that this happens with the little waves from
the paddles of a steam-boat. It is remarkable that

whilst Talcahuano and Callao (near Lima), both situated at the head of large shallow bays, have suffered
during every severe earthquake from great waves,
Valparaiso, seated close to the edge of profoundly
deep water, has never been overwhelmed, though so
often shaken by the severest shocks. From the great
wave not immediately following the earthquake, but
sometimes after the interval of even half an hour, and
from distant islands being affected similarly with the
coasts near the focus of the disturbance, it appears
that the wave first rises in the offing; and as this is of
general occurrence, the cause must be general: I suspect we must look to the line, where the less disturbed waters of the deep ocean join the water
nearer the coast, which has partaken of the movements of the land, as the place where the great wave
is first generated; it would also appear that the wave
is larger or smaller, according to the extent of shoal
water which has been agitated together with the
bottom on which it rested.

The most remarkable effect of this earthquake was
the permanent elevation of the land, it would probably be far more correct to speak of it as the cause.
There can be no doubt that the land round the Bay
of Concepcion was upraised two or three feet; but it
deserves notice, that owing to the wave having oblit-
erated the old lines of tidal action on the sloping
sandy shores, I could discover no evidence of this

fact, except in the united testimony of the inhabitants, that one little rocky shoal, now exposed, was
formerly covered with water. At the island of S.
Maria (about thirty miles distant) the elevation was
greater; on one part, Captain Fitz Roy founds beds
of putrid mussel-shells *still adhering to the rocks*, ten
feet above high-water mark: the inhabitants had formerly dived at lower water spring tides for these
shells. The elevation of this province is particularly
interesting, from its having been the theatre of several other violent earthquakes, and from the vast
numbers of sea-shells scattered over the land, up to a
height of certainly 600, and I believe, of 1000 feet.
At Valparaiso, as I have remarked, similar shells are
found at the height of 1300 feet: it is hardly possible
to doubt that this great elevation has been effected
by successive small uprisings, such as that which accompanied or caused the earthquake of this year, and
likewise by an insensibly slow rise, which is certainly
in progress on some parts of this coast.

The island of Juan Fernandez, 360 miles to the
N.E., was, at the time of the great shock of the 20th,
violently shaken, so that the trees beat against each
other, and a volcano burst forth under water close
to the shore: these facts are remarkable because this
island, during the earthquake of 1751, was then also
affected more violently than other places at an equal
distance from Concepcion, and this seems to show

some subterranean connection between these two points. Chiloe, about 340 miles southward of Concepcion, appears to have been shaken more strongly than the intermediate district of Valdivia, where the volcano of Villarica was noways affected, whilst in the Cordillera in front of Chiloe, two of the volcanos burst forth at the same instant in violent action. These two volcanos, and some neighbouring ones, continued for a long time in eruption, and ten months afterwards were again influenced by an earthquake at Concepcion. Some men, cutting wood near the base of one of these volcanos, did not perceive the shock of the 20th, although the whole surrounding Province was then trembling; here we have an eruption relieving and taking the place of an earthquake, as would have happened at Concepcion, according to the belief of the lower orders, if the volcano at Antuco had not been closed by witchcraft. Two years and three-quarters afterwards, Valdivia and Chiloe were again shaken, more violently than on the 20th, and an island in the Chonos Archipelago was permanently elevated more than eight feet. It will give a better idea of the scale of these phenomena, if (as in the case of the glaciers) we suppose them to have taken place at corresponding distances in Europe:—then would the land from the North Sea to the Mediterranean have been violently shaken, and at the same instant of time a large tract of the eastern coast of England would have been permanently elevated, together with some outlying islands,—a train of volcanos on the coast of Holland would have burst forth in action, and an eruption taken place at the bottom of the sea, near the northern extremity of Ireland—and lastly, the ancient vents of Auvergne, Cantal, and Mont d'Or would each have sent up to the sky a dark column of smoke, and have long remained in fierce action. Two years and three-quarters afterwards, France, from its centre to the English Channel, would have been again desolated by an earthquake and an island permanently upraised in the Mediterranean.

The space, from under which volcanic matter on the 20th was actually erupted, is 720 miles in one line, and 400 miles in another line at right angles to the first: hence, in all probability, a subterranean lake of lava is here stretched out, of nearly double the area of the Black Sea. From the intimate and complicated manner in which the elevatory and eruptive forces were shown to be connected during this train of phenomena, we may confidently come to the conclusion, that the forces which slowly and by little starts uplift continents, and those which at successive periods pour forth volcanic matter from open orifices, are identical. From many reasons, I believe that the frequent quakings of the earth on this line of coast are caused by the rending of the strata, necessarily consequent on the tension of the land when upraised, and their injection by fluidified rock. This rending and injection would, if repeated often enough (and we know that earthquakes repeatedly affect the same areas in the same manner), form a chain of hills;—and the linear island of S. Mary, which was upraised thrice the height of the neighbouring country, seems to be undergoing this process. I believe that the solid axis of a mountain, differs in its manner of formation from a volcanic hill, only in the molten stone having been repeatedly injected, instead of having been repeatedly ejected. Moreover, I believe that it is impossible to explain the structure of great mountain-chains, such as that of the Cordillera, where the strata, capping the injected axis of plutonic rock, have been thrown on their edges along several parallel and neighbouring lines of elevation, except on this view of the rock of the axis having been repeatedly injected, after intervals sufficiently long to allow the upper parts or wedges to cool and become solid;—for if the strata had been thrown into their present highly inclined, vertical, and even inverted positions, by a single blow, the very bowels of the earth would have gushed out; and instead of beholding abrupt mountain-axes of rock solidified under great pressure, deluges of lava would have flowed out at innumerable points on every line of elevation.

The Famous Perry
Expedition to Japan

[JOHN S. SEWALL]

A t last, on the second of July 1853, four of the fleet got underway for Japan. The *Saratoga* took her place in tow of the *Susquehanna* as before, and the *Plymouth* in tow of the *Mississippi*. The *Supply* storeship was left for the time at anchor in Napa harbor, and the *Caprice,* under command of Lieutenant William L. Maury, was sent to Shanghai. Our course followed the chain of island groups that extend to the northward and eastward from Lew Chew over to Nippon— some of the time in sight of them. One of the last we passed was Ohosima, a well-bred volcano that was enjoying a nice quiet smoke all by itself. It may wake up someday and start its furnaces, as its fiery neighbor Torisima has been doing while these pages have been in process of incubation. There is plenty of time; geology will furnish all it wants. And it may yet make its record in history and hold up its head with Vesuvius and Krakatoa and Mont Pelée. They are uncertain characters, these volcanoes; you can never be quite sure when any given island is preparing to burn out its chimney. The safest plan is to follow Confucius's advice about the gods—"Respect them, and keep out of their way."

We made moderate speed and reached Japan on the eighth of July. It was Friday, a memorable day in our calendar. That morning the lookouts at the masthead echoed through the fleet the rousing call, "Land ho!" We rushed on deck. There it was, at last. There it was, a dark silent cloud on the northern horizon, a *terra incognita* still shrouded in mystery, still inspiring the imagination with an indefinable awe, just as it had years ago in the studies of our childhood at school. We came up with it rapidly. But the rugged headlands and capes still veiled themselves in mist, as if resolved upon secrecy to the last. About noon the fog melted away, and there lay spread before us the Empire of the Rising Sun, a living picture of hills and valleys, of fields and hedges, groves, orchards, and forests that tufted the lawns and mantled the heights, villages with streets just a trifle wider, and houses a little less densely packed than those in China, defended by forts mounted with howitzers and "quakers," and fenced with long strips of black and white cotton, which signified that the fortifications were garrisoned and ready for business. On the waters were strange boats skimming about, impelled by strange boatmen, uncouth junks wafted slowly along by the breeze, vanishing behind the promontories and reappearing in the distance, or lowering their sails and dropping their four-fluked anchors in the harbors near us. And towering above all, forty miles inland, like a giant man-at-arms standing sentry over the scene, rose the snowy peak of Fusiyama, an extinct volcano fourteen thousand feet high, one of the most shapely cones in the world and well named "the matchless mountain."

Our squadron comprised, as already noted, two steam frigates and two sloops of war. For equipment we mustered sixty-one guns and 977 officers and men—a respectable force for the times, but soon eclipsed and forgotten in the vaster armaments of the Civil War and of our late scrimmage with Spain. Such a warlike apparition in the bay, small as it was, created a powerful sensation. A Japanese writer informs us that "the popular commotion in Yedo . . . was beyond description. The whole city was in an uproar. In all directions were seen mothers flying with children in their arms and men with mothers on their backs. Rumors of an immediate action, exaggerated each time they were communicated from mouth to mouth, added horror to the horror-stricken. The tramp of war-horses, the clatter of armed warriors, the noise of carts, the parade of firemen, the incessant tolling of bells, the shrieks of women, the cries of children, dinning all the streets of a city of more than a million souls, made confusion worse confounded."[1]

Of all this we were quite unconscious. We had no idea that we had frightened the empire so badly, the capital being some forty or fifty miles away from our anchorage. But that the town near us was thrown into convulsions by the big "black fireships of the barbarians," as the Japanese called us, was sufficiently evident. Before our anchors were fairly down, a battery on Cape Kamisaki sent a trio of bombshells to inquire after our health, or perhaps to consign us to perdition. But they exploded harmlessly astern, and we sent no bombshells back to explain how we were, or whether we intended going in the direction indicated. Our friends on shore knew something of guns and gunnery—that was plain. How much, we could not tell. But our glasses showed us that not all the black logs frowning at us from their portholes were genuine. Some at least were "quakers," that could not be fired except in a general conflagration; like the battery of a native guard boat in the harbor of Nagasaki that once

---

[1]Nitobe. *Intercourse between the United States and Japan,* p. 46.

upon a time capsized in a squall; various things went to the bottom, but most of her guns floated!

By the time we were well anchored and sails furled and men piped down, swarms of picturesque Mandarins came off to challenge the strange arrival and to draw around the fleet the customary cordon of guard boats. This looked like being in custody. The American ambassador had not come to Japan to be put under sentries. He notified the Mandarins that his vessels were not pirates and need not be watched. They pleaded Japanese law. He replied with American law. They still insisted. Whereupon he clinched the American side of the argument with the notice that if the boats were not off in fifteen minutes, he should be obliged to open his batteries and sink them. That was entirely convincing, and the guard boats stood not on the order of their going but betook themselves to the shelter of the shore.

I well remember that still starlit night that closed our first day in Yedo Bay. Nothing disturbed its peaceful beauty. The towering ships slept motionless on the water, and the twinkling lights of the towns along the shore went out one by one. A few beacon fires lighted upon the hilltops, the rattling cordage of an occasional passing junk, the musical tones of a distant temple bell that came rippling over the bay at intervals throughout the long night—these were to us the only tokens of life in the sleeping empire.

A sleeping empire truly; aloof from the world, shut in within itself and utterly severed from the general world-consciousness, not awake to the opportunities and privileges it was later so suddenly and so brilliantly to achieve as one of the world's powers, not even conscious that there was any such high position to be attained. While the expedition is resting a its anchors, and the empire around is asleep, let us take the chance to paint in a bit of the background. An historical reminiscence or two will enable us more fully to appreciate the aim and the ultimate success of the enterprise.

The Sunrise Kingdom, like the telescope, was discovered by accident. In 1542, when Henry VIII of England, Charles V of Germany, Knox, Calvin, and Luther were the chief characters on the European stage, a Portuguese vessel bound to Macao in China was driven by storms into Bungo, a port of Kiusiu. It was the first meeting of Japanese and Europeans. It seems to have been mutually agreeable. The accidental visitors were dazzled with the riches of the oriental paradise they had found, and the natives were pleased and entertained with their outlandish guests. When the news reached Europe, it started a crusade of adventurers to the eastern seas. There was gold fever; all the commercial nations of the West had even caught it. The flags of Portugal, England, Holland, France, and Spain soon waved in succession over the waters of the newly discovered empire. The Japanese were amiable, and a busy barter was maintained for some scores of years.

Traders and speculators were not the only visitors in that distant mart. Some ten years later the Jesuits resolved to signalize the beginnings of their new order by converting those rich and dissolute Gentiles. Their crusade, like many others, was successful. It is related that when the first missioners, as they were called, reached the field of their operations, some of the courtiers desired an edict against the propagation of the new faith. "How many religions have we now?" asked the emperor. "Thirty-five," was the answer. "Very well," said the tolerant monarch, "One more will hurt nobody—let them preach." And they did preach. And Xavier, the renowned Jesuit apostle and saint, though within the year he returned to China to die, lived long enough to baptize multitudes of the penitent pagans, grandees as well as commoners and peasantry. Other missioners flocked to the harvest. The Jesuits were then followed by Dominicans and Franciscans. The splendid robes and ritual of the church proved attractive and large numbers of the people were gathered into the Roman fold. Shrines were deserted and priests found their custom wasting away.

This was a result not entirely palatable to either the priesthood or the court. Several of the emperors recalled their apostate subjects to the mourning gods. Persecutions began. The foreign monks and friars were accused of political intrigue. The story is a bloody one and covers a whole generation of tragedy and horror. Let us turn the page and simply record the fact that Christianity was expunged from Japan.

The final catastrophe occurred in 1637 at the fall of Simabara and the massacre of some forty thousand Christians. The histories tell us that the bodies of the martyrs were tumbled together into one vast pit and over it was raised this defiant inscription: "So long as the sun shall warm the earth let no Christian be so bold as to come to Japan; and let all know that the King of Spain himself, or the Christian's God, or the most great God of all, if he violate this command, shall pay for it with his head."[2] Then the murderous empire wiped its sword, shut its gates, and barred itself in against all the world. One of the precautions by which it protected itself against Christianity and the civilization of the West was the famous ceremony of trampling on the cross; the astute pagans rightly divining that no foreigner would consent to such a sacrilege who had enough of the Christian religion about him to disturb the empire.

The ceremony was performed every year, as methodically as taking the census or collecting the

---

[2]MacFarlane, *Japan,* pp 49–50.

taxes, and was only abolished as late as 1853, after our first visit to Japan.[3] Once a year, officers went to every house with boxes containing the crucifix and images of the Virgin. These were laid on the floor, and all the household from octogenarians to infants in arms were required to tread upon them as a proof that they were not Christians. This law was enforced among the Dutch, the only western nation that maintained its foothold in the hermit land during all those darkened centuries. It is said that the cross was carved into the stone thresholds of their warehouses so that they could neither go nor come without trampling upon it. The placid Hollanders do not seem to have been much distressed by the requirement; their convenient religion was easily detached and left in Europe. One of them, we are told, one day wandered away from the warehouses on the island of Dezima across the bridge into the streets of Nagasaki and was suddenly halted by a Japanese patrol. "Are you a Christian?" was the challenge. "No, I am a Dutchman!" He was allowed to pass.

It is time to return to the ships. We left them sound asleep at anchor off Uraga the night of our arrival in Yedo Bay. Yet not all sound asleep, for a more vigilant watch has rarely been kept than was kept that night on board that fleet. Nothing happened however—

---

[3]Griffis, *Matthew Calbraith Perry,* p. 349.

except a brilliant display of meteoric light in the sky during the midwatch, an omen that terribly alarmed our friends on shore as portending that the very heavens themselves were enlisted on the side of these foreign barbarians. The commodore alludes to the phenomenon in his narrative and adds the devout wish, "The ancients would have construed this remarkable appearance of the heavens as a favorable omen for any enterprise they had undertaken; it may be so construed by us, as we pray God that our present attempt to bring a singular and isolated people into the family of civilized nations may succeed without resort to bloodshed."[4] In spite of the menacing sky we all survived, Yankees and natives, and in the morning were all alive and ready for business.

During the day, our new friends came off to visit the ships and some were admitted on board. These first interviews were a constant surprise to us; we found them so well-informed. They questioned us about the Mexican War, then recent; about General Taylor and General Santa Anna.[*] On board the *Susquehanna* one day, a Japanese gentleman asked the

---

[4]Official *Narrative of the Expedition,* &c. I: 236.

[*]For General Zachary Taylor and General Antonio Lopez de Santa Anna, see the Lakeside Classic by George Ballentine, *Autobiography of an English Soldier in the United States Army,* edited by William H. Goetzmann (Chicago: R.R. Donnelly & Sons Company, 1986).—Ed.

officer of the deck, "Where did you come from?"
"From America," the officer replied. "Yes, I know,"
he said, "Your whole fleet came from the United
States. But this ship—did she come from New York?
or Philadelphia? or Washington?" He knew enough
of our geography not to locate our seaports on our
western prairies or up among the Rockies—a pitch
of intelligence not yet too common among even
our European friends. One of them asked if the
monster gun on the quarter-deck was a "paixhan"
gun?** Yes, it was, but where and how could he ever
have heard the name? When two or three midship-
men were taking the sun at noon, one of them laid
his sextant down and a Japanese taking it up remarked that such instruments came from London
and Paris and the best were made in London. How
could a Japanese know that?

Our colloquies were carried on in Dutch through
our Dutch interpreter, Mr. Portman, the educated
Japanese being then accustomed to the use of that
language somewhat as we use French. We naturally
supposed, therefore, that all their information had
come through the Dutch, the only nation beside the
neighboring Chinese and Koreans that had for the
last three centuries kept its hold upon the good

**A gun named for its French inventor, General Henri Joseph
Paixhans (1783–1854).—Ed.

graces and the commerce of Japan. But we afterwards found that the Japanese printers were in the habit of republishing the textbooks prepared by our missionaries in China for use in their schools. The knowledge of America which we found thus diffused in Japan had come straight from Dr. Bridgeman's *History of the United States,* a manual written and published in China, which also had, what the good doctor never dreamed of, a wide circulation in the realm of the Mikado.* That book had already prepossessed its readers in our favor. The following winter it was my privilege to make the acquaintance of the author at his home in Shanghai and to sit often at his genial board. It has been one of the regrets of my life that I could not tell him and his accomplished wife that his little textbook was speeding its way within the Empire of the Rising Sun. But at that time, alas, none of use knew it. They have both long since gone home to the heaven they loved, and probably never learned in this world of the good they had thus unconsciously done.

The next day was Sunday. According to custom, divine service was held on board the flagship. The capstan on the quarterdeck was draped with the flag

---

*Elijah Coleman Bridgman (1801–61), the first American Protestant missionary to China; he arrived in 1830 and served there until his death.—Ed.

and the Bible was laid open upon it. Chaplain Jones took his station beside it. I do not know that any record was made of the service; presumably the chaplain followed the usual liturgical form and preached a brief sermon. But the hymn sung on the occasion has become historic; it was Watts' solemn lyric:

Before Jehovah's awful throne,
Ye nations, bow with sacred joy.

It was sung to the tune of "Old Hundred" and was led by the full band. The familiar strains poured in mighty chorus from two hundred or three hundred lusty throats with a peal that echoed through the fleet and wafted the gracious message to the distant shore. The Japanese listened with wonder; and their wonder deepened into amazement when they found that the whole day was to be observed as a day of rest and none of them could be admitted on board.[5]

On Monday the secular tide was turned on again and diplomatic overtures began in good earnest. In their official dealings with us it was interesting to see how the authorities clung to their time-honored policy of exclusion. It was a curious contest of steady nerve on one side, met by the most nimble

---

[5]Griffis, *Matthew Calbraith Perry,* p. 324. Official *Narrative of the Expedition,* &c. I: 240

parrying on the other. First they directed the commodore to go home; they wanted no letters from American presidents, nor any treaty. But the commodore would not go home. Then they ordered him to Nagasaki, where foreign business could be properly transacted through the Dutch. But the commodore declined to go to Nagasaki. If then this preposterous barbarian would not budge, and his letter must be received, they would receive it without ceremony on board ship. But his Western mightiness would not deliver it on board ship. Then they asked for time to consult the court at Yedo, and the commodore gave them three days—days big with fate; but exactly what happened at court we may never know. This much is certain, that our reluctant friends yielded at last; that pestilent letter would be received, and commissioners of suitable rank would come from court for the purpose. Even after all preliminaries had been settled, they begged to receive the letter on board ship, not on shore. But the Rubicon had been passed.

Some three miles below our anchorage a little semicircular harbor makes in on the western side of the bay, and at the head of it stands the village or hamlet of Kurihama. That was the spot selected for the meeting of the Western envoy and the imperial commissioners, and there the Japanese erected a temporary hall of audience. It was a memorable scene.

The two frigates steamed slowly down and anchored off the harbor. How big, black, and sullen they looked, masterful, accustomed to having their own way, full of pent-up force. Our little flotilla of fifteen boats landed under cover of their guns. We were not quite three hundred all told, but well befeathered in full uniform and armed to the teeth; a somewhat impressive lot, and yet of rather scant dimensions to confront five thousand native troops drawn up on the beach to receive us, with crowds of curious spectators lining the housetops and grouped on the hills in the rear. However, we were ready for anything and had no fear of treachery. The emblazonry of those Japanese regiments surpasses any powers of description that have been vouchsafed to the present deponent. Their radiant uniforms and trappings and ensigns must have been cut out of rainbows and sunsets; and the scores of boats fringing the shore heightened the effect with their fluttering plumage of flags. There was one thing not lively; the officers of these gorgeous troops sat in silent dignity on campstools in front of the line—a kind of military coma that the hustling regiments now tackling the great Northern Bear in Manchuria evidently have not inherited and could not comprehend.*

---

*Northern Bear signifies Russia, and "tackling" dates are Sewall's reference to the Russo-Japanese War of 1904–05.—Ed.

The situation was unique, not likely to be forgotten by any who participated in it, either American or Japanese. It was a clear and calm summer morning. As our lines disembarked and formed on the beach, the commodore stepped into his barge to follow us. Instantly the black "fireships" were wrapped in white clouds of smoke, and the thunder of their salute echoed among the hills and groves back of the village. To the startled spectators on shore they must have seemed suddenly transformed into floating volcanoes. And when the great man landed, they gazed with wonder, for no mortal eye (no Japanese mortal) had been permitted to look upon him before. In all the negotiations hitherto he had played their own game and veiled himself in mystery. They could communicate with so lofty a being only through his subordinates. This was not child's play. It was not an assumption of pomp inconsistent with republican simplicity. Commodore Perry was dealing with an oriental potentate according to oriental ideas. He showed his sagacity in doing so. At this time he was fifty-nine years old, a man of splendid physique and commanding presence. He had already lived through a varied experience that had helped to train him for this culminating achievement of his life. Endowed with strong native powers he had risen in mental capacity and executive force with every stage of his professional career.

The War of 1812, in which also his famous brother Oliver Hazard* and two younger brothers served, gave him his first baptism of fire; and later the Mexican War, service in various parts of the world civilized and savage, duties on naval boards at home, investigations and experiments in naval science, naval architecture, naval education—these and numberless other methods of serving his country both in the professional routine and in general affairs, had developed his judgment, his mental acumen, his breadth of vision, his knowledge of men; and thus had prepared him for his high mission as ambassador and diplomat. Unquestionably his insight into the oriental mind, his firmness and persistence, his stalwart physical presence, his portly bearing, his dignity, his poise, his stately courtesy were prime factors in his success as a negotiator with an Eastern court. He was the right kind of man for America to send on such an errand to such a people.

On his arrival we marched to the hall through an avenue of soldiers, our escort being formed of sailors and marines from the four ships. Leaving the escort drawn up on the beach, the forty officers entered. We found ourselves within a broad canopied

---

*Oliver Hazard Perry, U.S.N. (1785–1819), victor over the British in the Battle of Lake Erie in 1813. His report, "We have met the enemy and they are ours," made him famous.—Ed.

court of cotton hangings, carpeted with white, overlaid in the center with a scarlet breadth for a pathway leading to and extending up on the raised floor of the hall beyond. Many two-sworded officials in state robes were kneeling on either side of this flaming track. Within the hall sat—not in Japanese fashion but on chairs—the imperial commissioners, the princess Idzu and Iwami,* surrounded by their kneeling suite. They were both men of some years, fifty or sixty perhaps; Idzu a pleasant intellectual-looking man, Iwami's features narrow and somewhat disfigured by the smallpox; both were attired in magnificent robes richly embroidered in silver and gold. Vacant seats opposite the commissioners were taken by the commodore and his staff. Between the lines were the interpreters, on one side a native scholar on his knees, on the other erect and dignified the official interpreter of the squadron, S. Wells Williams LL.D., a well-known author and missionary in China. Behind them stood a scarlet lacquered chest that was destined to receive the fateful missive for conveyance to court. Overhead in rich folds drooped the purple silk hangings profusely decorated with the imperial arms and the national bird, the stork.

---

*The former is now transliterated in shorter form as Prince Izu; the latter's name remains unaltered as Prince Iwami.—Ed.

I had scarcely noted these few details and glanced at the genial face of Bayard Taylor as he stood behind the commodore taking notes, when the ceremony began. It was very brief. A few words between the interpreters, and then, at a signal, two boys in blue entered followed then by two stalwart Negroes, probably the first to be seen on the landscape of Japan. In slow and impressive fashion the two men brought in the rosewood boxes that contained the mysterious papers. These were opened in silence and laid on the scarlet coffer. Prince Iwami handed to the interpreters a formal receipt for the documents. The commodore announced that he should return the next spring for the reply. A brief conversation in answer to a question about the progress of the Taiping Rebellion in China, and the conference closed, having lasted not more than twenty minutes. A short ceremony, and witnessed by not more than fifty or sixty persons out of the entire populations of both the great countries engaged; but it was the opening of Japan. It brought together as neighbors and friends two nations that were the antipodes of each other not only in position on the globe but in almost every element of their two types of civilization.

That the Japanese have themselves appreciated the significance of this memorable meeting appears in the amazing historical developments that have followed all over the empire along the lines of commerce, industrial art, education, and religion, and is shown also by innumerable public utterances from the platform and press; and they have recently commemorated the occasion by erecting a monument at Kurihama in honor of the American commodore. But this later material can wait until the end of the chapter; we will keep on here with the main story.

This first act of the mission was now achieved, and the squadron rested from its labors. A great weight was lifted off its mind. The next day, with lightened conscience, it set itself to the easier task of surveying and sounding the bay, exploring future harbors, locating islands and rocks, measuring distances, and plotting charts. These uncanny operations were watched with some solicitude by the coast guards. They offered no active opposition, though once or twice we had occasion to show how thoroughly each boat was armed and ready for emergencies. The *Saratoga,* not willing to be outdone in this hydrographic work, located one shoal with undoubted accuracy by running upon it full tilt. Fortunately the wind was light and the bottom smooth; no harm was done to either ship or shoal. We were not proud of the achievement; but the commodore did us the honor to immortalize it and us by naming the sandbar the "Saratoga Spit"; and that title it bears to this day. Some years later it acquired a tragic interest when the U.S.S. *Oneida,* coming down the bay to sail for home, was run into in the night and sunk by the British mailship *Bombay*. She went down close by the "Saratoga Spit," carrying with her most of her hapless crew.

A few days after the Kurihama conference we left the Empire of the Rising Sun and returned to the Central Flowery Kingdom. On the seventeenth of July, as silently as they had entered nine days before, the two frigates steamed out of the bay with the two ships in tow. Outside they separated and went their several ways; the two steamers and the *Plymouth* back to Lew Chew and the *Saratoga* to Shanghai. We parted in a storm. If our Japanese friends could have seen our belabored ships scuttling away into the darkness and foam they would have taken it for a special interposition of their wind-god, wreaking vengeance on the Western barbarians for their temerity. The gale grew into a tempest, and the tempest into a typhoon, the largest through not the most vicious of the four encountered by the *Saratoga* in those uneasy seas. We compared the logbooks afterward of several ships that were caught in different sections of its enormous circuit and found that it was more than 1,000 miles in diameter and, in its progress, swept over the larger part of the north Pacific Ocean. It raged for several days, and every vessel in our fleet got entangled in some part of its vortex. Our own ship, the *Saratoga,* was under orders for Shanghai; and after the gale struck us, with battened hatches and sea-swept decks, we rode on the outer rim of that cyclone almost all the way back into the mouth of the Yang-tse-keang. It was riding a wild steed, as all sailors know who have tried it, but we got to Shanghai all the quicker. Six months we lay there at anchor off the American consulate. It was the time of the Taiping rebellion. As if to give us further object lessons in the oriental way of making history, one night the Taipings inside the walls rose and captured the city. The imperialist forces came down from Peking to retake it. And about once in three days we were treated to a Chinese battle—sometimes an assault by land, sometimes a bombardment by the fleet of forty or fifth junks; all very dramatic and spectacular, occasionally tragic, frequently funny. But, as Kipling says, that is another story and deserves a chapter of its own.

Meanwhile here is the place for a codicil in which to record the Kurihama celebration just referred to. During the autumn of 1900, Rear Admiral Beardslee, retired and traveling in Japan, took occasion to revisit the scene of the famous landing. In 1853 he was a young midshipman on board the *Plymouth,* and was in charge of one of the boats of the flotilla. He easily identified the spot and finding it neglected brought it to the attention of the *Beiyu-Kwai*—"Society of Friends of America"—who assumed the patriotic task of renovating the place and commemorating the event. The occasion truly was an inspiring one. On 14 July 1901, which was the forty-eighth anniversary of the conference, and on the spot where the hall of conference stood, there assembled a distinguished company of dignitaries of the empire, the officials of the *Beiyu-Kwai,* Admiral Beardslee and other representative Americans, together with many thousand interested spectators. Baron Kaneko presided and addressed the company. Other addresses followed, from the American minister Colonel Buck, from Viscount Katsura, from Admirals Rodgers and Beardslee, U.S.N., and also from the Governor of Kanagawa. It was felicitous circumstance that when the supreme moment came the monument was unveiled by Admiral Rodgers, a grandson of Commodore Perry and at that time commanding the American squadron in the East. The memorial is a shaft of unpolished granite standing on a massive base and rising to a height over all of thirty-three feet. The side facing the bay bears this inscription in Japanese:

> This monument marks the landing place of
> Commodore Perry of the United States of
> North America. Marquis Ito Hirobumi,
> Highest Order of Merit.

On the reverse is an inscription in English:

> This monument commemorates the
> first arrival of Commodore Perry,
> Ambassador from the United States of America,
> who landed at this place July 14, 1853.
> Erected July 14, 1901.

This solid memorial will forever dignify the little Japanese hamlet of Kurihama as the birthplace of the new Japan and the scene of the beginnings of a great international friendship.

In this epilogue belongs also the record of another celebration more recent and of a more personal flavor. The Japanese in foreign lands have a patriotic custom of strengthening the home ties by celebrating the birthday of their emperor, which falls on the third of November. The year 1903 marked a half century from the first landing of the Perry expedition on Japanese soil, and Mr. Uchida, the Japanese consul-general in New York, conceived the happy idea of adding still further prestige to the usual celebration by commemorating that famous event. Invitations were issued to the descendants of commodore Perry and to the now few survivors of the fleet. Out of the more than two thousand officers and men who composed the personnel of the expedition, less than a score are known to be living, three of whom were present at the reception.

To these three, who had not met for half a century, it may well be imagined the occasion was impressive, not to say thrilling. The forty or fifty Japanese gentlemen and the ladies present, and as many more Americans, some of them descendants of the famous commodore, and others who had been resident in the Mikado's dominions or were specially interested in the country and its people, made a most brilliant assemblage. The memories were indeed inspiring.

The half century had enlarged the dimensions of the event; rather had brought out and developed its natural results along the lines of trade, industrial art, commerce, education, intellectual and moral enlightenment, and so splendidly that the growing light reflected back on the original act and revealed its magnitude. With these sentiments were also mingled tender thoughts of shipmates long since gone and memories of scenes that made us sigh:

—for the touch of a vanished hand,
And the sound of a voice that is still.

On the walls hung a large old-time colored lithograph representing the landing at Kurihama, a print struck off soon after the return of the fleet and loaned for the occasion by one of the commodore's daughters. Near it was a companion picture of the same size, a photograph of the Perry monument at Kurihama.

After the social hour, the consul called his guests to order and made an address of welcome, alluding to the emperor, the expedition, and the presence of some who had been members of it. Two other brief speeches were made, one by Admiral Rodgers, a grandson of the old commodore, who spoke of his grandfather's mission in Japan, his own service in the East, and the unveiling of the Kurihama monument. The other was by one of the survivors and was, or course, largely reminiscent of those distant scene and descriptive of our famous old commander. It gives one a funny sensation to stand before a brilliant company as a relic of some ancient bit of history, and be watched by such curious eyes while you step out of your own past generation into the light of modern times to make your speech!

When the tables were brought in for the banquet, it fell to us three "relics" with three or four friends to surround the same board—a sumptuous improvement on a middies' mess in the steerage of a man-of-war and seasoned with high memories. As we broke bread together and the current of converse moved swiftly on, it seemed almost as if we were surrounded by the unseen forms of messmates who had long since sailed on to the haven beyond. And back of all was the thought of the Sunrise Kingdom herself, the hermit land of half a century ago, so exclusive, so mysterious, but now so teeming with the activities of a new civilization, the resources of a new power, and all the dignity and responsibility of a new place in the world. The occasion itself, the sentiments it inspired, and the distinguished company uniting in the celebration, all combined to make it a memorable evening.

Kit Carson and John Fremont

[EDWARD S. ELLIS]

K it Carson was astonished on reaching Bent's Fort to learn that Lieutenant Fremont had gone by on his second exploring expedition but a few days before. Carson felt a strong attachment for his old leader and galloped nearly a hundred miles to overtake him. Fremont gave the mountaineer most cordial greeting and insisted so strongly on his accompanying him that Carson could not refuse.

The object of Fremont's second exploration was to connect the survey of the previous year with those of Commander Wilkes on the Pacific coast. The first objective point was the Great Salt Lake of Utah, of which very little was known at that time.

Carson was sent back to the fort to procure a number of mules. He did as directed and rejoined Fremont at St. Vrain's Fort. The region traversed by these explorers is so well known today that it is hard to realize what a terra incognita it was but a short time since. Perhaps it will be most instructive at this point to quote the words of the great Pathfinder himself. The party arrived on the 21st of August on the Bear River, one of the principal tributaries of Great Salt Lake. The narrative of Fremont proceeds:

We were now entering a region, which for us possessed a strange and extraordinary interest. We were upon the waters of the famous lake which forms a salient point among the remarkable geographical features of the country, and around which the vague and superstitious accounts of the trappers had thrown a delightful obscurity, which we anticipated pleasure in dispelling, but which, in the meantime, left a crowded field for the exercise of our imagination.

In our occasional conversations with the few old hunters who had visited the region, it had been a subject of frequent speculation; and the wonders which they related were not the less agreeable because they were highly exaggerated and impossible.

Hitherto this lake had been seen only by trappers, who were wandering through the country in search of new beaver streams, caring very little for geography; its islands had never been visited; and none were to be found who had entirely made the circuit of its shores, and no instrumental observations, or geographical survey of any description, had ever been made anywhere in the neighboring region. It was generally supposed that it had no visible outlet; but, among the trappers, including those in my own camp, were many who believed that somewhere on its surface was a terrible whirlpool, through which its waters found their way to the ocean by some subterranean communication. All these things had been made a frequent subject of discussion in our desultory conversations around the fires at night; and my own mind had become tolerably well filled with their indefinite pictures, and insensibly colored with their romantic descriptions, which, in the pleasure of excitement, I was well disposed to believe, and half expected to realize.

In about six miles' travel from our encampment we reached one of the points in our journey to which we had always looked forward with great interest—the famous Beer Springs, which, on account of the effervescing gas and acid taste, had received their name from the voyageurs and trappers of the country, who, in the midst of their rude and hard lives, are fond of finding some fancied resemblance to the luxuries they rarely have the good fortune to enjoy.

Although somewhat disappointed in the expectations which various descriptions had led me to form of

unusual beauty of situation and scenery, I found it altogether a place of very great interest; and a traveller for
the first time in a volcanic region remains in a constant
excitement, and at every step is arrested by something
remarkable and new. There is a confusion of interesting
objects gathered together in a small space. Around the
place of encampment the Beer Springs were numerous
but, as far as we could ascertain, were entirely confined
to that locality in the bottom. In the bed of the river in
front, for a space of several hundred yards, they were
very abundant; the effervescing gas rising up and agitat-
ing the water in countless bubbling columns. In the
vicinity round about were numerous springs of an entirely different and equally marked mineral character. In
a rather picturesque spot, about 1,300 yards below our
encampment and immediately on the river bank, is the
most remarkable spring of the place. In an opening on
the rock, a white column of scattered water is thrown
up, in form, like a jet d'eau, to a variable height of about
three feet, and, though it is maintained in a constant supply, its greatest height is attained only at regular intervals,
according to the action of the force below. It is accompanied by a subterranean noise, which, together with the
motion of the water, makes very much the impression of
a steamboat in motion; and, without knowing that it had
been already previously so called, we gave to it the name
of the Steamboat Spring. The rock through which it is
forced is slightly raised in a convex manner, and gathered

at the opening into an urn mouthed form, and is evidently formed by continued deposition from the water, and colored bright red by oxide of iron.

It is a hot spring, and the water has a pungent, disagreeable metallic taste, leaving a burning effect on the tongue. Within perhaps two yards of the jet d'eau, is a small hole of about an inch in diameter, through which, at regular intervals escapes a blast of hot air with a light wreath of smoke, accompanied by a regular noise.

As they approached the lake, they passed over a country of bold and striking scenery, and through several 'gates,' as they called certain narrow valleys. The 'standing rock' is a huge column, occupying the centre of one of these passes. It fell from a height of perhaps 3,000 feet, and happened to remain in its present upright position.

At last, on the 6th of September, the object for which their eyes had long been straining was brought to view.

September 6.—This time we reached the butte without any difficulty; and ascending to the summit, immediately at our feet beheld the object of our anxious search, the waters of the Inland Sea, stretching in still and solitary grandeur, far beyond the limit of our vision. It was one of the great points of the exploration; and as we looked eagerly over the lake in the first emotions of excited pleasure, I am doubtful if the followers of Balboa felt more enthusiasm when, from the heights of the Andes, they saw for the first time the great Western Ocean. It was certainly a magnificent object, and a noble terminus to this part of our expedition; and to travellers so long shut up among mountain ranges, a sudden view over the expanse of silent waters had in it something sublime. Several large islands raised their high rocky heads out of the waves; but whether or not they were timbered was still left to our imagination, as the distance was too great to determine if the dark hues upon them were woodland or naked rock. During the day the clouds had been gathering black over the mountains to the westward, and while we were looking, a storm burst down with sudden fury upon the lake, and entirely hid the islands from our view.

On the edge of the stream a favorable spot was selected in a grove, and felling the timber, we made a strong corral, or horse pen, for the animals, and a little fort for the people who were to remain. We were now probably in the country of the Utah Indians, though none reside upon the lake. The India rubber boat was repaired with prepared cloth and gum, and filled with air, in readiness for the next day.

The provisions which Carson had brought with him being now exhausted, and our stock reduced to a small quantity of roots, I determined to retain with me only a sufficient number of men for the execution of our design; and accordingly seven were sent back to Fort Hall, under the guidance of Francois Lajeunesse, who, having been for many years a trapper in the country, was an experienced mountaineer.

We formed now but a small family. With Mr. Preuss and myself, Carson, Bernier, and Basil Lajeunesse had been selected for the boat expedition—the first ever attempted on this interior sea; and Badau, with Derosier, and Jacob (the colored man), were to be left in charge of the camp. We were favored with most delightful weather. Tonight there was a brilliant sunset of golden orange and green, which left the western sky clear and beautifully pure; but clouds in the east made me lose an occulation. The summer frogs were singing around us, and the evening was very pleasant, with a temperature of 60 degrees—a night of a more southern autumn. For our supper, we had yampak, the most agreeably flavored of the roots, seasoned by a small fat duck, which had come in the way of Jacob's rifle. Around our fire tonight were many speculations on what tomorrow would bring forth; and in our busy conjectures we fancied that we should find every one of the large islands a tangled wilderness of trees and shrubbery, teeming with game of every description that the neighboring region afforded, and which the foot of a white man or Indian had never violated. Frequently, during the day, clouds had rested on the summits of their lofty mountains, and we believed that we should find clear streams and springs of fresh water; and we indulged in anticipations of the luxurious repasts with which we were to indemnify ourselves for past privations. Neither, in our discussions, were the whirlpool and other mysterious dangers forgotten, which Indian and hunter's stories attributed to this unexplored lake. The men had discovered that, instead of being strongly sewed, (like that of the preceding year, which had so triumphantly rode the canyons of the Upper Great Platte), our present boat was only pasted together in a very insecure manner, the maker having been allowed so little time in the construction that he was obliged to crowd the labor of two months into several days. The insecurity of the boat was sensibly felt by us; and mingled with the enthusiasm and excitement that we all felt at the prospect of an undertaking which had never before been accomplished was a certain impression of danger, sufficient to give a serious character to our conversation. The momentary view which had been had of the lake the day before, its great extent and rugged islands, dimly seen amidst the dark waters in the obscurity of the sudden storm, were well calculated to heighten the idea of undefined danger with which the lake was generally associated.

September 8.—A calm, clear day, with a sunrise temperature of 41 degrees. In view of our present enterprise, a part of the equipment of the boat had been made to consist of three airtight bags, about three feet long, and capable each of containing five gallons. These had been filled with water the night before, and were now placed in the boat, with our blankets and instruments, consisting of a sextant, telescope, spyglass, thermometer, and barometer.

In the course of the morning we discovered that two of the cylinders leaked so much as to require one man constantly at the bellows, to keep them sufficiently full of air to support the boat. Although we had made a very early start, we loitered so much on the way—stopping every now and then, and floating silently along, to get a shot at a goose or a duck—that it was late in the day when he reached the outlet. The river here divided into several branches, filled with fluvials, and so very shallow that it was with difficulty we could get the boat along, being obliged to get out and wade. We encamped on a low point among rushes and young willows, where there was a quantity of driftwood, which served for our fires. The evening was mild and clear; we made a pleasant bed of the young willows; and geese and ducks enough had been killed for an abundant supper at night, and for breakfast next morning. The stillness of the night was enlivened by millions of waterfowl.

September 9.—The day was clear and calm; the thermometer at sunrise at 49 degrees. As is usual with the trappers on the eve of any enterprise, our people had made dreams, and theirs happened to be a bad one—one which always preceded evil—and consequently they looked very gloomy this morning; but we hurried through our breakfast, in order to make an early start, and have all the day before us for our adventure. The

channel in a short distance became so shallow that our
navigation was at an end, being merely a sheet of soft
mud, with a few inches of water, and sometimes none at
all, forming the low water shore of the lake. All this place
was absolutely covered with flocks of screaming plover.
We took off our clothes, and, getting overboard, commenced dragging the boat—making, by this operation,
a very curious trail, and a very disagreeable smell in stir-
ring up the mud, as we sank above the knee at every
step. The water here was still fresh, with only an insipid
and disagreeable taste, probably derived from the bed of
fetid mud. After proceeding in this way about a mile, we
came to a small black ridge on the bottom, beyond
which the water became suddenly salt, beginning gradually to deepen, and the bottom was sandy and firm. It was
a remarkable division, separating the fresh water of the
rivers from the briny water of the lake, which was entirely saturated with common salt. Pushing our little vessel across the narrow boundary, we sprang on board, and
at length were afloat on the waters of the unknown sea.

We did not steer for the mountainous islands, but directed our course towards a lower one, which it had
been decided we should first visit, the summit of which
was formed like the crater at the upper end of Bear
River Valley. So long as we could touch the bottom
with our paddles, we were very gay; but gradually, as the
water deepened, we became more still in our frail
bateau of gum cloth distended with air, and with pasted

seams. Although the day was very calm, there was a considerable swell on the lake; and there were white patches of foam on the surface, which were slowly moving to the southward, indicating the set of a current in that direction, and recalling the recollection of the whirlpool stories. The water continued to deepen as we advanced; the lake becoming almost transparently clear, of an extremely beautiful bright green color: and the spray which was thrown into the boat and over our clothes, was directly converted into a crust of common salt, which covered also our hands and arms. 'Captain,' said Carson, who for sometime had been looking suspiciously at some whitening appearances outside the nearest islands, 'what are those yonder?—won't you just take a look with the glass?' We ceased paddling for a moment, and found them to be the caps of the waves that were beginning to break under the force of a strong breeze that was coming up the lake. The form of the boat seemed to be an admirable one, and it rode on the waves like a water bird; but, at the same time, it was extremely slow in its progress. When we were a little more than half way across the reach, two of the divisions between the cylinders gave way, and it required the constant use of the bellows to keep in a sufficient quantity of air. For a long time we scarcely seemed to approach our island, but gradually we worked across the rougher sea of the open channel, into the smoother water under the lee of the island, and began to discover that what we took for a long row of pelicans, ranged on the beach, were only low cliffs whitened with salt by the spray of the waves; and about noon we reached the shore, the transparency of the water enabling us to see the bottom at a considerable depth.

The cliffs and masses of rock along the shore were whitened by an incrustation of salt where the waves dashed up against them; and the evaporating water, which had been left in holes and hollows on the surface of the rocks, was covered with a crust of salt about one eighth of an inch in thickness.

Carrying with us the barometer and other instruments, in the afternoon we ascended to the highest point of the island—a bare, rocky peak, 800 feet above the lake. Standing on the summit, we enjoyed an extended view of the lake, inclosed in a basin of rugged mountains, which sometimes left marshy flats and extensive bottoms between them and the shore, and in other places came directly down into the water with bold and precipitous bluffs.

As we looked over the vast expanse of water spread out beneath us, and strained our eyes along the silent shores over which hung so much doubt and uncertainty, and which were so full of interest to us, I could hardly repress the almost irresistible desire to continue our exploration; but the lengthening snow on the mountains was a plain indication of the advancing season, and our frail linen boat appeared so insecure that I was unwilling to trust our lives to the uncertainties of the lake. I therefore unwillingly resolved to terminate our survey here, and remain satisfied for the present with what we had been able to add to the unknown geography of the region. We felt pleasure also in remembering that we were the first who, in the traditionary annals of the country, had visited the islands, and broken, with the cheerful sound of human voices the long solitude of the place.

I accidentally left on the summit the brass cover to the object end of my spyglass and as it will probably remain there undisturbed by Indians, it will furnish matter of speculation to some future traveller. In our excursions about the island, we did not meet with any kind of animal: a magpie, and another larger bird, probably attracted by the smoke of our fire, paid us a visit from the shore, and were the only living things seen during our stay. The rock constituting the cliffs along the shore where we were encamped, is a talcous rock, or steatite, with brown spar.

At sunset, the temperature was 70 degrees. We had arrived just in time to obtain a meridian altitude of the sun, and other observations were obtained this evening, which placed our camp in latitude 41 degrees 10′ 42″ and longitude 112 degrees 21′ 05″ from Greenwich. From a discussion of the barometrical observations made during our stay on the shores of the lake, we have adopted 4,200 feet for its elevation above the Gulf of

Mexico. In the first disappointment we felt from the dissipation of our dream of the fertile islands, I called this Disappointment Island.

Out of the driftwood, we made ourselves pleasant little lodges, open to the water, and, after having kindled large fires to excite the wonder of any straggling savage on the lake shores, lay down, for the first time in a long journey, in perfect security; no one thinking about his arms. The evening was extremely bright and pleasant; but the wind rose during the night, and the waves began to break heavily on the shore, making our island tremble. I had not expected in our inland journey to hear the roar of an ocean surf; and the strangeness of our situation, and the excitement we felt in the associated interests of the place, made this one of the most interesting nights I remember during our long expedition.

In the morning, the surf was breaking heavily on the shore, and we were up early. The lake was dark and agitated, and we hurried through our scanty breakfast, and embarked—having first filled one of the buckets with water from which it was intended to make salt. The sun had risen by the time we were ready to start; and it was blowing a strong gale of wind, almost directly off the shore, and raising a considerable sea, in which our boat strained very much. It roughened as we got away from the island, and it required all the efforts of the men to make any head against the wind and sea; the gale rising with the sun; and there was danger of being blown into

one of the open reaches beyond the island. At the distance of half a mile from the beach, the depth of water
was sixteen feet, with a clay bottom; but, as the working
of the boat was very severe labor, and during the operation of sounding, it was necessary to cease paddling,
during which the boat lost considerable way, I was unwilling to discourage the men, and reluctantly gave up
my intention of ascertaining the depth and character of
the bed. There was a general shout in the boat when we
found ourselves in one fathom, and we soon after landed
on a low point of mud, where we unloaded the boat,
and carried the baggage to firmer ground.

The explorers remained in camp the next day and
boiled down some of the water from the lake,
thereby obtaining considerable salt. The following
morning was clear and beautiful and they returned
by the same route, ascending the valley of Bear
River toward the north.

The expected Fitzpatrick and the provisions did
not show themselves and the party began to suffer
for food. When their situation became serious, Fremont permitted a horse to be killed and then all enjoyed one of their old fashioned feasts.

But this supply could not last long, and still they
failed to meet their expected friends. After a time
they encountered an Indian who had killed an an-
telope, which they quickly purchased and another

feast made every heart glad. By way of dessert, a messenger galloped into camp with the news that Fitzpatrick was close at hand with an abundant supply of provisions.

The next morning the two parties united and continued the journey together. After leaving the Bear River Valley they crossed over to Lewis's Fork of the Columbia. At night the camp fires of the Indian twinkled like so many stars along the mountain side; but they were all friendly and the tired explorers slept peacefully.

Pushing onward they reached the upper waters of Lewis's Fork, where snow began to fall. However, they were quite near Fort Hall and they therefore went into camp, while Fremont rode to the fort and procured several horses and oxen.

The weather continued severe, but Fremont determined to push on, despite the hardships which he knew awaited them all. As a matter of prudence, however, he sent back eleven of his men, leaving about twenty with which he pursued his journey down the river valley in the direction of the Columbia. The Dalles was reached in safety where Kit Carson was left in command of the party, while Fremont with a few companions pushed on to Vancouver Island, where he procured some provisions. On his return, the whole party united and made their way to Klamath Lake, in what was then Oregon Territory.

When their observations were completed, they took up their march in the direction of California.

After a long and wearisome journey, attended by much suffering for the lack of food, they came in sight of the Sierra Nevada Mountains, which were seen to be covered with snow. The men were in a sorry plight. The provisions were nearly gone; they could not turn back, and there seemed but two alternatives before them: to push on through the mountains or remain where they were and starve to death. Such men were not the ones to fold their hands and lie down in helpless despair. Accordingly, they made their preparations for the terrible venture.

The snow was so deep that it was impossible to get forward without the aid of snowshoes. Devoting themselves to the manufacture of these indispensable articles, a few were sent ahead to learn how far it was necessary to break a path for the animals. After a laborious passage, it was found that nine miles would have to be prepared in that fashion. Carson was with this advance and when they halted, he saw in the distance the green Sacramento Valley. Although nearly twenty years had passed since he visited that section, he recognized it at once. Away beyond towered the white peaks of the Coast Range. Carson was the only man in the party who really knew where they were.

This passage of Fremont and his men through the Sierra Nevada Mountains is one of the most extraordinary achievements in American history. Carson himself took such a prominent part in it, that it seems only just that Fremont's thrilling account should be quoted.

The people were unusually silent; for every man knew that our enterprise was hazardous, and the issue doubtful.

The snow deepened rapidly, and it soon became necessary to break a road. For this service, a party of ten was formed, mounted on the strongest horses; each man in succession opening the road on foot, or on horseback, until himself and his horse became fatigued, when he stepped aside; and, the remaining number passing ahead, he took his station in the rear.

The camp had been all the day occupied in endeavoring to ascend the hill, but only the best horses had succeeded; the animals, generally, not having sufficient strength to bring themselves up without the packs; and all the line of road between this and the springs was strewed with camp stores and equipage, and horses floundering in snow. I therefore immediately encamped on the ground with my own mess, which was in advance, and directed Mr. Fitzpatrick to encamp at the springs, and send all the animals, in charge of Tabeau, with a strong guard, back to the place where they had been pastured the night before. Here was a small spot of level ground, protected on one side by the mountain, and on the other sheltered by a little ridge of rock. It was an open grove of pines, which assimilated in size to the grandeur of the mountain, being frequently six feet in diameter.

Tonight we had no shelter, but we made a large fire around the trunk of one of the huge pines; and covering the snow with small boughs, on which we spread our blankets, soon made ourselves comfortable. The night was very bright and clear, though the thermometer was only at 10 degrees. A strong wind which sprang up at sundown, made it intensely cold; and this was one of the bitterest nights during the journey.

Two Indians joined our party here; and one of them, an old man, immediately began to harangue us, saying that ourselves and animals would perish in the snow; and that, if we would go back, he would show us another and a better way across the mountain. He spoke in a very loud voice, and there was a singular repetition of phrases and arrangement of words, which rendered his speech striking, and not unmusical.

We had now begun to understand some words, and, with the aid of signs, easily comprehended the old man's simple ideas. 'Rock upon rock—rock upon rock—snow upon snow—snow upon snow,' said he; 'even if you get over the snow, you will not be able to get down from the mountains.' He made us the sign of precipices, and showed us how the feet of the horses would slip, and throw them off from the narrow trails led along their sides. Our Chinook, who comprehended even more readily than ourselves, and believed our situation hopeless, covered his head with his blanket, and began to weep and lament. 'I wanted to see the whites,' said he; 'I came away from my own people to see the whites, and I wouldn't care to die among them; but here' —and he looked around into the cold night and gloomy forest, and, drawing his blanket over his head, began again to lament.

Seated around the tree, the fire illuminating the rocks and the tall boils of the pines round about, and the old Indian haranguing, we presented a group of very serious faces.

February 5. —The night had been too cold to sleep, and we were up very early. Our guide was standing by the fire with all his finery on; and seeing him shiver in the cold, I threw on his shoulders one of my blankets. We missed him a few minutes afterwards, and never saw him again. He had deserted. His bad faith and treachery were in perfect keeping with the estimate of Indian character, which a long intercourse with this people had gradually forced upon my mind.

While a portion of the camp were occupied in bringing up the baggage to this point, the remainder were busied in making sledges and snowshoes. I had determined to explore the mountain ahead, and the sledges were to be used in transporting the baggage.

Crossing the open basin, in a march of about ten miles we reached the top of one of the peaks, to the left of the pass indicated by our guide. Far below us, dimmed by the distance, was a large, snowless valley, bounded on the western side, at the distance of about a hundred miles, by a low range of mountains, which Carson recognized with delight as the mountains bordering the coast. 'There,' said he, 'is the little mountain—it is fifteen years ago since I saw it; but I am just as sure as if I had seen it yesterday.' Between us, then, and this low coast range, was the valley of the Sacramento; and no one who had not accompanied us through the incidents of our life for the last few months, could realize the delight with which at last we looked down upon it. At the distance of apparently thirty miles beyond us were distinguished spots of prairie; and a dark line, which could be traced with the glass, was imagined to be the course of the river; but we were evidently at a great height above the valley, and between us and the plains extended miles of snowy fields and broken ridges of pine covered mountains.

It was late in the day when we turned towards the camp; and it grew rapidly cold as it drew towards night. One of the men became fatigued and his feet began to freeze, and building a fire in the trunk of a dry old cedar, Mr. Fitzpatrick remained with him until his clothes could be dried, and he was in a condition to come on. After a day's march of twenty miles, we straggled into camp, one after another, at nightfall; the greater number excessively fatigued, only two of the party having ever travelled on snowshoes before.

All our energies were now directed to getting our animals across the snow; and it was supposed that, after all the baggage had been drawn with the sleighs over the trail we had made, it would be sufficiently hard to bear our animals.

At several places, between this point and the ridge, we had discovered some grassy spots, where the wind and sun had dispersed the snow from the sides of the hills, and these were to form a resting place to support the animals for a night in their passage across. On our way across, we had set on fire several broken stumps and dried trees, to melt holes in the snow for the camp. Its general depth was five feet; but we passed over places where it was twenty feet deep, as shown by the trees.

With one party drawing sleighs loaded with baggage, I advanced today about four miles along the trail, and encamped at the first grassy spot, where we expected to bring our horses. Mr. Fitzpatrick, with another party, remained behind, to form an intermediate station between us and the animals.

Putting on our snowshoes, we spent the afternoon in exploring a road ahead. The glare of the snow, combined with great fatigue, had rendered many of the people nearly blind; but we were fortunate in having some black silk handkerchiefs, which, worn as veils, very much relieved the eye.

In the evening I received a message from Mr. Fitzpatrick, acquainting me with the utter failure of his attempt to get our mules and horses over the snow—the half hidden trail had proved entirely too slight to support them, and they had broken through, and were plunging about or lying half buried in snow. He was occupied in endeavoring to get them back to his camp; and in the mean time sent to me for further instructions. I wrote to him to send the animals immediately back to their old pastures; and, after having made mauls and shovels, turn in all the strength of his party to open and beat a road through the snow, strengthening it with branches and boughs of the pines.

February 12. —We made mauls, and worked hard at our end of the road all the day. The wind was high, but the sun bright, and the snow thawing. We worked down the face of the hill, to meet the people at the other end. Towards sundown it began to grow cold, and we shouldered our mauls, and trudged back to camp.

February 13. —We continued to labor on the road; and in the course of the day had the satisfaction to see the people working down the face of the opposite hill, about three miles distant. During the morning we had the pleasure of a visit from Mr. Fitzpatrick, with the information that all was going on well. A party of Indians had passed on snowshoes, who said they were going to the western side of the mountain after fish. This was an indication that the salmon were coming up the streams; and we could hardly restrain our impatience as we thought of them, and worked with increased vigor.

I was now perfectly satisfied that we had struck the stream on which Mr. Sutter lived, and turning about, made a hard push, and reached the camp at dark. Here we had the pleasure to find all the remaining animals, fifty-seven in number, safely arrived at the grassy hill near the camp; and here, also, we were agreeably surprised with the sight of an abundance of salt. Some of the horse guard had gone to a neighboring hut for pine nuts, and discovered unexpectedly a large cake of very white fine grained salt, which the Indians told them they had brought from the other side of the mountain; they used it to eat with their pine nuts, and readily sold it for goods.

On the 19th, the people were occupied in making a road and bringing up the baggage; and, on the afternoon of the next day, February 20, 1844, we encamped with all the materiel of the camp, on the summit of the pass in the dividing ridge, 1,000 miles by our travelled road from the Dalles of the Columbia.

February 21. —We now considered ourselves victorious over the mountain; having only the descent before us, and the valley under our eyes, we felt strong hope that we should force our way down. But this was a case in which the descent was not facile. Still, deep fields of snow lay between, and there was a large intervening space of rough looking mountains, through which we had yet to wind our way. Carson roused me this morning with an early fire, and we were all up long before day, in order to pass the snow fields before the sun should render the crust soft. We enjoyed this morning a scene at sunrise, which, even here, was unusually glorious and beautiful. Immediately above the eastern mountains was repeated a cloud formed mass of purple ranges, bordered with bright yellow gold; the peaks shot up into a narrow line of crimson cloud, above which the air was filled with a greenish orange; and over all was the singular beauty of the blue sky. Passing along a ridge which commanded the lake on our right, of which we began to discover an out-let through a chasm on the west, we passed over alternat-ing open ground and hard crusted snow fields which supported the animals, and encamped on the ridge after a journey of six miles. The grass was better than we had yet seen, and we were encamped in a clump of trees, twenty or thirty feet high, resembling white pine.

We had hard and doubtful labor yet before us, as the snow appeared to be heavier where the timber began fur-ther down, with few open spots. Ascending a height, we traced out the best line we could discover for the next day's march, and had at least the consolation to see that the mountain descended rapidly. The day had been one of April; gusty, with a few occasional flakes of snow; which, in the afternoon enveloped the upper mountains in clouds. We watched them anxiously, as now we dreaded a snow storm. Shortly afterwards we heard the roll of thunder, and looking toward the valley, found it all enveloped in a thunderstorm. For us, as connected with the idea of summer, it had a singular charm; and we watched its progress with excited feelings until nearly sunset, when the sky cleared off brightly, and we saw a shining line of water directing its course towards another, a broader and larger sheet. We knew that these could be no other than the Sacramento and the bay of San Francisco; but, after our long wandering in rugged mountains, where so frequently we had met with disappointments, and where the crossing of every ridge displayed some unknown lake or river, we were yet almost afraid to believe that we were at last to escape into the genial country of which we have heard so many glowing descriptions, and dreaded again to find some vast interior lake, whose bitter waters would bring us disappointment. On the southern shore of what appeared to be the bay, could be traced the gleaming line where entered another large stream; and again the Buenaventura rose up in our mind.

Carson had entered the valley along the southern side of the bay, but the country then was so entirely covered with water from snow and rain, that he had been able to form no correct impression of watercourses.

We had the satisfaction to know that at least there were people below. Fires were lit up in the valley just at night, appearing to be in answer to ours; and these signs of life renewed, in some measure, the gayety of the camp. They appeared so near, that we judged them to be among the timber of some of the neighboring ridges; but, having them constantly in view day after day, and night after night, we afterwards found them to be fires that had been kindled by the Indians among the tulares, on the shore of the bay, eighty miles distant.

Axes and mauls were necessary today to make a road through the snow. Going ahead with Carson to reconnoitre the road, we reached in the afternoon the river which made the outlet of the lake. Carson sprang over, clear across a place where the stream was compressed among rocks, but the parfleche sole of my moccasin glanced from the icy rock, and precipitated me into the river. It was some few seconds before I could recover myself in the current, and Carson, thinking me hurt, jumped in after me, and we both had an icy bath. We tried to search a while for my gun, which had been lost in the fall, but the cold drove us out; and making a large fire on the bank, after we had partially dried ourselves we went back to meet the camp. We afterwards found that the gun had been slung under the ice which lined the banks of the creek.

The sky was clear and pure, with a sharp wind from the northeast, and the thermometer 20 below the freezing point.

We continued down the south face of the mountain; our road leading over dry ground, we were able to avoid the snow almost entirely. In the course of the morning we struck a foot path, which we were generally able to keep; and the ground was soft to our animals' feet, being sandy or covered with mould. Green grass began to make its appearance, and occasionally we passed a hill scatteringly covered with it. The character of the forest continued the same; and, among the trees, the pine with sharp leaves and very large cones was abundant, some of them being noble trees. We measured one that had ten feet diameter, though the height was not more than one hundred and thirty feet. All along, the river was a roaring torrent, its fall very great; and, descending with a rapidity to which we had long been strangers, to our great pleasure oak trees appeared on the ridge, and soon became very frequent; on these I remarked unusually great quantities of mistletoe.

The opposite mountain side was very steep and continuous—unbroken by ravines, and covered with pines and snow; while on the side we were travelling, innumerable rivulets poured down from the ridge. Continuing on, we halted a moment at one of these rivulets, to admire some beautiful evergreen trees, resembling live oak, which shaded the little stream. They were forty to fifty feet high, and two in diameter, with a uniform tufted top; and the summer green of their beautiful foliage, with the singing birds, and the sweet summer wind which was whirling about the dry oak leaves, nearly intoxicated us with delight; and we hurried on, filled with excitement, to escape entirely from the horrid region of inhospitable snow, to the perpetual spring of the Sacramento.

February 25.—Believing that the difficulties of the road were passed, and leaving Mr. Fitzpatrick to follow slowly, as the condition of the animals required, I started ahead this morning with a party of eight, consisting (with myself) of Mr. Preuss, and Mr. Talbot, Carson, Derosier, Towns, Proue, and Jacob. We took with us some of the best animals, and my intention was to proceed as rapidly as possible to the house of Mr. Sutter, and return to meet the party with a supply of provisions and fresh animals.

Near night fall we descended into the steep ravine of a handsome creek thirty feet wide, and I was engaged in getting the horses up the opposite hill, when I heard a shout from Carson, who had gone ahead a few hundred yards. 'Life yet,' said he, as he came up, 'life yet; I have found a hillside sprinkled with grass enough for the night.' We drove along our horses, and encamped at the place about dark, and there was just room enough to make a place for shelter on the edge of the stream. Three horses were lost today—Proveau; a fine young horse from the Columbia, belonging to Charles Towns; and another Indian horse which carried our cooking utensils; the two former gave out, and the latter strayed off into the woods as we reached the camp: and Derosier knowing my attachment to Proveau, volunteered to go and bring him in.

Carson and I climbed one of the nearest mountains; the forest land still extended ahead, and the valley appeared as far as ever. The pack horse was found near the camp, but Derosier did not get in.

We began to be uneasy at Derosier's absence, fearing he might have been bewildered in the woods. Charles Towns, who had not yet recovered his mind, went to swim in the river, as if it was summer, and the stream placid, when it was a cold mountain torrent foaming among the rocks. We were happy to see Derosier appear in the evening. He came in, and sitting down by the fire, began to tell us where he had been. He imagined he had been gone several days, and thought we were still at the camp where he had left us; and we were pained to see that his mind was deranged. It appeared that he had been lost in the mountain, and hunger and fatigue, joined to weakness of body, and fear of perishing in the mountains had crazed him. The times were severe when stout men lost their minds from extremity of suffering—when horses died—and when mules and horses, ready to die of starvation, were killed for food. Yet there was no murmuring or hesitation. In the meantime Mr. Preuss continued on down the river, and unaware that we had encamped so early in the day, was lost. When night arrived and he did not come in, we began to understand what had happened to him; but it was too late to make any search.

March 3.—We followed Mr. Preuss's trail for a considerable distance along the river, until we reached a place where he had descended to the stream below and encamped. Here we shouted and fired guns, but received no answer; and we concluded that he had pushed on down the stream. I determined to keep out from the river, along which it was nearly impracticable to travel with animals, until it should form a valley. At every step the country improved in beauty; the pines were rapidly disappearing, and oaks became the principal trees of the forest. Among these, the prevailing tree was the evergreen oak (which, by way of distinction, we shall call the live oak); and with these, occurred frequently a new species of oak, bearing a long, slender acorn, from an inch to an inch and a half in length, which we now began to see formed the principal vegetable food of the inhabitants of this region. In a short distance we crossed a little rivulet, where were two old huts and near by were heaps of acorn hulls. The ground round about was very rich, covered with an exuberant sward of grass; and we sat down for a while in the shade of the oaks to let the animals feed. We repeated our shouts for Mr. Preuss; and this time we were gratified with an answer. The voice grew rapidly nearer, ascending from the river, but when we expected to see him emerge, it ceased entirely. We had called up some straggling

Indian—the first we had met, although for two days back we had seen tracks—who, mistaking us for his fellows, had been only undeceived by getting close up. It would have been pleasant to witness his astonishment; he would not have been more frightened had some of the old mountain spirits they are so much afraid of suddenly appeared in his path. Ignorant of the character of these people, we had now additional cause of uneasiness in regard to Mr. Preuss; he had no arms with him, and we began to think his chance doubtful. Occasionally we met deer, but had not the necessary time for hunting. At one of these orchard grounds, we encamped about noon to make an effort for Mr. Preuss. One man took his way along a spur leading into the river, in hope to cross his trail, and another took our own back. Both were volunteers; and to the successful man was promised a pair of pistols—not as a reward, but as a token of gratitude for a service which would free us all from much anxiety.

At the end of four days, Mr. Preuss surprised and delighted his friends by walking into camp. He had lived on roots and acorns and was in the last stages of exhaustion.

Shortly the advance party reached Sutter's Fort where they received the most hospitable treatment. All their wants were abundantly supplied, and provisions were sent back to Fitzpatrick and his party.

The Malay Archipelago

[ALFRED RUSSEL WALLACE]

In order not to omit so important a portion of my life as my eight years in the far East, I propose to give a general sketch of my various journeys and their results, told as far as possible in quotations from the few of my letters home that have been preserved, with such connecting facts as may serve to render them intelligible.

Ten days after my arrival at Singapore I wrote home as follows:

> After being a week in a hotel here, I at last got permission to stay with a French Roman Catholic missionary, who lives about eight miles out of town, in the centre of the island, and close to the jungle. The greater part of the inhabitants of Singapore are Chinese, many of whom are

very rich, and almost all the villages around are wholly Chinese, who cultivate pepper and gambier, or cut timber. Some of the English merchants have fine country houses. I dined with one, to whom I brought an introduction. His house was spacious, and full of magnificent China and Japan furniture. We are now staying at the mission of Bukit Tima. The missionary (a French Jesuit) speaks English, Malay, and Chinese, and is a very pleasant man. He has built a pretty church here, and has about three hundred Chinese converts.

A month later (May 28th) I wrote—

I am very comfortable here with the missionary. I and Charles go into the jungle every day for insects. The forest here is very similar to that of South America. Palms are very numerous, but they are generally small, and very spiny. There are none of the large majestic species so common on the Amazon. I am so busy with insects now that I have no time for anything else. I send now about a thousand beetles to Mr. Stevens, and I have as many other insects still on hand, which will form part of my next and principal consignment. Singapore is rich in beetles, and before I leave I think I shall have a beautiful collection of them. I will tell you how my day is now occupied. Get up at half-past five, bath, and coffee. Sit down to arrange and put away my insects of the day before, and set them in a safe place to dry. Charles mends

our insect-nets, fills our pin-cushions, and gets ready for
the day. Breakfast at eight; out to the jungle at nine. We
have to walk about a quarter mile up a steep hill to reach
it, and arrive dripping with perspiration. Then we wander about in the delightful shade along paths made by
the Chinese wood-cutters till two or three in the afternoon, generally returning with fifty or sixty beetles,
some very rare or beautiful and perhaps a few butterflies. Change clothes and sit down to kill and pin insects,
Charles doing the flies, wasps, and bugs; I do not trust
him yet with beetles. Dinner at four, then at work again
till six: coffee. Then read or talk, or, if insects very numerous, work again till eight or nine. Then to bed.

In July I wrote from "The Jungle, near Malacca:"

We have been here a week, living in a Chinese house or
shed, which reminds me of some of my old Rio Negro
habitations. We came from Singapore in a small trading
schooner, with about fifty Chinese, Hindoos, and Portuguese passengers, and were two days on the voyage
with nothing but rice and curry to eat, not having made
any special provision, it being our first experience of the
country vessels. Malacca is a very old Dutch city, but the
Portuguese have left the clearest marks of their possession of it in the common language of the place being
still theirs. I have now two Portuguese servants, a cook
and a hunter, and find myself almost back in Brazil,

owing to the similarity of the language, the people, and the general aspect of the forest. In Malacca we stayed only two days, being anxious to get into the country as soon as possible. I stayed with a Roman Catholic missionary; there are several here, each devoted to a particular portion of the population—Portuguese, Chinese, and wild Malays of the jungle. The gentleman we were with is building a large church, of which he is architect himself, and superintends the laying of every brick and the cutting of every piece of timber. Money enough could not be raised here, so he took a voyage round the world, and in the United States, California, and India got enough subscribed to finish it. It is a curious and not very creditable thing, that in the English possessions of Singapore and Malacca, there is not a single Protestant missionary; while the conversion, education, and physical and moral improvement of the non-European inhabitants is left entirely to these French missionaries, who, without the slightest assistance from our Government, devote their lives to christianizing and civilizing the varied population under our rule.

Here the birds are abundant and most beautiful, more so than on the lower Amazon, and I think I shall soon form a fine collection. They are, however, almost all common species, and are of little value, except that I hope they will be better specimens than usually reach England. My guns are both very good, but I find powder and shot actually cheaper in Singapore than in London, so I need not have troubled myself to bring any. So far both I and Charles have had excellent health. He can now shoot pretty well, and is so fond of it that I can hardly get him to do anything else.

The Chinese here are most industrious. They clear and cultivate the ground with a neatness which I have never seen equaled in the tropics, and they save every particle of manure, both from animals and men, to enrich the ground.

The country around Malacca is much more beautiful than near Singapore, it being an old settlement with abundance of old fruit and forest trees scattered about. Monkeys of many sorts are abundant; in fact, all animal life *seems* more abundant than in Brazil. Among the fruits I miss the delicious oranges of Para and the Amazon. Here they are scarce and not good, and there is nothing that can replace them.

I may as well state here that the "Charles" referred to in the preceding letter was a London boy, the son of a carpenter who had done a little work for my sister, and whose parents were willing for him to go with me to learn to be a collector. He was sixteen years old, but quite undersized for his age, so that no one would have taken him for more than thirteen or fourteen. He remained with me about a year and a half, and learned to shoot and to catch insects pretty well, but not to prepare them properly. He was rather of a religious turn, and when I left Borneo he decided to stay with the bishop and become a teacher. After a year or two, however, he returned to Singapore, and got employment on some plantations. About five years later he joined me in the Moluccas as a collector. He had grown to be a fine young man, over six feet. When I returned home he remained in Singapore, married, and had a family. He died some fifteen years since.

At the end of September I returned to Singapore, whence I wrote home as follows:—

I have now just returned to Singapore after two months' hard work. At Malacca I had a strong touch of fever, with the old 'Rio Negro' symptoms, but the Government doctor made me take large doses of quinine every day for a week, and so killed it, and in less than a fortnight I was quite well, and off to the jungle again. I never took half enough quinine in America to cure me.

Malacca is a pretty place. Insects are not very abundant there, still, by perseverance, I got a good number, and many rare ones. Of birds, too, I made a good collection. I went to the celebrated Mount Ophir, and ascended to the top, sleeping under a rock. The walk there was hard work, thirty miles through jungle in a succession of mud-holes, and swarming with leeches, which crawled all over us, and sucked when and where they pleased. We lived a week at the foot of the mountain, in a little hut built by our men, near a beautiful rocky stream. I got some fine new butterflies there, and hundreds of other new or rare insects. Huge centipedes and scorpions, some nearly a foot long, were common, but we none of us got bitten or stung. We only had rice, and a little fish and tea, but came home quite well. The mountain is over four thousand feet high. Near the top are beautiful ferns and pitcher-plants, of which I made a small collection. Elephants and rhinoceroses, as well as tigers, are abundant there, but we had our usual bad luck in seeing only their tracks. On returning to Malacca I found the accumulation of two or three posts—a dozen letters, and about fifty newspapers . . . I am glad to be safe in Singapore with my collections, as from here they can be insured. I have now a fortnight's work to arrange, examine, and pack them, and four months hence there will be work for Mr. Stevens.[1]

Sir James Brooke is here. I have called on him. He received me most cordially, and offered me every assistance at Sarawak. I shall go there next, as the missionary does not go to Cambodia for some months. Besides, I shall have some pleasant society at Sarawak, and shall get on in Malay, which is very easy; but I have had no practice yet, though I can ask for most common things.

---

[1]They were sent by sailing ship round the Cape of Good Hope, the overland route being too costly for goods.

I reached Sarawak early in November, and remained in Borneo fourteen months, seeing a good deal of the country. The first four months was the wet season, during which I made journeys up and down the Sarawak river, but obtained very scanty collections. In March I went to the Sadong river, where coal mines were being opened by an English mining engineer, Mr. Coulson, a Yorkshireman, and I stayed there nearly nine months, it being the best locality for beetles I found during my twelve years' tropical collecting, and very good for other groups. It was also in this place that I obtained numerous skins and skeletons of the orangutan, as fully described in my "Malay Archipelago."

In my first letter, dated May, 1855, I gave a sketch of the country and people:—

As far inland as I have yet seen this country may be described as a dead level, and a lofty and swampy forest. It would, therefore, be very uninviting were it not for a few small hills which here and there rise abruptly—oases in the swampy wilderness. It is at one of these that we are located, a hill covering an area of, perhaps, three or four square miles, and less than a thousand feet high. In this hill there are several coal seams; one of these three feet and a half thick, of very good coal for steamers, crops out round three-fourths of the hill, dipping down at a moderate angle. We have here near a hundred men, mostly Chinese; ground has been cleared, and houses built, and a road is being made through the jungle, a distance of two miles, to the Sadong river, where the coal will be shipped.

The jungle here is exceedingly gloomy and monotonous; palms are scarce, and flowers almost wanting, except some species of dwarf gingerworts. It is only high overhead that flowers can be seen. There are many find orchids of the genus caelogyne, with great drooping spikes of white or yellow flowers, and occasionally bunches of the scarlet flowers of a magnificent creeper, a species of aeschynanthus. Oak trees are rather common, and I have already noticed three species having large acorns of a red, brown, and black colour respectively.

Our mode of life here is very simple, and we have a continual struggle to get enough to eat, as all fowls and vegetables grown by the Dyaks go to Sarawak, and I have been obliged to send there to buy some.

The old men here relate with pride how many 'heads' they took in their youth; and though they all acknowledge the goodness of the present rajah, yet they think that if they were allowed to take a few heads, as of old, they would have better crops. The more I see of uncivilized people, the better I think of human nature on the whole, and the essential differences between civilized and savage man seem to disappear. Here we are, two Europeans, surrounded by a population of Chinese,

Malays, and Dyaks. The Chinese are generally considered, and with some amount of truth, to be thieves, liars, and reckless of human life, and these Chinese are coolies of the lowest and least educated class, though they can all read and write. The Malays are invariably described as being barbarous and bloodthirsty; and the Dyaks have only recently ceased to think head-taking a necessity of their existence. We are two days' journey from Sarawak, where, though the government is nominally European, it only exists with the consent and by the support of the native population. Yet I can safely say that in any part of Europe where the same opportunities for crime and disturbance existed, things would not go so smoothly as they do here. We sleep with open doors, and go about constantly unarmed; one or two petty robberies and a little fighting have occurred among the Chinese, but the great majority of them are quiet, honest, decent sort of people. They did not at first like the strictness and punctuality with which the English manager kept them to their work, and two or three ringleaders tried to get up a strike for shorter hours and higher wages, but Mr. Coulson's energy and decision soon stopped this by discharging the ringleaders at once, and calling all the Malays and Dyaks in the neighbourhood to come up to the mines in case any violence was attempted. It was very gratifying to see how rapidly they obeyed the summons, knowing that Mr. Coulson represented the rajah, and this display of power did much good, for since then everything has gone on smoothly. Preparations are now making for building a 'joss-house,' a sure sign that the Chinese have settled down contentedly.

In my next letter, a month latter, I gave the following account of an interesting episode:—

I must now tell you of the addition to my household of an orphan boy, a curious little half-nigger baby, which I have nursed now more than a month. I will tell you presently how I came to get it, but must first relate my inventive skill as a nurse. The little innocent was not weaned, and I had nothing proper to feed it with, so was obliged to give it rice-water. I got a large-mouthed bottle, making two holes in the cork, through one of which I inserted a large quill so that the baby could suck. I fitted up a box for a cradle with a mat for it to lie upon, which I had washed and changed every day. I feed it four times a day, and wash it and brush its hair every day, which it likes very much, only crying when it is hungry or dirty. In about a week I gave it the rice-water a little thicker, and always sweetened it to make it nice. I am afraid you would call it an ugly baby, for it has dark brown skin and red hair, a very large mouth, but very pretty little hands and feet. It has not cut its two lower front teeth, and the uppers are coming. At first it would not sleep alone at night, but cried very much; so I made it a pillow of an old stocking, which it likes to hug, and now sleeps very soundly. It has powerful lungs, and sometimes screams tremendously, so I hope it will live.

But I must now tell you how I came to take charge of it. Don't be alarmed; I was the cause of its mother's death. It happened as follows:—I was out shooting in the jungle and saw something up a tree which I thought was a large monkey or orang-utan, so I fired at it, and down fell this little baby—in its mother's arms. What she did up in the tree of course I can't imagine, but as she ran about the branches quite easily, I presume she was a wild 'woman of the woods;' so I have preserved her skin and skeleton, and am trying to bring up her only daughter, and hope some day to introduce her to fashionable society at the Zoological Gardens. When its poor mother fell mortally wounded, the baby was plunged head over ears in a swamp about the consistence of pea soup, and when I got it out looked very pitiful. It clung to me very hard when I carried it home, and having got its little hands unawares into my beard, it clutched so tight that I had great difficulty in extricating myself. Its mother, poor creature, had very long hair, and while she was running about the trees like a mad woman, the little baby had to hold fast to prevent itself from falling, which accounts for the remarkable strength of its little fingers and toes, which catch hold of anything with the firmness of a vice. About a week ago I bought a little monkey with a long tail, and as the baby was very lonely while we were out in the daytime, I put the little monkey into the cradle to keep it warm. Perhaps you will say that this was not proper. 'How could you do such a thing?' But, I assure you, the baby likes it exceedingly, and they are excellent friends. When the monkey wants to run away, as he often does, the baby clutches him by the tail or ears and drags him back; and if the monkey does succeed in escaping, screams violently till he is brought back again. Of course, baby cannot walk yet, but I let it crawl about on the floor to exercise its limbs; but it is the most wonderful baby I ever saw, and has such strength in its arms that it will catch hold of my trousers as I sit at work, and hang under my legs for a quarter of an hour at a time without being the least tired, all the time trying to suck, thinking, no doubt, it has got hold of its poor dear mother. When it finds no milk is to be had, there comes another scream, and I have to put it back in its cradle and give it 'Toby'—the little monkey—to hug, which quiets it immediately. From this short account you will see that my baby is no common baby, and I can safely say, what so many have said before with much less truth, 'There never was such a baby as my baby,' and I am sure nobody ever had such a dear little duck of a darling of a little brown hairy baby before.

In a letter dated Christmas Day, 1855, I gave my impressions of the Dyaks, and of Sir James Brooke, as follows:—

I have now lived a month in a Dyak's house, and spent a day or two in several others, and I have been very much pleased with them. They are a very kind, simple, and hospitable people, and I do not wonder at the great interest Sir James Brooke takes in them. They are more communicative and more cheerful than the American Indians, and it is therefore more agreeable to live with them. In moral character they are far superior to either the Malays or the Chinese, for though head-taking was long a custom among them, it was only as a trophy of war. In their own villages crimes are very rare. Ever since Sir James Brooke has been rajah, more than twelve years, there has only been one case of murder in a Dyak tribe, and that was committed by a stranger who had been adopted into the tribe. One wet day I produced a piece of string to show them how to play 'cat's cradle,' and was quite astonished to find that they knew it much better than I did, and could make all sorts of new figures I had never seen. They were also very clever at tricks with string on their fingers, which seemed to be a favourite amusement. Many of the remoter tribes think the rajah cannot be a man. They ask all sorts of curious questions about him—Whether he is not as old as the mountains; whether he cannot bring the dead to life; and I have no doubt, for many years after his death, he will be held to be a deity and expected to come back again.

I have now seen a good deal of Sir James, and the more I see of him the more I admire him. With the highest talents for government he combines in a high degree goodness of heart and gentleness of manner. At the same time, he has so much self-confidence and determination that he has put down with the greatest ease the conspiracies of one or two of the Malay chiefs against him. It is a unique case in the history of the world for a private English gentleman to rule over two conflicting races—a superior and an inferior—with their own consent, without any means of coercion, but depending solely upon them both for protection and support, while at the same time he introduces some of the best customs of civilization, and checks all crimes and barbarous practices that before prevailed. Under his government 'running-a-muck,' so frequent in other Malay countries, has never taken place, and in a population of about 30,000 Malays, almost all of whom carry their *kris,* and were accustomed to revenge an insult with a stab, murders only occur once in several years. The people are never taxed except with their own consent, and in the manner most congenial to them, while almost the whole of the rajah's private fortune has been spent in the improvement of the country or for its benefit. Yet this is the man who has been accused in England of wholesale murder and butchery of unoffending tribes to secure his own power!

In my next letter (from Singapore in February, 1856) I say—"I have now left Sarawak, where I began to feel quite at home, and may perhaps never return to it again, but I shall always look back with pleasure to my residence there and to my acquaintance with Sir James Brooke, who is a gentleman and a nobleman in the truest and best sense of those words."

At the end of this letter I make some remarks on the Crimean War, then almost concluded, and though I afterwards saw reason to change my opinion as regards this particular war, my views then as to the menace of Russian power to civilization are not altogether inapplicable at the present day. I say— "The warlike stores found in Sebastopol are alone a sufficient justification of the war. For what purpose were four thousand cannon and other stores in proportion accumulated there for if not to take Constantinople, get a footing in the Mediterranean, and ultimately to subjugate Europe? And why do such tremendous fortresses exist in every part of the frontiers of Russia, if not to render herself invulnerable from the attacks which she has determined by her ambitious designs to bring upon her? Russia is perpetually increasing her means both of defence and of aggression; if she had continued unmolested for a few years longer, it would have cost still greater sacrifices to subdue her. The war, therefore, is absolutely necessary as the only means of teaching Russia that Europe will not submit to the indefinite increase of her territory and power, and the constant menace of her thousands of cannons and millions of men. It is the only means of saving Europe from a despotism as much worse than that of Napoleon as the Russian people are behind the French in civilization."

There is a certain amount of truth in this, but to avoid misconception I wish to state that I think the danger does not arise from the Russian Government being any worse than our own, or than the Governments of Germany or France. All have the same insatiable craving for extending their territories and ruling subject peoples for the benefit of their own upper classes. Russia is only the most dangerous because she is already so vast, and each fresh extension of her territory adds to her already too large population, from which to create enormous armies, which she can and will use for further aggrandizement. It is a disgrace to Europe that they have allowed Russia to begin the dismemberment of China, and to leave to Japan the tremendous task of putting a check to her progress.

A later letter from Singapore touches on two matters of some interest.

I quite enjoy being a short time in Singapore again. The scene is at once so familiar and yet so strange. The half-naked Chinese coolies, the very neat shopkeepers, the clean, fat, old, long-tailed merchants, all as pushing and full of business as any Londoners. Then the handsome, dark-skinned *klings* from southern India, who always ask double what they will take, and with whom it is most amusing to bargain. The crowd of boatmen at the ferry, a dozen begging and disputing for a farthing fare; the tall, well-dressed Armenians; the short, brown Malays in their native dress; and the numerous Portuguese clerks in black, make up a scene doubly interesting to me now that I know something about them, and can talk to them all in the common language of the place—Malay. The streets of Singapore on a fine day are as crowded and busy as Tottenham Court Road, and from the variety of nationalities and occupations far more interesting. I am more convinced than ever that no one can appreciate a new country by a short visit. After two years in the East I only now begin to understand Singapore, and to thoroughly appreciate the life and bustle, and the varied occupations of so many distinct nationalities on a spot which a short time ago was an uninhabited jungle. A volume might

be written upon it without exhausting its humours and
its singularities . . .

I have been spending three weeks with my old friend
the French Jesuit missionary at Bukit Tima, going daily
into the jungle, and every Friday fasting on omelet
and vegetables, a most wholesome custom, which the
protestants erred in leaving off I have been reading
Huc's 'Travels' in French, and talking a good deal with
one of the missionaries just arrived from Tonquin, who
can speak no English. I have thus obtained a good deal
of information about these countries, and about the
extent of the Catholic missions in them, which is really
astonishing. How is it that they do their work so much
more thoroughly that most Protestant missions? In
Cochin China, Tonquin, and China, where Christian
missionaries are obliged to live in secret, and are subject to persecution, expulsion, or death, every province,
even those farthest in the interior of China, has its regular establishment of missionaries constantly kept up
by fresh supplies, who are all taught the languages of
the countries they are going to at Penang or Singapore.
In China there are near a million of Catholics, in Tonquin and Cohin China more than half a million. One
secret of their success is their mode of living. Each
missionary is allowed about £30 a year, on which he
lives in whatever counry he may be. This has two good

results. A large number of missionaries can be kept on limited funds, and the people of the country in which they reside, seeing that they live in poverty and with none of the luxuries of life, are convinced that they are sincere. Most of them are Frenchmen, and those I have seen or heard of are well-educated men, who give up their lives to the good of the people they live among. No wonder they make converts, among the lower orders principally; for it must be a great blessing to these poor people to have a man among them to whom they can go in any trouble or distress, whose sole object is to advise and help them, who visits them in sickness and relieves them in want, and whom they see living in continual danger of persecution and death only for *their* benefit.

Before leaving Singapore I wrote a long letter to my old fellow traveler and companion, Henry Walter Bates, then collecting on the Upper Amazon, almost wholly devoted to entomology, and especially giving my impressions of the comparative richness of the two countries. As this comparison is of interest not only to entomologists but to all students of the geographical distribution of animals, I give it here almost entire. The letter is dated April 30, 1856:—

I must first inform you that I have just received the *Zoologist* containing your letters up to September 14,

1855 (Ega), which have interested me greatly, and have almost made me long to be again on the Amazon, even at the cost of leaving the unknown Spice Islands still unexplored. I have been here since February waiting for a vessel to Macassar (Celebes), a country I look forward to with the greatest anxiety and with expectations of vast treasures in the insect world. Malacca, Sumatra, Java, and Borneo form but one zoological province, the *majority* of the species in all classes of animals being common to two or more of these countries. There is decidedly less difference between them than between Para and Santarem or Barra. I have therefore as yet only visited the best known portion of the Archipelago, and consider that I am now about to commence my real work. I have spent six months in Malacca and Singapore, and fifteen months in Borneo (Sarawak), and have therefore got a good idea of what this part of the Archipelago is like. Compared with the Amazon valley, the great and striking feature here is the excessive poverty of the Diurnal Lepidoptera. The glorious Heliconidae are represented here by a dozen or twenty species of generally obscure-coloured Euplaeas, the Nymphalidae containing nothing comparable with Epicalias, Callitheas, Catagrammas, etc., either in variety or abundance to make up for their want of brilliancy. A few species of Adolias, Limentis, and Charaxes are the most notable forms. The Satyridae have nothing to be placed by the side of the lovely Haeteras of the Amazon. Your glorious

Erycinidae are represented by half a dozen rather in-conspicuous species, and even the Lycaenidae, though more numerous and comprising some lovely species, do not come up to the Theclas of Para. Even the dull Hesperidae are almost wanting here, for I do not think I have yet exceeded a dozen species of this family. All this is very miserable and discouraging to one who has wandered in the forest-paths around Para or on the sandy shores of the Amazon or Rio Negro. The only group in which we may consider the two counties to be about equal is that of the true Papillios (including Ornithoptera), though even in these I think you have more species. Including Ornithoptera and Leptocircus, I have found as yet only thirty species, five of which I believe are new. Among these is the magnificent *Ornithoptera Brookeana,* perhaps the most elegant butterfly in the world.

To counterbalance this dearth of butterflies there should be an abundance of other orders, or you will think I have made a change for the worse, and compared with Para only perhaps there is, though it is doubtful whether at Ega you have not found Coleoptera quite as abundant as they are here. But I will tell you my experience so far and then you can decide the question, and let me know *how* you decide it. You must remember that it is now just two years since I reached Singapore, and out of that time I have lost at least six months by voyages and sickness, besides six months of an un-

usually wet season at Sarawak. However, during the dry
weather at Sarawak I was very fortunate in finding a
good locality for beetles, at which I worked hard for
five or six months. At Singapore and Malacca I collected about a thousand species of beetles, at Sarawak
about two thousand, but as about half my Singapore
species occurred also at Sarawak, I reckon that my total
number of species may be about 2500. The most numerous group is (as I presume with you) the Rhyno-
cophora (weevils, etc.), of which I have at least 600
species, perhaps many more. The majority of these are
very small, and all are remarkably obscure in their
colours, being in this respect inferior to some of our
British species. There are, however, many beautiful and
interesting forms, especially among the Ahthribidae, of
one of which—a new genus—I send a rough sketch.
The group next in point of numbers and, to me, of the
highest interest are the Longicorns. Of these I obtained
fifty species in the first ten days at Singapore, and when
in a good locality I seldom passed a day without getting
a new one. At Malacca and Singapore I collected about
160 species, at Sarawak 290, but as only about fifty from
the former places occurred at the latter, my Longicorns
must now reach about 400 species. . . . As to size, I have
only about thirty species which exceed an inch in
length, the majority being from one half to three quarters of an inch, while a considerable number are two
or three lines only. I see you say you must have near

500 species of Longicorns; but I do not know if this refers to Ega only, or to your whole South American collections.

The Geodephaga, always rare in the tropics, we must expect to be still more so in a level forest country so near the equator, yet I have found more species than I anticipated—as nearly as I can reckon, a hundred—twenty-four being Cicindelidae (tiger beetles) of various groups.

Lamellicorns are very scarce, about one hundred and forty species in all, of which twenty-five are Cetoniidae, all rare, and about the same number of Lucanidae. Elaters are rather plentiful, but with few exceptions small and obscure. I have one hundred and forty species, one nearly three inches long, and several of one and a half inch. The Buprestidae are exceedingly beautiful, but the larger and finer species are very rare. I have one hundred and ten species, of which half are under one-third of an inch long, though one, *Catoxantha bicolor,* is two and a half inches. Two genera of Cleridae are rather abundant, others rare; but I have obtained about fifty species, which, compared with the very few previously know, is very satisfactory. Of the remaining groups, in which I took less interest, I have not accurately noted the number of species.

The individual abundance of beetles is not, however, so large as the number of species would indicate. I hardly collect on an average more than fifty beetles a day, in which number there will be from thirty to forty species. Often, in fact, twenty or thirty beetles are as much as I can scrape together, even when giving my whole attention to them, for butterflies are too scarce to distract it. Of the other orders of insects, I have no accurate notes; the species, however, of all united (excluding Lepidoptera) about equal those of the beetles. I found one place only where I could collect moths, and have obtained altogether about one thousand species, mostly of small or average size. My total number of species of insects, therefore, I reckon at about six thousand, and of specimens collected about thirty thousand. From these data I think you will be able to form a pretty good judgment of the comparative entomological riches of the two countries. The matter, however, will not be definitely settled till I have visited Celebes, the Moluccas, etc., which I hope to find as much superior to the western group of islands as the Upper is to the Lower Amazon.

In other branches of Natural History I have as yet done little. The birds of Malacca and Borneo, though beautiful, are too well known to be worth collecting largely. With the orang-utans I was successful, obtaining fifteen skins and skeletons, and proving, I think, the existence of two species, hitherto a disputed question. The forests here are scarcely to be distinguished from those of Brazil, except by the frequent presence of various species of Calamus (Rattan palms) and the Pandani

(Screw pines), and by the rarity of those Leguminous trees with finely divided foliage, which are so frequent in the Amazonian forests. The people and their customs I hardly like as well as those of Brazil, but the comparatively new settlements of Singapore and Sarawak are not quite comparable with the older towns of the Amazon. Here provisions and labour are dear, and travelling is both tedious and expensive. Servants' wages are high, and the customs of the country do not permit you to live in the free-and-easy style of Brazil.

I must tell you that the fruits of the East are a delusion. Never have I seen a place where fruits are more scarce and poor than at Singapore. In Malacca and Sarawak they are more abundant, but there is nothing to make up for the deficiency of oranges, which are so poor and sour that they would hardly be eaten even in England. There are only two good fruits, the mangosteen and the durian. The first is a very delicate juicy fruit, but hardly worthy of the high place that has been given it; the latter, however, is a wonderful fruit, quite unique of its kind, and worth coming to the Malay Archipelago to enjoy; it is totally unlike every other fruit. A thick glutinous, almond-flavoured custard is the only thing it can be compared to, but which it far surpasses. These two fruits, however, can only be had for about two months in the year, and everywhere, except far into the interior, they are dear. The plantains and bananas even are poor, like the worst sorts in South America.

May 10th.—The ship for which I have been waiting nearly three months is in at last, and in about a week I hope to be off for Macassar. The monsoon, however, is against us, and we shall probably have a long passage, perhaps forty days. Celebes is quite as unknown as was the Upper Amazon before your visit to it, perhaps even more so. In the British Museum catalogues of Cetoni-idae, Buprestidae, Longicorns, and Papilionidae, not a single specimen is recorded from Celebes, and very few form the Moluccas; but the fine large species described by the old naturalists, some of which have recently been obtained by Madame Reiffer, give promise of what sys-tematic collection may produce."

Before giving a general sketch of my life and work in less known parts of the Archipelago, I must refer to an article I wrote while in Sarawak, which formed my first contribution to the great question of the origin of species. It was written during the wet season, while I was staying in a little house at the mouth of the Sarawak river, at the foot of the Santuabong mountain. I was quite alone, with one Malay boy as cook, and during the evenings and wet days I had nothing to do but to look over my books and ponder over the problem which was rarely absent from my thoughts. Having always been interested in the geographical distribution of animals and plants, having studied Swainson and Humboldt, and having now myself a vivid impression of the fundamental differences between the Eastern and Western tropics; and having also read through such books as Bonaparte's "Conspectus," already referred to, and several catalogues of insects and reptiles in the British Museum (which I almost knew by heart), giving a mass of facts as to the distribution of animals over the whole world, it occurred to me that these facts had never been properly utilized as indications of the way in which species had come into existence. The great work of Lyell had furnished me with the main features of the succession of species in time, and by combining the two I thought that some valuable conclusions might be reached. I accordingly put my facts and ideas on paper, and the result seeming to me to be of some importance, I sent it to *The Annals and Magazine of Natural History,* in which it appeared in the following September (1855). Its title was "On the Law which has regulated the Introduction of New Species," which law was briefly stated (at the end) as follows: *"Every species has come into existence coincident both in space and time with a pre-existing closely-allied species."* This clearly pointed to some kind of evolution. It suggested the *when* and the *where* of its occurrence, and that it could only be through natural generation, as was also suggested in the "Vestiges"; but the *how* was still a secret only to be penetrated some years later.

Soon after this article appeared, Mr. Stevens wrote me that he had heard several naturalists express regret that I was "theorizing," when what we had to do was to collect more facts. After this, I had in a letter to Darwin expressed surprise that no notice appeared to have been taken of my paper, to which he replied that both Sir Charles Lyell and Mr. Edward Blyth, two very good men, specially called his attention to it. I was, however, rewarded later, when in Huxley's chapter, "On the Reception of the Origin of Species," contributed to the "Life and Letters," he referred to this paper as—"his powerful essay," adding—"On reading it afresh I have been astonished to recollect how small was the impression it made" (vol. ii. p. 185). The article is reprinted in my "Natural Selection and Tropical Nature."

Down Through Italy by Rail

[MARK TWAIN]

ome of the *Quaker City's* passengers had arrived in Venice from Switzerland and other
lands before we left there, and others were
expected every day. We heard of no casualties among
them and no sickness.

We were a little fatigued with sightseeing, and so
we rattled through a good deal of country by rail
without caring to stop. I took few notes. I find no
mention of Bologna in my memorandum book, except that we arrived there in good season, but saw
none of the sausages for which the place is so justly
celebrated.

Pistoria awoke but a passing interest.

Florence pleased us for a while. I think we appreciated the great figure of David in the grand square,

and the sculptured group they call the Rape of the Sabines. We wandered through the endless collections of paintings and statues of the Pitti and Ufizzi galleries, of course. I make that statement in self-defense; there let it stop. I could not rest under the imputation that I visited Florence and did not traverse its weary miles of picture galleries. We tried indolently to recollect something about the Guelphs and Ghibellines and the other historical cutthroats whose quarrels and assassinations make up so large a share of Florentine history, but the subject was not attractive. We had been robbed of all the fine mountain scenery on our little journey by a system of railroading that had three miles of tunnel to a hundred yards of daylight, and we were not inclined to be sociable with Florence. We had seen the spot, outside the city somewhere, where these people had allowed the bones of Galileo to rest in unconsecrated ground for an age because his great discovery that the world turned around was regarded as a damning heresy by the Church; and we know that long after the world had accepted his theory and raised his name high in the list of its great men, they had still let him rot there. That we had lived to see his dust in honored sepulture in the Church of Santa Croce we owed to a society of *literati,* and not to Florence or her rulers. We saw Dante's tomb in that church also, but we were glad to know that his body was not in it; that

the ungrateful city that had exiled him and perse-
cuted him would give much to have it there, but
need not hope to ever secure that high honor to
herself. Medicis are good enough for Florence. Let
her plant Medicis and build grand monuments over
them to testify how gratefully she was wont to lick
the hand that scourged her.

Magnanimous Florence! Her jewelry marts are
filled with artists in mosaic. Florentine mosaics are
the choicest in all the world. Florence loves to have
that said. Florence is proud of it. Florence would foster this specialty of hers. She is grateful to the artists
that bring to her this high credit and fill her coffers
with foreign money, and so she encourages them
with pensions. With pensions! Think of the lavish-
ness of it. She knows that people who piece together the beautiful trifles die early because the
labor is so confining and so exhausting to hand and
brain, and so she has decreed that all these people
who reach the age of sixty shall have a pension after
that! I have not heard that any of them have called
for their dividends yet. One man did fight along till
he was sixty and started after his pension, but it appeared that there had been a mistake of a year in his
family record, and so he gave it up and died.

These artists will take particles of stone or glass no
larger than a mustard seed, and piece them together
on a sleeve button or a shirt stud, so smoothly and

with such nice adjustment of the delicate shades of color the pieces bear as to form a pygmy rose with stem, thorn, leaves, petals complete, and all as softly and as truthfully tinted as though Nature had builded it herself. They will counterfeit a fly or a high-toned bug or the ruined Coliseum, within the cramped circle of a breast pin, and do it so deftly and so neatly that any man might think a master painted it.

I saw a little table in the great mosaic school in Florence—a little trifle of a center table—whose top was made of some sort of precious polished stone, and in the stone was inlaid the figure of a flute, with bell mouth and a mazy complication of keys. No painting in the world could have been softer or richer; no shading out of one tint into another could have been more perfect; no work of art of any kind could have been more faultless than this flute, and yet to count the multitude of little fragments of stone of which they swore it was formed would bankrupt any man's arithmetic! I do not think one could have seen where two particles joined each other with eyes of ordinary shrewdness. Certainly *we* could detect no such blemish. This tabletop cost the labor of one man for ten long years, so they said, and it was for sale for thirty-five thousand dollars.

We went to the Church of Santa Croce, from time to time, in Florence, to weep over the tombs of

Michelangelo, Raphael, and Machiavelli (I suppose they are buried there, but it may be that they reside elsewhere and rent their tombs to other parties—such being the fashion in Italy), and between times we used to go and stand on the bridges and admire the Arno. It is popular to admire the Arno. It is a great historical creek with four feet in the channel and some scows floating around. It would be a very plausible river if they would pump some water into it. They all call it a river, and they honestly think it *is* a river, do these dark and bloody Florentines. They even help out the delusion by building bridges over it. I do not see why they are too good to wade.

How the fatigues and annoyances of travel fill one with bitter prejudices sometimes! I might enter Florence under happier auspices a month hence and find it all beautiful, all attractive. But I do not care to think of it now at all, nor of its roomy shops filled to the ceiling with snowy marble and alabaster copies of all the celebrated sculptures in Europe—copies so enchanting to the eye that I wonder how they can really be shaped like the dingy petrified nightmares they are the portraits of. I got lost in Florence at nine o'clock one night, and stayed lost in that labyrinth of narrow streets and long rows of vast buildings that look all alike until toward three o'clock in the morning. It was a pleasant night and at first there were a good many people abroad, and there were cheerful lights about. Later I grew accustomed to prowling about mysterious drifts and tunnels and astonishing and interesting myself with coming around corners expecting to find the hotel staring me in the face, and not finding it doing anything of the kind. Later still, I felt tired. I soon felt remarkably tired. But there was no one abroad now—not even a policeman. I walked till I was out of all patience and very hot and thirsty. At last, somewhere after one o'clock, I came unexpectedly to one of the city gates. I knew then that I was very far from the hotel. The soldiers thought I wanted to leave the city, and they sprang up and barred the way with their muskets. I said:

"Hotel d'Europe!"

It was all the Italian I knew, and I was not certain whether that was Italian or French. The soldiers looked stupidly at each other and at me, and shook their heads and took me into custody. I said I wanted to go home. They did not understand me. They took me into the guardhouse and searched me, but they found no sedition on me. They found a small piece of soap (we carry soap with us now), and I made them a present of it, seeing that they regarded it as a curiosity. I continued to say Hotel d'Europe and they continued to shake their heads, until at last a young soldier nodding in the corner roused up and said something. He said he knew where the hotel was, I suppose, for the officer of the guard sent him away with me. We walked a hundred or a hundred and fifty miles, it appeared to me, and then *he* got lost. He turned this way and that, and finally gave it up and signified that he was going to spend the remainder of the morning trying to find the city gate again. At that moment it struck me that there was something familiar about the house over the way. It was the hotel!

It was a happy thing for me that there happened to be a soldier there that knew even as much as he did; for they say that the policy of the government is to change the soldiery from one place to another constantly and from country to city, so that they cannot become acquainted with the people and grow lax in their duties and enter into plots and conspiracies with friends. My experiences of Florence were chiefly unpleasant. I will change the subject.

At Pisa we climbed up to the top of the strangest structure the world has any knowledge of—the Leaning Tower. As everyone knows, it is in the neighborhood of one hundred and eighty feet high—and I beg to observe that one hundred and eighty feet reach to about the height of four ordinary three-story buildings piled one on top of the other and is a very considerable altitude for a tower of uniform thickness to aspire to, even when it stands upright, yet this one leans more than thirteen feet out of the perpendicular. It is seven hundred years old, but neither history or tradition say whether it was built as it is purposely or whether one of its sides has settled. There is no record that it ever stood straight up. It is built of marble. It is an airy and a beautiful structure, and each of its eight stories is encircled by fluted columns, some of marble and some of granite, with Corinthian capitals that were handsome when they were new. It is a bell tower, and in its top hangs a chime of ancient bells. The winding staircase within is dark, but one always knows which side of the tower he is on because of his naturally gravitating from one side to the other of the staircase with the rise or dip of the tower. Some of the stones steps are footworn only on one end; others only on the other end; others only in the middle. To look down into the tower from the top is like looking down into a tilted well. A rope that hangs from the center of the top touches the wall before it reaches the bottom. Standing on the summit, one does not feel altogether comfortable when he looks down from the high side; but to crawl on your breast to the verge on the lower side and try to stretch your neck out far enough to see the base of the tower makes your flesh creep, and convinces you for a single moment, in spite of all your philosophy, that the building is falling. You handle yourself very carefully all the time, under the silly impression that if it is *not* falling, your trifling weight will start it unless you are particular not to "bear down" on it.

The Duomo, close at hand, is one of the finest cathedrals in Europe. It is eight hundred years old. Its grandeur has out-lived the high commercial prosperity and the political importance that made it a necessity, or rather, a possibility. Surrounded by poverty, decay, and ruin, it conveys to us a more tangible impression of the former greatness of Pisa than books could give us.

The Baptistery, which is a few years older than the Leaning Tower, is a stately rotunda of huge dimensions, and was a costly structure. In it hangs the lamp whose measured swing suggested to Galileo the pendulum. It looked an insignificant thing to have conferred upon the world of science and mechanics such a mighty extension of their dominions as it has. Pondering, in its suggestive presence, I seemed to see a crazy universe of swinging disks, the toiling children of this sedate parent. He appeared to have an intelligent expression about him of knowing that he was not a lamp at all; that he was a Pendulum; a pendulum disguised, for prodigious and inscrutable purposes of his own deep devising, and not a common pendulum either, but the old original patriarchal Pendulum—the Abraham Pendulum of the world.

This Baptistery is endowed with the most pleasing echo of all the echoes we have read of. The guide sounded two sonorous notes, about half an octave apart; the echo answered with the most enchanting, the most melodious, the richest blending of sweet sounds that one can imagine. It was like a long-drawn chord of a church organ, infinitely softened by distance. I may be extravagant in this matter, but if this be the case my ear is to blame—not my pen. I am describing a memory—and one that will remain long with me.

The peculiar devotional spirit of the olden time, which placed a higher confidence in outward forms of worship than in the watchful guarding of the heart against sinful thoughts and the hands against sinful deeds, and which believed in the protecting virtues of inanimate objects made holy by contact with holy things, is illustrated in a striking manner in one of the cemeteries of Pisa. The tombs are set in soil brought in ships from the Holy Land ages ago. To be buried in such ground was regarded by the ancient Pisans as being more potent for salvation than many masses purchased of the Church and the vowing of many candles to the Virgin.

Pisa is believed to be about three thousand years old. It was one of the twelve great cities of ancient Etruria, that commonwealth which has left so many monuments in testimony of its extraordinary advancement and so little history of itself that is tangible and comprehensible. A Pisan antiquarian gave me an ancient tear jug which he averred was full four thousand years old. It was found among the ruins of one of the oldest of the Etruscan cities. He said it came from a tomb, and was used by some bereaved family in that remote age when even the pyramids of Egypt were young. Damascas a village, Abraham a prattling infant, and ancient Troy not yet dreamt of, in weaving the tears wept for some lost idol of a household. It spoke to us in a language of its own; and with a pathos more tender than any words might bring, its mute eloquence swept down the long roll of the centuries with its tale of a vacant chair, a familiar footstep missed from the threshold, a pleasant voice gone from the chorus, a vanished form!—a tale which is always so new to us, so startling, so terrible, so benumbing to the senses, and behold how threadbare and old it is! No shrewdly worded history could have brought the myths and shadows of that old dreamy age before us clothed with human flesh and warmed with human sympathies so vividly as did this poor little unsentient vessel of pottery.

Pisa was a republic in the Middle Ages, with a government of her own, armies and navies of her own, and a great commerce. She was a warlike power and inscribed upon her banners many a brilliant fight with Genoese and Turks. It is said that the city once numbered a population of four hundred thousand;

but her scepter has passed from her grasp now, her ships and her armies are gone, her commerce is dead. Her battle flags bear the mold and the dust of centuries, her marts are deserted, she has shrunken far within her crumbling walls, and her great population has diminished to twenty thousand souls. She had but one thing left to boast of, and that is not much, viz.: she is the second city of Tuscany.

We reached Leghorn in time to see all we wished to see of it long before the city gates were closed for the evening, and then came on board the ship.

We felt as though we had been away from home an age. We never entirely appreciated before what a very pleasant den our stateroom is, nor how jolly it is to sit at dinner in one's own seat in one's own cabin and hold familiar conversation with friends in one's own language. Oh, the rare happiness of comprehending every single word that is said, and knowing that every word one says in return will be understood as well! We would talk ourselves to death now, only there are only about ten passengers out of the sixty-five to talk to. The others are wandering we hardly know where. We shall not go ashore in Leghorn. We are surfeited with Italian cities for the present, and much prefer to walk the familiar quarterdeck and view this one from a distance.

The stupid magnates of this Leghorn government cannot understand that so large a steamer as ours could cross the broad Atlantic with no other purpose than to indulge a party of ladies and gentlemen in a pleasure excursion. It looks too improbable. It is suspicious, they think. Something more important must be hidden behind it all. They cannot understand it, and they scorn the evidence of the ship's papers. They have decided at last that we are a battalion of incendiary, blood-thirsty Garibaldians in disguise! And in all seriousness they have set a gunboat to watch the vessel night and day, with orders to close down on any revolutionary movement in a twinkling! Police boats are on patrol duty about us all the time, and it is as much as a sailor's liberty is worth to show himself in a red shirt. These policemen follow the executive officer's boat from shore to ship and from ship to shore and watch his dark maneuvers with a vigilant eye. They will arrest him yet unless he assumes an expression of countenance that shall have less of carnage, insurrection, and sedition in it. A visit paid in a friendly way to General Garibaldi yesterday (by cordial invitation) by some of our passengers has gone far to confirm the dread suspicions the government harbors toward us. It is thought the friendly visit was only the cloak of a bloody conspiracy. These people draw near and watch us when we bathe in the sea from the ship's side. Do they think we are communing with a reserve force of rascals at the bottom?

It is said that we shall probably be quarantined at Naples. Two or three of us prefer not to run this risk. Therefore, when we are rested, we propose to go in a French steamer to Civitavecchia, and from thence to Rome, and by rail to Naples. They do not quarantine the cars, no matter where they got their passengers from.

Stanley's Last Great Expedition

[HON. J. T. HEADLEY]

S tanley, after he had found Livingstone, naturally thought much of the latter's explorations. Africa had become to him an absorbing
subject, till he began to imbibe the spirit of Livingstone. This was natural, for he had won fame there,
and why should he not win still greater laurels in
the same field? This feeling was much increased
after the death of the great explorer, with his work
unfinished, and he longed to complete it. True,
Cameron was on the ground to accomplish this
very object, but Stanley knew the difficulties he
would have to contend with without a boat of his
own. The matter was talked over a good deal, and
finally the proprietors of the New York *Herald* and

London *Telegraph* determined to send him out. The vast lake region, embracing some six degrees of longitude and extending from the equator to fifteen degrees south latitude, had become a region of the greatest interest to explorers. On this vast water-shed lived a mighty population, and these lakes, with the rivers running into and out of them, must furnish the roads to commerce and be the means by which Africa would be lifted out of its barbarism into the light of civilization.

The large lakes Nyassa and Tanganika had been more or less explored, but the one possessing the greatest interest—the Victoria Nyanza, on account of the general impression that it was the head of the Nile—was almost wholly unknown. The persistence with which the Nile had mocked all the efforts to find its source, had imparted a mystery to it and caused efforts to be made to unlock the secret, apparently wholly disproportioned to its value or real importance. This lake, therefore, was to be Stanley's first objective point. Livingstone, Speke and Burton, and others had seen it—*he* would sail round it in a boat which he would take with him. This he had made in sections, so that it could be carried the nearly one thousand miles through the jungles of Africa to its destination.

Everything being completed he started on his route, and in the latter part of 1874 found himself once more at Zanzibar. Here, in organizing his expedition, he discovered that the builder had made his boat, which he had christened the Lady Alice, a great deal heavier than he had ordered; but he luckily found a man in Zanzibar who was able to reduce its weight so that it could be transported by the carriers. It is not necessary to go into a description of how he organized the new expedition, nor of his journey along his old route to Unyanyembe. His force consisted in all of a little over three hundred men, and he took with him this time several powerful dogs. The interest of the expedition begins when he struck off from the regular route of the caravans going west, and entered an entirely new country and encountered a new race of people. Instead of moving directly westward, he turned off to the north, and at length reached the western frontier of Ugogo, on the last day of the year 1874. The country at this point stretched before him in one vast plain, which some of the natives said extended clear to Nyanza. He found that his course led him along the extremity of Whumba, which he was glad to know, as he thought his march would now be unmolested. Two days' march brought them to the borders of Usandawa, a country abounding in elephants. Here he turned to the north-west and entered Ukimbu or Uyonzi on its eastern extremity. The guides he had hired in Ugogo to take him as far as Iramba here deserted him. Hiring fresh ones, he continued two days in the same direction, when these deserted him also, and Stanley found himself one morning on the edge of a vast wilderness without a guide. The day before, the guides had told him that three days' march would bring him to Urimi. Relying on the truth of this statement, he had purchased only two days' provisions. Thinking, therefore, that they would be there by evening of the next day, he thought little of the desertion and moved off with confidence. But the next morning, the track, which was narrow and indistinct at the best, became so inextricably mixed up with the paths made by elephants and rhinoceros, that they were wholly at loss what course to take. Halting, Stanley sent out men to seek the lost path, but they returned unable to find it. They then, of course, had nothing left to do but to march by compass, which they did.

As might be expected, it brought them, after a few hours' march, into a dense jungle of acacias and euphorbias, through which they could make their way only by crawling, scrambling and cutting the entangling vines. Now pushing aside an obstructing branch—now cutting a narrow lane through the matted mass, and now taking advantage of a slight opening, this little band of three hundred struggled painfully forward toward what they thought was open country, and an African village with plenty of provisions.

In this protracted struggle the third night overtook them in the wilderness, and there they pitched their lonely, starving camp. To make it more gloomy, one of the men died and was buried; his shallow grave seeming to be a sad foreboding of what awaited them in the future. The want of provisions now began to tell terribly on the men, but there was nothing to do but go forward, trusting to some outbreak to this apparently interminable wilderness. But human endurance has its limit, and although Stanley kept his little force marching all day, they made but fourteen miles. It was a continual jungle, with not a drop of water on the route. The poor carriers, hungry and thirsty, sunk under their loads and lagged behind the main force for many miles, until it became a straggling, weary, despondent crowd, moving without order and without care through the wilderness. The strong endeavored to help the weak, and did relieve them of their burdens and encourage them to hold on, so that most of them were able to reach the camp at night. But in despite of all effort five sick, despairing men, strayed from the path, which was only a blind trail made by those in advance. After the camp for the night was pitched, Stanley sent back scouts to find them, who explored the woods for a mile each side of the track they had made, but only one man was found, and he full a mile from the trail and dead. The other four had wandered off beyond reach and were never heard of more. This was getting to be fearful marching— five men in one day was a death roll that could not be kept up long, and Stanley began to cast about anxiously to determine what step he should next take. But there was but one course left open to him, to attempt to retrace his steps was certain death by famine, to advance could not be worse, while it might bring relief, so push on was the order, and they did push on weary, thirsty, starving, and on the fifth day came to a little village recently established, and which consisted of only four huts, occupied by four men with their wives and children. These had scarcely provisions enough to keep themselves, and hence could give nothing to Stanley's starving men. It was useless to attempt further marching without food, for the men staggered into camp exhausted, and would rather die there than attempt to move again.

Stanley's experience had taught him how far he could urge on these African carriers and soldiers, and he saw they had now become desperate and would not budge another inch until they had some-thing to eat. He, therefore, ordered a halt, and se-lecting twenty of his strongest men, sent them off in search of food. They were to press on to a village called Suna, about thirty miles distant, of which the natives told him, and where they said food was in abundance. As soon as they had disappeared in the forest, Stanley took his gun and strolled out in search of game. But, filled as the country seemed with it, he could find nothing to shoot. One of his men, however, came across a lion's den, in which were two cubs, which he brought to Stanley. The latter skinned them and took them back to camp. As he entered it, the pinched and worn faces of his faithful men, as they sat hungry and despairing, moved him so deeply that he would have wept, but for fear of adding to their despondency. The two cubs would go but a little way toward feeding some two hundred and twenty men, if cooked as ordinary meat, so he resolved to make a soup of them, which would go much farther. But the question was where to get a kettle large enough to make a soup for such a large body of men. Luckily, he bethought himself of a sheet-iron trunk which he had among his baggage, and which was water-tight. He quickly dumped out of it its contents, and filling it with water, set it over a fire which he had ordered to be made. He then broke open his medical stores, and taking out five pounds of Scotch oatmeal and three one-pound tins of revalenta Arabica, he made with it and the two young lions a huge trunk full of gruel, that would give even two hundred and twenty men a good bowl apiece. He said it was a rare sight to see those hungry, famished men gather around that Torquay dress-trunk and pile on the fuel, and in every way assist to make the contents boil, while with greedy eyes, with gourds in their hands, full of water, they stood ready to pour it in the moment it threatened to boil over and waste the precious contents. But he adds, "it was a rarer sight still to watch the famished wretches, as, with these same gourds full of the precious broth, they drank it down as only starving men swallow food. The weak and sick got a larger portion, and another tin of oat-meal being opened for their supper and breakfast, they waited patiently the return of those who had gone in quest of food."

Stanley's position now became painfully trying. He was five days' march from where he could obtain food, if he attempted to go back, which, in the present condition of his men, they could never make, and if any survived, it would be on the terrible condition of the living eating the dead.

The only hope lay in reaching supplies in advance. But what if those twenty strong men he had sent on to find them never returned, having been ambushed and killed on the way, or what if they, at the end of several days, returned and reported nothing but an unbroken wilderness and impassable jungle or swamps in front, and themselves famished, ready to die? These were questions that Stanley anxiously put to himself and dared not contemplate the answer. The hours of painful anxiety and suspense, the maddening thoughts and wild possibilities that fire the brain and oppress the heart in such crises as these cannot be imagined, they can be known only by him who suffers the pangs they inflict. This is a portion of the history of the expedition that Stanley can never write, though it is written on his heart in lines that will never be effaced.

The empty trunk lay on one side, and the night came down and the stars burned bright and tranquilly above, and all was silent in the wide solitude as Stanley sat and listened for the return of his men. But they came not, and the morning broke and the sun rode once more the tropical heavens in his splendor, but no musket shot from the forest told of the returning scouts. The weary hours wore on and the emaciated men lay around in silent suffering. To Stanley those hours seemed days. Night again darkened the forest and still no sign of the returning party. Would they ever return, was the terrible question Stanley was perpetually putting to himself, and if not, what desperate movement should he attempt? The third morning broke as calm and peaceful as the rest; he was beginning to despair, when, suddenly, a musket shot broke over the forest, and then another and another, sending sudden life and activity throughout the despairing camp. The men, as they emerged into view laden with food, were greeted with a loud shout, and the hungry wretches fell on the provisions they brought like ravening wolves. The report of abundance ahead so excited the men that they forgot their feebleness and clamored to be led on that very afternoon. Stanley was quite willing to get away from the jungle, filled with such painful associations, and cheerfully ordered the march, but before they could get away two men breathed their last in the camp and were left to sleep alone in the wilderness.

That night they encamped at the base of a rocky hill, from which stretched away a broad plain. The hill—lifting itself into the clear air—the open plain seemed like civilization compared with the gloomy jungle in which they had been starving for the last two days, and where they had left two of their number, and they awoke next morning cheerful and refreshed. Starting off with the prospect of abundant provisions ahead, they made a steady march of twenty miles and reached the district of Suna in Urimi.

Stanley was surprised, on entering the rude village, to see a new type of African life. Men and women of great beauty and fine physical proportions met his astonished sight. They stood before him in all their naked beauty, unabashed; the women bearing children alone wearing a covering of goat skins, designed evidently as a protection against external injury, and not caused by any notions of modesty. Their fine appearance seemed to indicate a greater mental development than any other tribes which they had met. Whether this were so or not, it would be difficult to tell, for they were the most suspicious, reserved people Stanley had ever met, being greatly disinclined to barter provisions, of which they had more than they wanted, for cloth and beads, of which they apparently had none. They had no chief, but seemed to be governed in their actions by the old men. With these Stanley therefore treated for permission to pass through their land. It required great tact to secure this, and still more to obtain the required food. Stanley bore this silent hostility patiently, for though he could have taken all he wanted by force, he wished to avoid all violence. While lingering here, two more of his exhausted company gave out and died, while his sick list swelled up to thirty. Among the latter was Edward Pocoke, who, with his brother, Stanley had engaged in England to accompany him as attendants. This compelled him to halt for four days, but finding that the hostile feeling of the natives increased the longer he stayed, he determined, dangerous as it was to the sick, especially to Pocoke, to leave. Dysentery and diarrhoea was prevailing to an alarming extent, and rest was especially necessary for these, if they hoped to recover; but he was afraid matters would become dangerously complicated if he remained, and he turned his soldiers into carriers and slung the sick into hammocks. Encouraging them with the prospect of plenty and comfort ahead, he gave the order to march, and they passed out and entered upon a clear, open and well cultivated country. Reaching a village at ten o'clock they halted, and here young Pocoke breathed his last "to the great grief of all." In speaking of the sad event that cast a gloom over the camp, Stanley says: "We had finished the four hundredth mile of our march from the sea and had reached the base of the water-shed, where the trickling streams and infant waters began to flow Nileward, when this noble young man died." They buried him at night under a tree, with the stars shining down on the shallow-made grave—Stanley reading the burial service of the Church of England over the body. Far from home and friends in that distant, lonely land he sleeps to-day, a simple wooden cross marking his burial place. Stanley sent the following letter home to his father, describing his sickness and death:

Letter to Pocoke's father.

Kagehyi, on the Victoria Nyanza,
March 4th, 1875.

Dear Sir:—A most unpleasant, because sad, task devolves upon me, for I have the misfortune to have to report to you the death of your son Edward, of typhoid fever. His service with me was brief, but it was long enough for me to know the greatness of your loss, for I doubt that few fathers can boast of such sons as yours. Both Frank and Ted proved themselves sterling men, noble and brave hearts and faithful servants. Ted had endeared himself to the members of the expedition by his amiable nature, his cheerfulness and by various qualifications which brought him into high favor with the native soldiers of this force. Before daybreak we were accustomed to hear the cheery notes of his bugle, which woke us to a fresh day's labor; at night, around the camp-fires, we were charmed with his sweet, simple songs, of which he had an inexhaustible *répertoire*. When tired also with marching, it was his task to announce to the tired people the arrival of the vanguard at camp, so that he had become quite a treasure to us all; and I must say, I have never know men who could bear what your sons have borne on this expedition so patiently and uncomplainingly. I never heard one grumble either from Frank or Ted; have never heard them utter an illiberal remark, or express any wish that the expedition had never set foot in Africa, as many men would have done in their situation, so that you may well imagine, that if the loss of one of your sons causes grief to your paternal heart, it has been no less a grief to us, as we were all, as it were, one family, surrounded as we are by so much that is dark and forbidding.

On arriving at Suna, in Urina, Ted came to me, after a very long march, complaining of pain in his limbs and loins. I did not think it was serious at all, nor anything uncommon after walking twenty miles, but told him to go and lie down, that he would be better on the morrow, as it was very likely fatigue. The next morning I visited him, and he again complained of pains in the knees and back, at which I ascribed it to rheumatism, and treated him accordingly. The third day he complained of pain in the chest, difficulty of breathing and sleeplessness, from which I perceived he was suffering from some other malady than rheumatism, but what it could be I could not divine. He was a little feverish, so I gave him a mustard-plaster and some aperient medicine. Toward night he began to wander in his head, and on examining his tongue I found it was almost black and coated with dark-gray fur. At these symptoms I thought he had a severe attack of remittent fever, from which I suffered in Ujiji, in 1871, and therefore I watched for an opportunity to administer quinine—that is, when the fever should abate a little. But, on the fourth day, the patient still wandering in his mind, I suggested to Frank that he should sponge him with cold water and change his clothing, during which operation I noticed that the chest of the patient was covered with spots like pimples or small-pox pustules, which perplexed me greatly. He could not have caught the small-pox, and what the disease was I could not imagine; but, turning to my medical books, I saw that your son was suffering from typhoid, the description of which was too clear to be longer mistaken, and both Frank and I devoted our attention to him. He was nourished with arrow-root and brandy, and everything that was in our power to do was done; but it was very evident that the case was serious, though I hoped that his constitution would brave it out

On the fifth day we were compelled to resume our journey, after a rest of four days. Ted was put in a hammock and carried on the shoulders of four men. At ten o'clock on the 17th of January we halted at Chiwyn, and the minute that he was laid down in the camp he breathed his last. Our companion was dead.

We buried him that night under a tree, on which his brother Frank had cut a deep cross, and read the beautiful service of the Church of England over him as we laid the poor worn-out body in its final resting-place.

Pease be to his ashes. Poor Ted deserved a better fate they dying in Africa, but it was impossible that he could have died easier. I wish that my end may be as peaceful and painless as his. He was spared the stormy scenes we went through afterwards in our war with the Waturn; and who knows how much he has been saved from? But I know that he would have rejoiced to be with us at this hour of our triumph, gazing on the laughing waters of the vast fountain of old Nile. None of us would have been more elated at the prospect before us than he, for he was a true sailor, and loved the sight of water. Yet again I say peace be to his ashes; be consoled, for Frank still lives, and, from present appearances, is likely to come home to you with honor and glory, such as he and you may well be proud of. Believe me, dear sir, with true sincerity, your well-wisher,

Henry M. Stanley.

Stanley still traveled in a north-west direction, and the farther he advanced the more he was convinced that the rivulets he encountered flowed into the Nile, and he became elated with the hope that he should soon stand on the shores of the great lake that served as the reservoir of the mighty river.

Two days' march now brought them to Mongafa, where one of his men who had accompanied him on his former expedition was murdered. He was suffering from the asthma, and Stanley permitted him to follow the party slowly. Straggling thus behind alone, he was waylaid by the natives and murdered. It was impossible to ascertain who committed the deed, and so Stanley could not avenge the crime.

Keeping on they at length entered Itwru, a district of Northern Urimi. The village where they camped was called Vinyata, and was situated in a broad and populous valley, containing some two thousand to three thousand souls, through which flowed a stream twenty feet wide. The people here received him in a surly manner, but Stanley was very anxious to avoid trouble and used every exertion to conciliate them. He seemed at last to succeed, for at evening they brought him milk, eggs and chickens, taking cloth in exchange. This reached the ears of the great man of the valley, a magic doctor, who, there being no king over the people, is treated with the highest respect and honor by them. The next day he brought Stanley a fat ox, for which the latter paid him twice what it was worth in cloth and beads, besides making a rich present to his brother and son. To all his requests he cheerfully consented in his anxiety to conciliate him and the natives.

That day, taking advantage of the bright sun to dry the bales and goods, he exposed his rich stores, an imprudence which he very quickly deeply regretted, for he saw that the display awoke all the greedy feelings of the natives, as was evinced by their eager looks. But the day passed quietly, and on the third morning the great man made his appearance again and begged for more beads, which were given him and he departed apparently very much pleased, and Stanley congratulated himself that he would be allowed to depart in peace.

Major Burnham,
Chief of Scouts

[RICHARD HARDING DAVIS]

A mong the Soldiers of Fortune whose stories have been told in this book were men who are no longer living, men who, to the United States, are strangers, and men who were of interest chiefly because in what they attempted they failed.

The subject of this article is none of these. His adventures are as remarkable as any that ever led a small boy to dig behind the barn for buried treasure, or stalk Indians in the orchard. But entirely apart from his adventures he obtains our interest because in what he has attempted he has not failed, because he is one of our own people, one of the earliest and best types of American, and because, so

far from being dead and buried, he is at this moment very much alive, and engaged in Mexico in
searching for a buried city. For exercise, he is alternately chasing, or being chased by, Yaqui Indians.

In his home in Pasadena, Cal., where sometimes he
rests quietly for almost a week at a time, the neighbors know him as "Fred" Burnham. In England the
newspapers crowned him "The King of Scouts."
Later, when he won an official title, they called him
"Major Frederick Russell Burnham, D. S. O."

Some men are born scouts, others by training become scouts. From his father Burnham inherited his
instinct for wood-craft, and to this instinct, which in
him is as keen as in a wild deer or a mountain lion,
he has added, in the jungle and on the prairie and
mountain ranges, years of the hardest, most relentless
schooling. In those years he has trained himself to en-
dure the most appalling fatigues, hunger, thirst, and
wounds; has subdued the brain to infinite patience,
has learned to force every nerve in his body to ab-
solute obedience, to still even the beating of his heart.
Indeed, than Burnham no man of my acquaintance
to my knowledge has devoted himself to his life's
work more earnestly, more honestly, and with such
single-mindedness of purpose. To him scouting is as
exact a study as is the piano to Paderewski, with the
result that to-day what the Pole is to other pianists,
the American is to all other "trackers," woodmen, and

scouts. He reads "the face of Nature" as you read your morning paper. To him a movement of his horse's ears is as plain a warning as the "Go SLOW" of an automobile sign; and he so saves from ambush an entire troop. In the glitter of a piece of quartz in the firelight he discovers King Solomon's mines. Like the horned cattle, he can tell by the smell of it in the air the near presence of water, and where, glaring in the sun, you can see only a bare kopje, he distinguishes the muzzle of a pompom, the crown of a Boer sombrero, the levelled barrel of a Mauser. He is the Sherlock Holmes of all out-of-doors.

Besides being a scout, he is soldier, hunter, mining expert, and explorer. Within the last ten years the educated instinct that as a younger man taught him to follow the trail of an Indian, or the "spoor" of the Kaffir and the trek wagon, now leads him as a mining expert to the hiding-places of copper, silver, and gold, and, as he advises, great and wealthy syndicates buy or refuse tracts of land in Africa and Mexico as large as the State of New York. As an explorer in the last few years in the course of his expeditions into undiscovered lands, he has added to this little world many thousands of square miles.

Personally, Burnham is as unlike the scout of fiction, and of the Wild West Show, as it is possible for a man to be. He possesses no flowing locks, his talk is not of "greasers," "grizzly b'ars," or "pesky redskins."

In fact, because he is more widely and more thoroughly informed, he is much better educated than many who have passed through one of the "Big Three" universities, and his English is as conventional as though he had been brought up on the borders of Boston Common, rather than on the borders of civilization.

In appearance he is slight, muscular, bronzed; with a finely formed square jaw, and remarkable light blue eyes. These eyes apparently never leave yours, but in reality they see everything behind you and about you, above and below you. They tell of him that one day, while out with a patrol on the veldt, he said he had lost the trail and, dismounting, began moving about on his hands and knees, nosing the ground like a bloodhound, and pointing out a trail that led back over the way the force had just marched. When the commanding officer rode up, Burnham said:

"Don't raise your head, sit. On that kopje to the right there is a commando of Boers."

"When did you see them?" asked the officer.

"I see them now," Burnham answered.

"But I thought you were looking for a lost trail?"

"That's what the Boers on the kopje think," said Burnham.

In his eyes, possibly, owing to the uses to which they have been trained, the pupils, as in the eyes of animals that see in the dark, are extremely small. This feature of his eyes is obvious, and that he can see in the dark the Kaffirs of South Africa firmly believe. In manner he is quiet, courteous, talking slowly but well, and, while without any of that shyness that comes from self-consciousness, extremely modest. Indeed, there could be no better proof of his modesty than the difficulties I have encountered in gathering material for this article, which I have been five years in collecting. And even now, as he reads it by his camp-fire, I can see him squirm with embarrassment.

Burnham's father was a pioneer missionary in a frontier hamlet called Tivoli on the edge of the Indian reserve of Minnesota. He was a stern, severely religious man, born in Kentucky, but educated in New York, where he graduated from the Union Theological Seminary. He was wonderfully skilled in wood-craft. Burnham's mother was a Miss Rebecca Russell of a well-known family in Iowa. She was a woman of great courage, which, in those days on that skirmish line of civilization, was a very necessary virtue; and she was possessed of a most gentle and sweet disposition. That was her gift to her son Fred, who was born on May 11, 1861.

His education as a child consisted in memorizing many verses of the Bible, the "Three R's," and woodcraft. His childhood was strenuous. In his mother's arms he saw the burning of the town of New Ulm, which was the funeral pyre for the women and children of that place when they were massacred by Red Cloud and his braves.

On another occasion Fred's mother fled for her life from the Indians, carrying the boy with her. He was a husky lad, and knowing that if she tried to carry him farther they both would be overtaken, she hid him under a shock of corn. There, the next morning, the Indians having been driven off, she found her son sleeping as soundly as a night watchman. In these Indian wars, and the Civil War which followed, of the families of Burnham and Russell, twenty-two of the men were killed. There is no question that Burnham comes of fighting stock.

In 1870, when Fred was nine years old, his father moved to Los Angeles, Cal., where two years later he died; and for a time for both mother and boy there was poverty, hard and grinding. To relieve this young Burnham acted as a mounted messenger. Often he was in the saddle from twelve to fifteen hours, and even in a land where every one rode well, he gained local fame as a hard rider. In a few years a kind uncle offered to Mrs. Burnham and a younger brother a home in the East, but at the last moment Fred refused to go with them, and chose to make his own way. He was then thirteen years old, and he had determined to be a scout.

At that particular age many boys have set forth determined to be scouts, and are generally brought
home the next morning by a policeman. But Burnham, having turned his back on the cities, did not re-
pent. He wandered over Mexico, Arizona, California.
He met Indians, bandits, prospectors, hunters of all
kinds of big game; and finally a scout who, under
General Taylor, had served in the Mexican War. This
man took a liking to the boy; and his influence upon
him was marked and for his good. He was an educated man, and had carried into the wilderness a few
books. In the cabin of this man Burnham read "The
Conquest of Mexico and Peru" by Prescott, the lives
of Hannibal and Cyrus the Great, of Livingstone the
explorer, which first set his thoughts toward Africa,
and many technical works on the strategy and tactics
of war. He had no experience of military operations
on a large scale, but, with the aid of the veteran of
the Mexican War, with corn-cobs in the sand in front
of the cabin door, he constructed forts and made
trenches, redoubts, and traverses. In Burnham's life
this seems to have been a very happy period. The big
game he hunted and killed he sold for a few dollars
to the men of Nadean's freight outfits, which in those
days hauled bullion from Cerro Gordo for the man
who is now Senator Jones of Nevada.

At nineteen Burnham decided that there were
things in this world he should know that could not

be gleaned from the earth, trees, and sky; and with the few dollars he had saved he came East. The visit apparently was not a success. The atmosphere of the town in which he went to school was strictly Puritanical, and the townspeople much given to religious discussion. The son of the pioneer missionary found himself unable to subscribe to the formulas which to the others seemed so essential, and he returned to the West with the most bitter feelings, which lasted until he was twenty-one.

"It seems strange now," he once said to me, "but in those times religious questions were as much a part of our daily life as to-day are automobiles, the Standard Oil, and the insurance scandals, and when I went West I was in an unhappy, doubting frame of mind. The trouble was I had no moral anchors; the old ones father had given me were gone, and the time for acquiring new ones had not arrived." This bitterness of heart, or this disappointment, or whatever the state of mind was that the dogmas of the New England town had inspired in the boy from the prairie, made him reckless. For the life he was to lead this was not a handicap. Even as a lad, in a land-grant war in California, he had been under gunfire, and for the next fifteen years he led a life of danger and of daring; and studied in a school of experience than which, for a scout, if his life be spared, there can be none better. Burnham came out of it a quiet, manly, gentleman. In those fifteen years he roved the West from the Great Divide to Mexico. He fought the Apache Indians for the possession of waterholes, he guarded bullion on stage-coaches, for days rode in pursuit of Mexican bandits and American horse thieves, took part in county-seat fights, in rustler wars, in cattle wars; he was cowboy, miner, deputy-sheriff, and in time throughout the name of "Fred" Burnham became significant and familiar.

During this period Burnham was true to his boy-hood ideal of becoming a scout. It was not enough that by merely living the life around him he was being educated for it. He daily practised and re-hearsed those things which some day might mean to himself and others the difference between life and death. To improve his sense of smell he gave up smoking, of which he was extremely fond, nor, for the same reason, does he to this day use tobacco. He accustomed himself also to go with little sleep, and to subsist on the least possible quantity of food. As a deputy-sheriff this educated faculty of not requiring sleep aided him in many important captures. Some-times he would not strike the trail of the bandit or "bad man" until the other had several days the start of him. But the end was the same; for, while the murderer snatched a few hours' rest by the trail, Burnham, awake and in the saddle, would be clos-ing up the miles between them.

That he is a good marksman goes without telling. At the age of eight his father gave him a rifle of his own, and at twelve, with either a "gun" or a Winchester, he was an expert. He taught himself to use a weapon either in his left or right hand and to shoot, Indian fashion, hanging by one leg from his pony and using it as a cover, and to turn in the saddle and shoot behind him. I once asked him if he really could shoot to the rear with a galloping horse under him and hit a man.

"Well," he said, "maybe not to hit him, but I can come near enough to him to make him decide my pony's so much faster than his that it really isn't worth while to follow me."

Besides perfecting himself in what he tolerantly calls "tricks" of horsemanship and marksmanship, he studied the signs of the trail, forest and prairie, as a sailing-master studies the waves and clouds. The knowledge he gathers from inanimate objects and dumb animals seems little less than miraculous. And when you ask him how he knows these things he always gives you a reason founded on some fact or habit of nature that shows him to be a naturalist, mineralogist, geologist, and botanist, and not merely a seventh son of a seventh son.

In South Africa he would say to the officers: "There are a dozen Boers five miles ahead of us riding Basuto ponies at a trot, and leading five others. If we hurry we should be able to sight them in an hour." At first the officers would smile, but not after a half-hour's gallop, when they would see ahead of them a dozen Boers leading five ponies. In the early days of Salem, Burnham would have been burned as a witch.

When twenty-three years of age he married Miss Blanche Blick, of Iowa. They had known each other from childhood, and her brothers-in-law have been Burnham's aids and companions in every part of Africa and the West. Neither at the time of their marriage nor since did Mrs. Burnham "lay a hand on the bridle rein," as is witnessed by the fact that for nine years after his marriage Burnham contin-ued his career as sheriff, scout, mining prospector. And in 1893, when Burnham and his brother-in-law, Ingram, started for South Africa, Mrs. Burnham went with them, and in every part of South Africa shared her husband's life of travel and danger.

In making this move across the sea, Burnham's original idea was to look for gold in the territory owned by the German East African Company. But as in Rhodesia the first Matabele uprising had bro-ken out, he continued on down the coast, and vol-unteered for that campaign. This was the real beginning of his fortunes. The "war" was not unlike the Indian fighting of his early days, and although the country was new to him, with the kind of war-fare then being waged between the Kaffirs under

King Lobengula and the white settlers of the British South Africa Company, the chartered company of Cecil Rhodes, he was intimately familiar.

It does not take big men long to recognize other big men, and Burnham's remarkable work as a scout at once brought him to the notice of Rhodes and Dr. Jameson, who was personally conducting the campaign. The war was their own private war, and to them, at such a crisis in the history of their settlement, a man like Burnham was invaluable.

The chief incident of this campaign, the fame of which rang over all Great Britain and her colonies, was the gallant but hopeless stand made by Major Alan Wilson and his patrol of thirty-four men. It was Burnham's attempt to save these men that made him known from Buluwayo to Cape Town.

King Lobengula and his warriors were halted on one bank of the Shangani River, and on the other Major Forbes, with a picked force of three hundred men, was coming up in pursuit. Although at the moment he did not know it, he also was being pursued by a force of Matabeles, who were gradually surrounding him. At nightfall Major Wilson and a patrol of twelve men, with Burnham and his brother-in-law, Ingram, acting as scouts, were ordered to make a dash into the camp of Lobengula and, if possible, in the confusion of their sudden attack, and under cover of a terrific thunder-storm that was raging, bring him back a prisoner.

With the king in their hands the white men believed the rebellion would collapse. To the number of three thousand the Matabeles were sleeping in a succession of camps, through which the fourteen men rode at a gallop. But in the darkness it was difficult to distinguish the trek wagon of the king, and by the time they found his laager the Matabeles from the other camps through which they had ridden had given the alarm. Through the underbrush from every side the enemy, armed with assegai and elephant guns, charged toward them and spread out to cut off their retreat.

At a distance of about seven hundred yards from the camps there was a giant ant-hill, and the patrol rode toward it. By the aid of the lightning flashes they made their way through a dripping wood and over soil which the rain had turned into thick black mud. When the party drew rein at the ant-hill it was found that of the fourteen three were missing. As the official scout of the patrol and the only one who could see in the dark, Wilson ordered Burnham back to find them. Burnham said he could do so only by feeling the hoof-prints in the mud and that he would like some one with him to lead his pony. Wilson said he would lead it. With his fingers Burnham followed the trail of the eleven horses to where, at right angles, the hoof-prints of the three others separated from it, and so came upon the three men. Still, with nothing but the mud of the jungle to guide him, he brought them back to their comrades. It was this feat that established his reputation among British, Boers, and black men in South Africa.

Throughout the night the men of the patrol lay in the mud holding the reins of their horses. In the jungle about them, they could hear the enemy splashing through the mud, and the swishing sound of the branches as they swept back into place. It was still raining. Just before the dawn there came the sounds of voices and the welcome clatter of accoutrements. The men of the patrol, believing the column had joined them, sprang up rejoicing, but it was only a second patrol, under Captain Borrow, who had been sent forward with twenty men as re-enforcements. They had come in time to share in a glorious immortality. No sooner had these men joined than the Kaffirs began the attack; and the white men at once learned that they were trapped in a complete circle of the enemy. Hidden by the trees, the Kaffirs fired point-blank, and in a very little time half of Wilson's force was killed or wounded. As the horses were shot down the men used them for breastworks. There was no other shelter. Wilson called Burnham to him and told him he must try and get through the lines of the enemy to Forbes.

"Tell him to come up at once," he said; "we are nearly finished." He detailed a trooper named Gooding and Ingram to accompany Burnham. "One of you may get through," he said. Gooding was but lately out from London, and knew nothing of scouting, so Burnham and Ingram warned him, whether he saw the reason for it or not, to act exactly as they did. The three men had barely left the others before the enemy sprang at them with their spears. In five minutes they were being fired at from every bush. Then followed a remarkable ride, in which Burnham called to his aid all he had learned in thirty years of border warfare. As the enemy rushed after them, the three doubled on their tracks, rode in triple loops, hid in dongas to breathe their horses; and to scatter their pursuers, separated, joined again, and again separated. The enemy followed them to the very bank of the river, where, finding the "drift" covered with the swollen waters, they were forced to swim. They reached the other bank only to find Forbes hotly engaged with another force of the Matabeles.

"I have been sent for re-enforcements," Burnham said to Forbes, "but I believe we are the only survivors of that party." Forbes himself was too hard pressed to give help to Wilson, and Burnham, his errand over, took his place in the column, and began firing upon the new enemy.

Six weeks later the bodies of Wilson's patrol were found lying in a circle. Each of them had been shot many times. A son of Lobengula, who witnessed their extermination, and who in Buluwayo had often heard the Englishmen sing their national anthem, told how the five men who were the last to die stood up and, swinging their hats defiantly, sang "God Save the Queen." The incident will long be recorded in song and story; and in London was re-produced in two theatres, in each of which the man who played "Burnham, the American Scout," as he rode off for re-enforcements, was as loudly cheered by those in the audience as by those on the stage.

Hensman, in his "History of Rhodesia," says: "One hardly knows which to most admire, the men who went on this dangerous errand, through brush swarming with natives, or those who remained behind battling against overwhelming odds."

For his help in this war the Chartered Company presented Burnham with the campaign medal, a gold watch engraved with words of appreciation; and at the suggestion of Cecil Rhodes gave him, Ingram, and the Hon. Maurice Clifford, jointly, a tract of land of three hundred square acres.

After this campaign Burnham led an expedition of ten white men and seventy Kaffirs north of the

Zambesi River to explore Barotzeland and other regions to the north of Mashonaland, and to establish the boundaries of the concession given him, Ingram, and Clifford.

In order to protect Burnham on the march the Chartered Company signed a treaty with the native king of the country through which he wished to travel by which the king gave him permission to pass freely and guaranteed him against attack.

But Latea, the son of the king, refused to recognize the treaty and sent his young men in great numbers to surround Burnham's camp. Burnham had been instructed to avoid a fight, and was torn between his desire to obey the Chartered Company and to prevent a massacre. He decided to make it a sacrifice either of himself or of Latea. As soon as night fell, with only three companions and a missionary to act as a witness of what occurred, he slipped through the lines of Latea's men, and, kicking down the fence around the prince's hut, suddenly appeared before him and covered him with his rifle.

"Is it peace or war?" Burnham asked. "I have the king your father's guarantee of protection, but your men surround us. I have told my people if they hear shots to open fire. We may all be killed, but you will be the first to die."

The missionary also spoke urging Latea to abide by the treaty. Burnham says the prince seemed much more impressed by the arguments of the missionary than by the fact that he still was covered by Burnham's rifle. Whichever argument moved him, he called off his warriors. On this expedition Burnham discovered the ruins of great granite structures fifteen feet wide, and made entirely without mortar. They were of a period dating before the Phoenicians. He also sought out the ruins described to him by F. C. Selous, the famous hunter, and by Rider Haggard as King Solomon's Mines. Much to the delight of Mr. Haggard, he brought back for him from the mines of his imagination real gold ornaments and a real gold bar.

On this same expedition, which lasted five months, Burnham endured one of the severest hardships of his life. Alone with ten Kaffir boys, he started on a week's journey across the dried-up basin of what once had been a great lake. Water was carried in goat-skins on the heads of the bearers. The boys, finding the bags an unwieldy burden, and believing, with the happy optimism of their race, that Burnham's warnings were needless, and that at a stream they soon could refill the bags, emptied the water on the ground.

The tortures that followed this wanton waste were terrible. Five of the boys died, and after several days, when Burnham found water in abundance, the tongues of the others were so swollen that their jaws could not meet.

On this trip Burnham passed through a region ravaged by the "sleeping sickness," where his nostrils were never free from the stench of dead bodies, where in some of the villages, as he expressed it, "the hyenas were mangy with overeating, and the buzzards so gorged they could not move out of our way." From this expedition he brought back many ornaments of gold manufactured before the Christian era, and made several valuable maps of hitherto uncharted regions. It was in recognition of the information gathered by him on this trip that he was elected a Fellow of the Royal Geographical Society.

He returned to Rhodesia in time to take part in the second Matabele rebellion. This was in 1896. By now Burnham was a very prominent member of the "vortrekers" and pioneers at Buluwayo, and Sir Frederick Carrington, who was in command of the forces, attached him to his staff. This second outbreak was a more serious uprising than the one of 1893, and as it was evident the forces of the Chartered Company could not handle it, imperial troops were sent to assist them. But with even their aid the war dragged on until it threatened to last to the rainy season, when the troops must have gone into winter quarters. Had they done so, the cost of keeping them would have fallen on the Chartered Company, already a sufferer in pocket from the ravages of the rinderpest and the expenses of the investigation which followed the Jameson raid.

Accordingly, Carrington looked about for some measure by which he could bring the war to an immediate end.

It was suggested to him by a young Colonial, named Armstrong, the Commissioner of the district, that this could be done by destroying the "god," or high priest, Umlimo, who was the chief inspiration of the rebellion.

This high priest had incited the rebels to a general massacre of women and children, and had given them confidence by promising to strike the white soldiers blind and to turn their bullets into water. Armstrong had discovered the secret hiding-place of Umlimo, and Carrington ordered Burnham to penetrate the enemy's lines, find the god, capture him, and if that were not possible to destroy him.

The adventure was a most desperate one. Umlimo was secreted in a cave on the top of a huge kopje. At the base of this was a village where were gathered two regiments, of a thousand men each, of his fighting men.

For miles around this village the country was patrolled by roving bands of the enemy.

Against a white man reaching the cave and returning, the chances were a hundred to one, and the difficulties of the journey are illustrated by the fact that Burnham and Armstrong were unable to move faster than at the rate of a mile an hour. In making the last mile they consumed three hours. When they reached the base of the kopje in which Umlimo was hiding, they concealed their ponies in a clump of bushes, and on hands and knees began the ascent.

Directly below them lay the village, so close that they could smell the odors of cooking from the huts, and hear, rising drowsily on the hot, noonday air, voices of the warriors. For minutes at a time they lay as motionless as the granite boulders around or squirmed and crawled over loose stones which a miss of hand or knee would have dislodged and sent clattering into the village. After an hour of this tortuous climbing the cave suddenly opened before them, and they beheld Umlimo. Burnham recognized that to take him alive from his stronghold was an impossibility, and that even they themselves would leave the place was equally doubtful. So, obeying orders, he fired, killing the man who had boasted he would turn the bullets of his enemies into water. The echo of the shot aroused the village as would a stone hurled into an ant-heap. In an instant the veldt below was black with running men, and as, concealment being no longer possible, the white men rose to fly a great shout of anger told them they were discovered. At the same moment two women, returning from a stream where they had gone for water, saw the ponies, and ran screaming to give the alarm. The race that followed lasted two hours, for so quickly did the Kaffirs spread out on every side that it was impossible for Burnham to gain ground in any one direction, and he was forced to dodge, turn, and double. At one time the white men were driven back to the very kopje from which the race had started.

But in the end they evaded assegai and gunfire, and in safety reached Buluwayo. This exploit was one of the chief factors in bringing the war to a close. The Matabeles, finding their leader was only a mortal like themselves, and so could not, as he had promised, bring miracles to their aid, lost heart, and when Cecil Rhodes in person made overtures of peace, his terms were accepted. During the hard days of the siege, when rations were few and bad, Burnham's little girl, who had been the first white child born in Buluwayo, died of fever and lack of proper food. This with other causes led him to leave Rhodesia and return to California. It is possible he then thought he had forever turned his back on South Africa, but, though he himself had departed, the impression he had made there remained behind him.

Burnham did not rest long in California. In Alaska the hunt for gold had just begun, and, the old restlessness seizing him, he left Pasadena and her blue skies, tropical plants, and trolley-car strikes for the new raw land of the Klondike. With Burnham it has always been the place that is being made, not the place in being, that attracts. He has helped to make straight the ways of several great communities—Arizona, California, Rhodesia, Alaska, and Uganda. As he once said: "It is the constructive side of frontier life that most appeals to me, the building up of a country, where you see the persistent drive and force of the white man; when the place is finally settled I don't seem to enjoy it very long."

In Alaska he did much prospecting, and, with a sled and only two dogs, for twenty-four days made one long fight against snow and ice, covering six hundred miles. In mining in Alaska he succeeded well, but against the country he holds a constant grudge, because it kept him out of the fight with Spain. When war was declared he was in the wilds and knew nothing of it, and though on his return to civilization he telegraphed Colonel Roosevelt volunteering for the Rough Riders, and at once started south, by the time he had reached Seattle the war was over.

Several times has he spoken to me of how bitterly he regretted missing this chance to officially fight for his country. That he had twice served with English forces made him the more keen to show his loyalty to his own people.

That he would have been given a commission in the Rough Riders seems evident from the opinion President Roosevelt has publicly expressed of him.

"I know Burnham," the President wrote in 1901. "He is a scout and a hunter of courage and ability, a man totally without fear, a sure shot, and a fighter. He is the ideal scout, and when enlisted in the military service of any country he is bound to be of the greatest benefit."

The truth of this Burnham was soon to prove.

In 1899 he had returned to the Klondike, and in January of 1900 had been six months in Skagway. In that same month Lord Roberts sailed for Cape Town to take command of the army, and with him on his staff was Burnham's former commander, Sir Frederick, now Lord, Carrington. One night as the ship was in the Bay of Biscay, Carrington was talking of Burnham and giving instances of his marvellous powers as a "tracker."

"He is the best scout we ever had in South Africa!" Carrington declared.

"Then why don't we get him back there?" said Roberts. What followed is well known.

From Gibraltar a cable was sent to Skagway, offering Burnham the position, created especially for him, of chief of scouts of the British army in the field.

Probably never before in the history of wars has one nation paid so pleasant a tribute to the abilities of a man of another nation.

The sequel is interesting. The cablegram reached Skagway by the steamer City of Seattle. The purser left it at the post-office, and until two hours and a half before the steamer was listed to start on her return trip there it lay. Then Burnham, in asking for his mail, received it. In two hours and a half he had his family, himself, and his belongings on board the steamer, and had started on his half-around-the-world journey from Alaska to Cape Town.

A Skagway paper of January 5, 1900, published the day after Burnham sailed, throws a side light on his character. After telling of his hasty departure the day before, and of the high compliment that had been paid to "a prominent Skagwayan," it adds: "Although Mr. Burnham has lived in Skagway since last August, and has been North for many months, he has said little of his past, and few have known that he is the man famous over the world as 'the American scout' of the Matabele wars."

Many a man who went to the Klondike did not, for reasons best known to himself, talk about his past. But it is characteristic of Burnham that, though he lived there two years, his associates did not know, until the British Government snatched him from among them, that he had not always been a prospector like themselves.

I was on the same ship that carried Burnham the latter half of his journey, from Southampton to Cape Town, and every night for seventeen nights was one of a group of men who shot questions at him. And it was interesting to see a fellow-countryman one had heard praised so highly so completely make good. It was not as though he had a credulous audience of commercial tourists. Among the officers who each evening gathered around him were Colonel Gallilet of the Egyptian cavalry, Captain Frazer commanding the Scotch Gillies, Captain Mackie of Lord Roberts's staff, each of whom was later killed in action; Colonel Sir Charles Hunter of the Royal Rifles, Major Bagot, Major Lord Dudley, and Captain Lord Valentia. Each of these had either held command in border fights in India or the Sudan or had hunted big game, and the questions each asked were the outcome of his own experience and observation.

Not for a single evening could a faker have submitted to the midnight examination through which they put Burnham and not have exposed his ignorance. They wanted to know what difference there is in a column of dust raised by cavalry and by trek wagons, how to tell whether a horse that has passed was going at a trot or a gallop, the way to throw a diamond hitch, how to make a fire without at the

same time making a target of yourself, how—
why—what—and how?

And what made us most admire Burnham was
that when he did not know he at once said so.

Within two nights he had us so absolutely at his
mercy that we would have followed him anywhere;
anything he chose to tell us, we would have accepted. We were ready to believe in flying foxes, flying squirrels, that wild turkeys dance quadrilles—
even that you must never sleep in the moonlight.
Had he demanded: "Do you believe in vampires?"
we would have shouted "Yes." To ask that a scout
should on an ocean steamer prove his ability was
certainly placing him under a severe handicap.

As one of the British officers said: "It's about as
fair a game as though we planted the captain of this
ship in the Sahara Desert, and told him to prove he
could run a ten-thousand-ton liner."

Burnham continued with Lord Roberts to the
fall of Pretoria, when he was invalided home.

During the advance north he was a hundred
times inside the Boer laagers, keeping Headquarters
Staff daily informed of the enemy's movements; was
twice captured and twice escaped.

He was first captured while trying to warn the
British from the fatal drift at Thaba'nchu. When re-
connoitring alone in the morning mist he came
upon the Boers hiding on the banks of the river,

toward which the English were even then advancing. The Boers were moving all about him, and cut him off from his own side. He had to choose between abandoning the English to the trap or signalling to them, and so exposing himself to capture. With the red kerchief the scouts carried for that purpose he wigwagged to the approaching soldiers to turn back, that the enemy were awaiting them. But the column, which was without an advance guard, paid no attention to his signals and plodded steadily on into the ambush, while Burnham was at once made prisoner. In the fight that followed he pretended to receive a wound in the knee and bound it so elaborately that not even a surgeon would have disturbed the carefully arranged bandages. Limping heavily and groaning with pain, he was placed in a trek wagon with the officers who really were wounded, and who, in consequence, were not closely guarded. Burnham told them who he was and, as he intended to escape, offered to take back to head-quarters their names or any messages they might wish to send to their people. As twenty yards behind the wagon in which they lay was a mounted guard, the officers told him escape was impossible. He proved otherwise. The trek wagon was drawn by sixteen oxen and driven by a Kaffir boy. Later in the evening, but while it still was moonlight, the boy descended from his seat and ran forward to belabor the first spans of oxen. This was the opportunity for which Burnham had been waiting.

Slipping quickly over the driver's seat, he dropped between the two "wheelers" to the disselboom, or tongue, of the trek wagon. From this he lowered himself and fell between the legs of the oxen on his back in the road. In an instant the body of the wagon had passed over him, and while the dust still hung above the trail he rolled rapidly over into the ditch at the side of the road and lay motionless.

It was four days before he was able to re-enter the British lines, during which time he had been lying in the open veldt, and had subsisted on one biscuit and two handfuls of "mealies," or what we call Indian corn.

Another time when out scouting he and his Kaffir boy while on foot were "jumped" by a Boer commando and forced to hide in two great ant-hills. The Boers went into camp on every side of them, and for two days, unknown to themselves, held Burnham a prisoner. Only at night did he and the Cape boy dare to crawl out to breathe fresh air and to eat the food tablets they carried in their pockets. On five occasions was Burnham sent into the Boer lines with dynamite cartridges to blow up the railroad over which the enemy was receiving supplies and ammunition. One of these expeditions nearly ended his life.

On June 2, 1901, while trying by night to blow up the line between Pretoria and Delagoa Bay, he was surrounded by a party of Boers and could save himself only by instant flight. He threw himself Indian fashion along the back of his pony, and had all but got away when a bullet caught the horse and, without even faltering in its stride, it crashed to the ground dead, crushing Burnham beneath it and knocking him senseless. He continued unconscious for twenty-four hours, and when he came to, both friends and foes had departed. Bent upon carrying out his orders, although suffering the most acute agony, he crept back to the railroad and destroyed it. Knowing the explosion would soon bring the Boers, on his hands and knees he crept to an empty kraal, where for two days and nights he lay insensible. At the end of that time he appreciated that he was sinking and that unless he found aid he would die.

Accordingly, still on his hands and knees, he set forth toward the sound of distant firing. He was indifferent as to whether it came from the enemy or his own people, but, as it chanced, he was picked up by a patrol of General Dickson's Brigade, who carried him to Pretoria. There the surgeons discovered that in his fall he had torn apart the muscles of the stomach and burst a blood-vessel. That his life was saved, so they informed him, was due only to the fact that for three days he had been without food.

Had he attempted to digest the least particle of the "staff of life " he would have surely died. His injuries were so serious that he was ordered home.

On leaving the army he was given such hearty thanks and generous rewards as no other American ever received from the British War Office. He was promoted to the rank of major, presented with a large sum of money, and from Lord Roberts received a personal letter of thanks and appreciation.

In part the Field-Marshal wrote: "I doubt if any other man in the force could have successfully carried out the thrilling enterprises in which from time to time you have been engaged, demanding as they did the training of a lifetime, combined with exceptional courage, caution, and powers of endurance." On his arrival in England he was commanded to dine with the Queen and spend the night at Osborne, and a few months later, after her death, King Edward created him a member of the Distinguished Service Order, and personally presented him with the South African medal with five bars, and the cross of the D. S. O. While recovering his health Burnham, with Mrs. Burnham, was "passed on" by friends he had made in the army from country house to country house; he was made the guest of honor at city banquets, with the Duke of Rutland rode after the Belvoir hounds, and in Scotland made mild excursions after grouse. But after six months of convalescence he was off again, this time to the hinterland of Ashanti, on the west coast of Africa, where he went in the interests of a syndicate to investigate a concession for working gold mines.

With his brother-in-law, J. C. Blick, he marched and rowed twelve hundred miles, and explored the Volta River, at that date so little visited that in one day's journey they counted eleven hippopotamuses. In July, 1901, he returned from Ashanti, and a few months later an unknown but enthusiastic admirer asked in the House of Commons if it were true Major Burnham had applied for the post of Instructor of Scouts at Aldershot. There is no such post, and Burnham had not applied for any other post. To the Timer he wrote: "I never have thought myself competent to teach Britons how to fight, or to act as an instructor with officers who have fought in every corner of the world. The question asked in Parliament was entirely without my knowledge, and I deeply regret that it was asked." A few months later, with Mrs. Burnham and his younger son, Bruce, he journeyed to East Africa as director of the East African Syndicate.

During his stay there the African Review said of him: "Should East Africa ever become a possession for England to be proud of, she will owe much of her prosperity to the brave little band that has faced hardships and dangers in discovering her hidden resources. Major Burnham has chosen men from England, Ireland, the United States, and South Africa for sterling qualities, and they have justified his choice. Not the least like a hero is the retiring, diffident little major himself, though a finer man for a friend or a better man to serve under would not be found in the five continents."

Burnham explored a tract of land larger than Germany, penetrating a thousand miles through a country, never before visited by white men, to the borders of the Congo Basin. With him he had twenty white men and five hundred natives. The most interesting result of the expedition was the discovery of a lake forty-nine miles square, composed almost entirely of pure carbonate of soda, forming a snowlike crust so thick that on it the men could cross the lake.

It is the largest, and when the railroad is built—the Uganda Railroad is now only eighty-eight miles distant—it will be the most valuable deposit of carbonate of soda ever found.

A year ago, in the interests of John Hays Hammond, the distinguished mining engineer of South Africa and this country, Burnham went to Sonora, Mexico, to find a buried city and to open up mines of copper and silver.

Besides seeking for mines, Hammond and Burnham, with Gardner Williams, another American who also made his fortune in South Africa, are working together on a scheme to import to this country at their own expense many species of South African deer.

The South African deer is a hardy animal and can live where the American deer cannot, and the idea in importing him is to prevent big game in this country from passing away. They have asked Congress to set aside for these animals a portion of the forest reserve. Already Congress has voted toward the plan $15,000, and President Roosevelt is one of its most enthusiastic supporters.

We cannot leave Burnham in better hands than those of Hammond and Gardner Williams. Than these three men the United States has not sent to British Africa any Americans of whom she has better reason to be proud. Such men abroad do for those at home untold good. They are the real ambassadors of their country.

The last I learned of Burnham is told in [a] snapshot of him . . . which shows him, barefoot, in the Yaqui River, where he has gone, perhaps, to conceal his trail from the Indians. It came a month ago in a letter which said briefly that when the picture was snapped the expedition was "trying to cool off." There his narrative ended. Promising as it does adventures still to come, it seems a good place in which to leave him.

Meanwhile, you may think of Mrs. Burnham after a year in Mexico keeping the house open for her husband's return to Pasadena, and of their first son, Roderick, studying woodcraft with his father, forestry with Gifford Pinchot, and playing right guard on the freshman team at the University of California.

But Burnham himself we will leave "cooling off" in the Yaqui River, maybe, with Indians hunting for him along the banks. And we need not worry about him. We know they will not catch him.